HOLLYWOOD DESTINIES

D1260175

HOLLYWOOD DESTINIES

EUROPEAN DIRECTORS IN AMERICA, 1922-1931

—— o ——

Revised Edition

Graham Petrie

Wayne State University Press
Detroit

Contemporary Film and Television Series
A complete listing of the books in this series can be found at the back of this volume.

General Editor
Barry Keith Grant
Brock University

Advisory Editors
Patricia B. Erens
Dominican University

Lucy Fischer
University of Pittsburgh

Peter Lehman
Arizona State University

Caren J. Deming
University of Arizona

Robert J. Burgoyne
Wayne State University Press

Tom Gunning
University of Chicago

Copyright © 2002 by Wayne State University Press,
Detroit, Michigan 48201. All rights are reserved.
No part of this book may be reproduced without formal permission.

Manufactured in the United States of America.

06 05 04 03 02   5 4 3 2 1

Library of Congress Cataloging-in-Publication Data

Petrie, Graham.
  Hollywood destinies : European directors in America, 1922-1931 /
Graham Petrie.— Rev. ed.
      p. cm. — (Contemporary film and television series)
Includes index.
  ISBN 0-8143-2958-6 (pbk. : alk. paper)
  1. Motion pictures—United States—History. 2. Motion picture
producers and directors—Europe—Biography.   I. Title. II. Series.
  PN1993.5.U6 P47 2002
    791.43'0973'09042—dc21
                        2001004771

Contents

Acknowledgments

T his study could not have been completed without the generous coopera-tion of many individuals and institutions. For the financial assistance that enabled me to travel to archives and to spend time in Britain working with the British Film Institute's magazine and periodical holdings, I would like to thank the Social Sciences and Humanities Research Council of Canada. I would also like to thank McMaster University for allowing me some time free of teaching duties to carry out this research. I am grateful to the staff of the following film archives for their courtesy and cooperation in answering queries and permitting me to make use of their facilities during the original research process: Charles Silver and the Museum of Modern Art Film Department; Marshall Deutelbaum and the George Eastman House, Rochester, New York; Barbara Humphries and the Motion Picture Section of the Library of Congress, Washington, D.C.; the late Jacques Ledoux and the Royal Film Archive of Belgium; Jiri Levy and the Czechoslovak Film Archive; Per Calum and the Danish Film Museum; Anna-Lena Wibom and the Swedish Film Institute; Enno Patalas and the Munich Film Museum, Mrs. Lita Osmundsen and the Wenner-Gren Foundation, New York; Frank Grisbrook and Bellevue/MGM Film Distributors, Toronto; and Elaine Burrows and the British Film Institute Viewing Service, as well as the staff of the British Film Institute Book Library. I am grateful to Vladimir Opela and the Národni Filmovy Archiv in Prague for enabling me to see Lubitsch's *Three Women* and *Eternal Love*, which I had been unable to view for the orig-inal edition. Many other people contributed their knowledge and expertise to this book, either by answering my questions or putting me in touch with sources of information previously unknown to me. I am particularly indebted to the following: Gerald Pratley, the late Clive Denton, Tony Thomas, David Shepard, Philippe Haudiquet, Lothar Wolff, and the late John Gillett, who encouraged and assisted this project from the beginning. For the revised edition, I would like to thank Richard Allen, Barry Grant, Patrice Petro, Catherine Portuges and Catherine Surowiec for advice and encouragement. I would also like to thank Bengt Forslund and Peter Cowie for allowing me to make use of Cowie's translation of Forslund's authoritative biography of Victor Sjöström prior to its publication in 1988, and I am grateful to Jane Ehrlich for providing factual information concerning Sjöström's career.

Kevin Brownlow, who saw this book at the final proof stage, has kindly pointed out that one reel of Sjöström's *The Divine Woman* (discussed on p. 149) has been rediscovered, and says that it indicates that the film "might have been exceptional." He also mentions that "most" of one of Paul Leni's German-made films, *Diary of Dr Hart* (1916), still exists, and that Carl Mayer's original script for *Sunrise* has no comedy scenes in it. Murnau apparently had a "comedy constructor" during the filming, but whether or not this indicates that the comedy scenes were forced on him remains unclear.

The stills for this book are printed courtesy of the Museum of Modern Art/Film Stills Archive, AB Svensk Filmindustri, the Danish Film Museum, the Academy of Motion Picture Arts and Sciences and the Academy Foundation, the Wisconsin Center for Film and Theater Research, and Gerhard Ullman. Most of these are production stills rather than the frame enlargements that are correctly being used with increasing frequency to illustrate books of this kind. The difficulties of making frame enlargements from prints scattered all over Europe and North America ruled these out in all but one or two cases; I have endeavored, however, to choose production stills that correspond as closely as possible to the actual images that appear on the screen.

Quotations from *Variety* are reprinted with the permission of Variety, Inc.

Graham Petrie
(1985, revised 2001)

Introduction

Since the early 1920s it has been commonplace for "foreign" (i.e., non-American) film directors and stars who make any impression at all on the American market to receive, at one time or another, an invitation to work in Hollywood. Few, however, especially among the directors, survive for long enough to become permanent fixtures on the American film scene. For every Alfred Hitchcock or Milos Forman there are perhaps dozens who sink into oblivion after one or two films, or who return, frustrated and disillusioned, to resume work in their homelands. The list of such "failures" is almost endless: over the past two or three decades it would include Michelangelo Antonioni, Bo Widerberg, Lina Wertmüller, Ivan Passer, Jerzy Skolimowski, Krzysztof Zanussi, Emir Kusturica, Andrei Konchalovsky, Bill Forsyth, and countless others.

The word "failure" in this context is both instructive and prejudicial, for such films as Passer's *Cutter's Way* or Widerberg's *Joe Hill* received considerable critical acclaim on their release, even in America; their "failure" is in terms of box-office success rather than inadequate artistry. In this respect, perhaps, they are no different from American-born directors such as Robert Altman, whose insistence on making films that have puzzled and even alienated the mass audience while delighting the critics, led to his increasing marginalization and risked destroying his career—until he was saved by the unexpected success of *The Player*. It might therefore be argued that there is no particular distinction between "difficult" American directors and "difficult" foreign ones: both are victims of a shift in audience tastes that has moved sharply away from the enthusiasm for foreign films and art cinema that reached its peak in the mid-1970s.

The inability of so many foreign filmmakers to establish themselves permanently in Hollywood is not a recent phenomenon, for it has occurred with almost monotonous regularity since the first wave of European directors arrived in the United States in the early 1920s. Though individual Europeans such as Maurice Tourneur and Erich von Stroheim were prominent figures on the American film scene by 1920, in the following decade the major Hollywood studios made a concerted attempt to undermine the film industries of their major European competitors. Their strategies included buying up the services of the people most responsible for the success of, in particular, German and Scandinavian films, and attempting to use American financial power to gain increased influence on film production and distribution in countries such as Germany.[1]

During the first wave in the 1920s many directors were brought to Hollywood who had already established themselves both in their home countries and in the American marketplace: Ernst Lubitsch, F. W. Murnau, Paul Leni, and E. A. Dupont from Germany; Victor Sjöström and Mauritz Stiller from Sweden; and Benjamin Christensen from Denmark. In addition, several directors arrived without any specific invitation from a Hollywood studio, finding their way there as a result of political upheavals in their own countries. Among these were Hungarians Alexander Korda, Michael Curtiz, and Paul Fejös.[2] Yet, by the beginning of the 1930s, only Lubitsch and Curtiz had any future to look forward to in Hollywood; the others had moved elsewhere, usually back to their own countries, or, like Murnau and Leni, had died. This latter group left behind several films now recognized as classics of American cinema—*The Wind* and *The Scarlet Letter* from Sjöström, *Sunrise* and *Tabu* from Murnau, *Hotel Imperial* from Stiller, *The Cat and the Canary* from Leni—as well as a host of lesser-known but still important works. But, by the time they left, the stigma of failure had already attached itself to them, and few critics or filmgoers seemed to regret their disappearance.

The pattern established in the 1920s essentially repeated itself in the two subsequent decades. In the late 1930s and early 1940s major influxes of foreign talent were brought into Hollywood, including refugees from Nazi-dominated Europe, such as Billy Wilder, Otto Preminger, Robert Siodmak, Max Ophüls, Jean Renoir, and René Clair. Though Wilder, Preminger, and Siodmak stayed on after 1945 to become important figures on the American film scene, Renoir, Clair, and Ophüls were only too happy to return to Europe after decidedly mixed experiences in Hollywood, leaving behind some films that have since gained classic status, such as Ophüls's *Letter from an Unknown Woman*. In the late 1960s and 1970s Hollywood attempted, as in the 1920s, to entice some of the people responsible for the remarkable revival of interest in European cinema that began in the late 1950s. At the same time, as in both the 1920s and 1930s, filmmakers such as Roman Polanski and Forman, who felt unable to work freely in their own countries, were also welcomed. Despite the critical and popular acclaim for such films as *Chinatown* and *One Flew Over the Cuckoo's Nest*, the survival rate for recent arrivals has probably been little higher than in previous decades, and the greatest commercial success in recent years has been achieved by directors such as Dutchman Paul Verhoeven who have unashamedly and enthusiastically adjusted to the imperatives of the American entertainment industry.[3]

Some interesting paradoxes emerge from a consideration of the fates of these various directors. Those specifically invited to work in Hollywood are brought over because their films are considered to be *different* from the standard Hollywood fare: they are more adventurous, daring, or unorthodox in style and theme; they are works of art produced by individual artists rather than preprogrammed mass entertainment. Yet, often after an initially enthusiastic response, their works begin to be condemned for being *too* artistic, *too* different, *too* individual, *too* disconcerting; they don't fit into the mainstream of everyday audience expectations; they are boring, obscure, depressing, puzzling, not *entertaining* enough, not *American* enough. The exceptions are those who manage to adapt to mainstream American taste, sometimes, like Forman, retaining enough self-conscious artistry to appear different, yet not different enough to shock or alienate. A few, like Wilder, were intelligent and shrewd enough to appear to accommodate themselves to American genre expectations while subtly subverting them; others, like Verhoeven, embrace them wholesale. Those who survive, in other words, generally do so by discarding the foreignness that made them interesting in the first place and adapting to the imperatives of the Hollywood machine.

The origins of this process can be found in the overall subject of this book: the fates of the major European directors brought over to Hollywood in the 1920s. The issues raised, however, are still relevant, perhaps even more so today than seventy or eighty years ago. In the 1970s, as in the 1920s, European cinema provided an invigorating challenge to Hollywood mainstream fare, and the result, especially in the 1970s, was the infusion of new life and excitement into the American cinema, and the opportunity for some directors to experiment, quite self-consciously, with creating works of art as well as entertainment. (An older generation of directors, such as Hitchcock, John Ford, Howard Hawks, and Wilder robustly denied that this was their intention, even when it was, in fact, the result.) In both decades, however, the renewal lasted for barely a decade until business as usual resumed, and the innovators found themselves forced to adapt or be marginalized or even silenced.

Since 1980 foreignness has been safely domesticated or assimilated into the mainstream of American cinema once more. The audience for foreign films in their original form has shrunk alarmingly in recent years, and European and Asian filmmakers who desire success in today's market-place generally attempt this by adapting their work to recognized American formulas or even by making their films in English. Alternatively, a European film that received a degree of recognition in its art cinema incarnation will be remade in an American setting with its potentially disturbing "foreignness" removed, such as *The Vanishing* or *The Return of Martin Guerre.* (A similar process is evident in television, where British programs that achieve popularity in the ghetto of public television are duly "Americanized" and remade for the mass audience—a process that usually ends in destroying all their original virtues.)

The origins of all this can be found in the 1920s, for, as is illustrated in the first chapter of this book, the challenge of foreign films and filmmakers during this decade forced American critics and audiences to decide, for perhaps the first time, what kind of filmmaking they were comfortable with and what did or did not suit American tastes. The result was an overall agreement on what was "American" and thus acceptable, versus what was "foreign" and thus not acceptable. Behind this lay a not always unspoken assumption that American standards of entertainment were both self-evident and universally valid and that anything failing to conform to these could safely be ignored. A similar response can be observed in post-1980s cinema as a whole.

One major theme of this book is a study of this process as it first worked itself out in the reception of the films of Lubitsch, Murnau, Sjöström and others after their arrival in America in the early 1920s. Another major concern, however, is the rehabilitation of some of the work they produced, which has too often been assumed to be largely unsuccessful and of little lasting significance. Though an exception is always made for Lubitsch and for individual films such as *The Wind* or *Sunrise*, the overall impression given by most film histories is that the foreign incursion had little wider impact beyond these isolated examples, apart from creating a relatively transient interest in unusual lighting effects and unorthodox camerawork.

There are many reasons for this generally dismissive attitude. Until recently, silent films have tended to be relegated by film historians and teachers alike to a ghetto of received "classics" largely established in the 1930s and 1940s by historians such as Lewis Jacobs and Paul Rotha. There were many, often quite valid, reasons for this, including the fact that the works of von Stroheim, D. W. Griffith, Sergei Eisenstein, Charles Chaplin, Buster Keaton, and Fritz Lang were among the few from the silent period that were easily available for rental from commercial distributors or film museums. These films were routinely shown in classrooms and film societies in conditions that seldom did justice to their original qualities. They were scratched, mutilated, and poor-quality 16mm prints, shown without musical accompaniment and generally at the wrong speed, with the result that the finest silent films were made to look like embarrassing curiosities rather than works of considerable visual subtlety and beauty.

Recently, however, Kevin Brownlow's restoration of Abel Gance's *Napoleon* and his own work as an indefatigable historian and champion of silent cinema have prompted an astonishing increase in interest in early cinema. This interest is fueled by the renewed availability of works that, previously inaccessibly hidden away in archives or considered lost, have been lovingly restored to something like their original condition and screened at film festivals and cinémathèques worldwide. The result has been a thorough rethinking of the standard silent film canon and the whole history of early cinema that, while not necessarily dislodging *The Birth of a Nation* or *The Passion of Joan of Arc* from their established pedestals, has placed them in a much wider and richer context than before. Festivals devoted entirely or largely to silent cinema, such as those in Pordenone and Bologna, regularly bring to light previously neglected or forgotten works, and a new generation of film historians, such as Tom Gunning, Douglas Gomery, David Shipman, and Brownlow, has provided a whole new perspective from which to view them.

The problem of more widespread availability of these "rediscovered" films still remains; many of the films discussed in this study can still be seen only in the archives that possess what is sometimes the only surviving copy, or by those who regularly visit the festivals mentioned above or the specialized screenings organized by cinémathèques, film museums, and annual gatherings such as Cinefest in Syracuse, New York. This relatively small-scale study involved, in its original form, visits to archives in Sweden, Denmark, Germany, Belgium, the Czech Republic, Britain, and the United States merely to carry out the primary task of viewing the relevant films. Many of the most interesting of these—such as *Phantom, The Oyster Princess, He Who Gets Slapped, Masterman, So This Is Paris, Lonesome,* and *City Girl* (to take a few examples entirely at random)—are still largely inaccessible to a wider public.

I hope, therefore, that my discussion of these still relatively unknown films will help to stimulate greater interest in them, while offering a new perspective on the careers of their creators both before and, especially, after their arrival in the United States. Lubitsch, for example, while invited to America on the strength of the success of *Passion (Madame Dubarry)* and *Deception (Anna Boleyn),* was already an accomplished director of comedies that have seldom received their full due from English-language critics of his work; an understanding of this helps to explain the direction taken by his career in the United States, which moved abruptly away from the large-scale historical epics that had established his initial reputation there.[4] Murnau and Sjöström likewise were known before their arrival in America only for a small, and to some extent unrepresentative, sample of their earlier work; a fuller understanding of this will help to establish greater continuity than is often recognized between their European and American careers, while sympathetic attention to their American films as a whole should help explain, for example, why Sjöström was hailed, at the time, as "The Greatest Director in the World" and, more recently, by David Shipman as "The Screen's First Master."

An essential basis for such reassessments is a study of the often difficult process of adjustment to American filmmaking methods and conditions that these and other directors underwent. Though there is some truth in the still common assumption that most of them were unable or unwilling to adapt totally to these, the reasons for this are worth examining in more depth than standard film histories are prepared to offer, while the very real successes enjoyed by most of them are still too often overlooked. To this end I have devoted a good deal of attention to the opinions of their work offered by the most influential film magazines and periodicals of the time. Though these seldom contain particularly sophisticated film criticism, their judgments are often surprisingly perceptive, and in cases where they are not, the prejudices and assumptions expressed about the true nature of American cinema and the tastes of the American audience are central to the whole development of that cinema since its inception, as well as being decisive in determining the fates of Lubitsch, Sjöström, and Stiller, among many others. The first chapter, therefore, tries to establish what might be called "the horizon of expectations" within which the newcomers had to work, in terms of what they might be expected to contribute to American cinema and of the demands made on them to conform to American taste. The result was often cruelly paradoxical, on the one hand welcoming the Europeans in their promise to bring something artistically adventurous and thematically daring to American cinema, and then all too often berating and condemning them for attempting to do just that.

Chapters 2 through 4 look at the overall careers of Lubitsch, Murnau, and Sjöström, partly because their achievements are among the most significant of the period, and partly because they were enthusiastically welcomed on their arrival, with great things expected of them, and their films were almost always singled out for particular attention and discussion.

They were widely recognized as creators with something special and individual to offer, and their films were viewed and judged with this in mind. The fifth chapter adopts a more thematic approach when dealing with directors who either were not so well known on their arrival or unable to establish themselves quite as forcefully on the American film scene. In their case, I felt that a treatment examining the main film genres to which they contributed during their time in America would help to illustrate and clarify the nature of the problems they faced in attempting to adjust to working methods and cultural assumptions so very different from those to which they had been accustomed. Despite the frustration and setbacks they all suffered, they succeeded in contributing something distinctive to the American cinema.

I make no claims to providing hitherto unknown biographical information about the directors discussed, though I have made every effort to consult the most reliable and up-to-date sources about their careers and to offer correct factual data in what is still too often a swamp of misinformation. If mistakes still exist, I apologize for them and will be happy to receive corrections. My main intention has been to examine the films themselves at firsthand and to avoid the procedure—all too common in the past but now thankfully rare—of relying on secondhand and often inaccurate descriptions or vague memories of screenings from a distant past. Where a film is now considered lost or I have been unable to see a copy myself, I have attempted to give a sense of its contents and its reception by quoting reviews and criticism of the time. All the relevant information about the film careers of Murnau, Lubitsch, and Sjöström is contained in the chapters dealing with them; but readers who might wish an overview that covers their earlier and later (post-1930) lives will find this provided, briefly, in Appendix C.

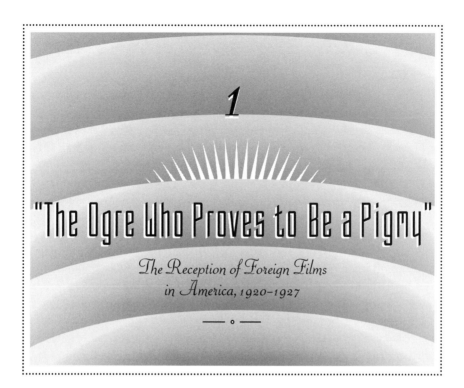

1

"The Ogre Who Proves to Be a Pigmy"

The Reception of Foreign Films in America, 1920–1927

— ∘ —

In the years immediately following the American entry into the First World War, the growing hatred toward German, Russian, Japanese, Italian, and Jewish immigrants, coupled with the increasing clamor to restrict immigration of all kinds, resulted in the Immigration Act of 1924, which drastically reduced the number of new arrivals. Hostility to foreigners and foreign ideas was fueled by an almost hysterical emphasis on patriotism and "Americanism"; the Ku Klux Klan flourished and "100 percent" Americans attempted, with increasing desperation, to defend what they saw as the purity of their native heritage against the onslaught of evil and alien influences dedicated to the destruction of American ideas.[1] During this same period films from Europe, Germany and Scandinavia in particular, began to make a significant impact on the American market. Hollywood's ultimate solution to the influx of foreign films was to buy up and attempt to assimilate the most successful of its foreign competitors. While this process has been chronicled often enough by film historians, the various stages, and the controversies and debates that were involved, have been given little attention. The often heated discussions over the merits of imported films versus American films reveal deep-rooted assumptions about the "natural" characteristics of American cinema that have profoundly affected its overall development, in both its strengths and weaknesses; these assumptions were

[]

perhaps more clearly articulated in a context in which the topic of "Americanism" was receiving constant attention.

The initial impulse toward an aggressive patriotism accompanied, and in some cases even preceded, American participation in the war. Films such as the 1917 *War and the Woman* reflected a widespread popular mythology of a country swarming with German spies and undercover agents, all busily undermining American institutions and eagerly awaiting the signal to reveal themselves and take over the machinery of government. Local officials, encouraged by the press and, in some cases, supported by the government itself, reflected the growing anti-German hysteria by attempting to eliminate all traces of German culture and even, in a few states, banning the teaching of the German language in schools. By 1918 widespread vigilante violence against individuals of German origin included destruction of property, public floggings and tar-and-featherings, and at least one lynching. The Wilson administration, under persistent attack from extremists for failing to act firmly enough against spies and traitors, did little to counteract such behavior and contented itself with trying to appease it.[2]

Hostility toward Germans died down with the ending of the war, only to be replaced almost immediately with an equally hysterical fear of the Bolshevik and radical ideas fostered by the Russian Revolution. Though the red scare of 1919–1921 came to be directed toward radicals, anarchists, and "agitators" of all kinds, whatever their native origins, it was inspired by a political fundamentalism that appealed to patriotism and the defense of basic American ideals that first manifested itself in attacks on Russian and Eastern European immigrants. Alarmed by increasing labor unrest, and in particular a national coal strike, Attorney General Palmer, a supporter of "100 percent" Americanism, took advantage of President Wilson's illness to authorize the arrest, on 7 November 1919, of hundreds of members of the Union of Russian Workers, 249 of whom were deported to Russia a month later, leaving wives and children in America. On 20 January 1920 Palmer ordered the arrest of thousands of members of the Communist and Communist Labor Parties (neither of them illegal) and recommended that almost 3,000 Eastern European aliens be deported. Though the full accomplishment of his intention was thwarted, several hundred Communists were eventually forced to leave the country.[3]

Next came the turn of Italians, Japanese, and Jews. In early August 1920 a mob in the southern Illinois mining town of West Frankfort went on a three-day rampage against Italian immigrants, beating and stoning them and burning their houses. In 1920 the California State Legislature passed a

law forbidding Japanese ownership of land, and in May of that year Henry Ford launched a propaganda campaign against Jews, many of whom were of German origin and thus doubly suspect. On the wider political scene "a general revulsion against European entanglements was crystallizing," and along with isolationism and hostility to European influences came increasing alarm at the post-war influx of foreign immigrants with the demand that restrictions more stringent than a simple reading test be applied to them. The immigrants "collided with an unemployment problem" and a business depression; and a combination of popular fears and prejudices along with agitation from the press, encouraged Congress to suspend immigration temporarily for one year. Various proposals to curtail immigration on a more permanent basis through the introduction of national quotas were next put forward, and these culminated in a law of 1921 that "imposed the first sharp and absolute numerical limits on European immigration" and "established a nationality quota system based on the pre-existing composition of the American population."[4] The subsequent Immigration Act of 1924 put the seal on this policy by eliminating all but a trickle of privileged new arrivals.[5]

During this period of widespread and often irrational hostility to foreign influences European films—after a hiatus of some ten years—began to be widely shown and commented on in the United States. Foreign films had already aroused concern for their suspect moral content ("many European features depict sexual problems with candor and a crudeness intolerable outside a clinic or a psychiatric hospital") and their lack of acceptable American subject-matter; but as they became directed toward a middle-class clientele and lost the association with the entertainment tastes and dubious morality of a largely working-class or immigrant audience, the proportion of foreign films fell from over fifty percent of those shown in 1908 to ten percent in 1913.[6]

The new influx of foreign films after the First World War spurred a renewed debate about moral values in the cinema, made more urgent by the social changes and the questioning of accepted standards that gathered strength throughout the decade. Though the discussions centered mostly on the foreign films shown in the United States and their impact both on audiences and the American film industry as a whole, the "invasion," as it was often characterized, followed a determined move in the opposite direction, as American film companies sought, as soon as possible after the ending of hostilities, to secure a foothold in the German, Austrian and Balkan markets before such countries as France, Italy and Britain, the traditional suppliers

of films to those areas before the war, had the chance to re-establish themselves.[7]

On 9 August 1919 *Moving Picture World* published a lengthy report on a recent visit to Central Europe by Ben Blumenthal, president of the Import and Export Film Company, who commented with some surprise on his discovery that the German film industry had maintained a high level of productivity throughout the war years. He added that the proliferation of German films created a major obstacle to American attempts to move smoothly into supposedly virgin territory. Not only were the Germans producing enough films to meet the needs of their domestic market, but they were woefully ignorant of the vast advances made in the technique and quality of American films since 1914 and reluctant "to see the light" in this respect, as most other European nations had done. Blumenthal showed little enthusiasm for a possible compromise by means of which anyone selling films to Germany would be paid by being given an equivalent number of German films for distribution in his own country, concluding that this would force the unfortunate American dealer to "run a series of Hun bargain days every week." Though the immediate outlook was gloomy, Blumenthal trusted that the overall quality of American films would finally ensure their acceptance, even if it promised to be a long and uphill struggle.[8]

While the Americans were encountering unexpected difficulties finding an outlet for their films in Germany, the tide began to run rapidly in the opposite direction, prompted by the huge popular and critical success of Ernst Lubitsch's *Passion (Madame Dubarry)*, the first German film to be shown in America after the war, and released in December 1920. The critical acclaim for German films was soon matched by cries of alarm and outrage from American producers who saw their livelihood threatened and from patriots who felt that it was far too soon to forgive and forget where German culture was concerned. The language used to describe the influx of German imports parallels that concurrently employed by opponents of unrestricted immigration: the imagery of "floods," "deluges," and "tidal waves" was common to both.

One of the earliest notes of warning (though it also contained a warm endorsement of the best European films) was sounded by Erich von Stroheim in an interview with *Moving Picture World* on 8 May 1920. After suggesting that "American producers had better look out for foreign picture makers" who would soon be at least their equals in both craftsmanship and quality, von Stroheim went on to offer some thoughts on the essential differences between European and American films: "Just as foreign literature is different from American literature, so are foreign plays different from American plays. Foreign writers go more into the deeper relationships of mankind than do American authors. They depict more emotion and less of the frivolities of life. This is reflected on the European screen." Von Stroheim, who was supervising the final editing of *The Devil's Pass Key* at the time of the interview, was clearly trying here to establish a basis for his own "European" style of filmmaking (as with his later recommendations that there should be "no limit of footage for master film productions" and that "when certain moving picture theatres are recognized as the home of certain classes of screen productions, then American producers will produce selected pictures for selective classes"). Nevertheless, his comments on the intrinsic differences between European and American taste, and the possible incompatibility between them, were to be heard with increasing frequency elsewhere.[9]

A mood of cautious self-interest led some American businessmen to offer a guarded welcome to imported films. Paul Cromelin, president and general manager of the Inter-Ocean Film Corporation, reported after a trip to Europe:

> Eventually the time will come when [the foreign producer's] pictures will be of sufficient quality to compete with the American product . . . If we show by our neglect to import the foreign-made productions that we are not anxious for their product, foreign producers will eventually cease to purchase American productions. . . . The English picture, the French production, and the offerings of our foreign producers should be given an opportunity to demonstrate their value to the American public.[10]

It was not long, however, before *Variety* (18 April 1921) was complaining about the "dumping" of German films in the United States: forty-six arrived in New York within one week and there were fears that their cheapness could undercut American production. A few days later, parallel to wider concern about the impact of foreign immigrants on the American economy, *Variety* (22 April 1921) reported that Equity, First National, Famous Players, and the American Legion had called for a ban on *all* foreign films (particularly German ones) on the grounds that they contributed to unemployment in the American film industry. The American Legion soon emphasized its dislike of foreign intrusions by participating in a riot at a showing of *The Cabinet of Dr. Caligari* in Los Angeles and sponsoring parades against the subsequent showing of German films there. One result was that

the offending cinema promptly withdrew *Caligari* and promised not to screen any more German films (*Variety*, 13 May 1921).

Though these activities did little to hinder the importation of foreign films overall (*Moving Picture World* reported the first screening of a Czech film in the United States on 29 May 1921, following after "British, French, German, Italian and even Danish pictures"), supporters of European imports tended to become somewhat defensive about the films' impact on the American scene, arguing that either a mere fraction of those bought for American screening were ever actually shown and that only a few even of these achieved commercial success, or that they appealed primarily to sophisticated city audiences and were ignored in rural and small-town areas. *Variety* on 29 April 1921 took much the same line as Paul Cromelin had earlier, claiming that restrictions on the showing of foreign films would invite retaliation against American films abroad and that the competition would be healthy for the native industry.

In November 1921 *Variety* reported one of the first moves toward what would be—from the American point of view at any rate—the perfect solution to the problem:

> After testing out French and English territory as a home for a foreign production studio, Famous Players has finally concentrated on Germany as the most advantageous center for European activity. . . . This scheme . . . is to educate American directors abroad and foreign directors here. Ernst Lubitsch and Pola Negri sail for this country Jan. 1. Both De Milles, Penrhyn Stanlaws and other Paramount directors are going one by one to Europe to make productions there. By this program it is hoped to interweave the best of both systems into one.
>
> Artistically foreign pictures have much to recommend them, and if Americans can absorb German ideas of picture making, it is felt American productions will improve to such an extent that their domination of the world market will be assured. But Germans have even more, from the world market standpoint, to learn here than our directors can get there. This is demonstrated by the selling power in this country of the German productions. 'The Golem,' for example, has followed in the trail of its predecessors. A hit in New York, it has flopped in out-of-town territory. This was true also of "Passion," "Deception," and "Caligari," all sponsored by different companies.[11]

This plan did not work out quite as anticipated. Lubitsch paid a short visit to the United States in December and January of 1921 and 1922, but did not return to work there until almost a year later, in December 1922, and the eventual traffic was primarily one way, with German directors abandoning their own industry to work in Hollywood. The article, however, accurately reflects the common assumption of the time that while the Germans might have "art," the Americans have commercial know-how.

The often self-serving and racially prejudiced complaints about the economic impact of foreign films on the American industry took on much of their coloring from the anti-immigrant mood of 1920 and 1921 and were less significant in the long run than the controversy over the artistic merits of the films as opposed to the native product. By 19 August 1921 *Variety* could report that Famous Players were having little success in attempting to "unload" thirty German films on to the American public, and reviewers who had been overawed by the earliest imported films to have an influence (Lubitsch's *Passion* and *Deception,* Robert Wiene's *Caligari* and Paul Wegener's *The Golem*) were becoming much more carping. Unfavorable reviews almost always drew attention to flaws that were assumed to be characteristic of "European" films as opposed to American ones and maintained that the subject matter, treatment, or moral tone of these films were unsuited to American tastes and possibly even pernicious to an American audience. The films, in other words, were rarely judged by their artistic merits or entertainment value, but were placed in a framework that took for granted that there was a "correct," "American" way of making films and were condemned for deviating from it.

Moving Picture World's review of Abel Gance's *J'accuse* (21 May 1921) found fault with its alleged technical inadequacies, though it condescendingly acknowledged that the acting was satisfactory in the "excessively animated and florid French school." The magazine returned to the attack a few months later when it reviewed a "Norwegian" production of *Hamlet* (actually a Danish-German coproduction) starring Asta Nielsen, and commented unfavorably on the "continental habit of over-accentuating every gesture and expression" (*Moving Picture World [MPW]*, 19 November 1921). An interesting, if unintentional, admission that foreign films were judged in terms of preconceived national stereotypes is found in a review of Lubitsch's *Eyes of the Mummy* where, for once, the acting is praised and the camerawork applauded for differing from the normal American style, but "the atmosphere of a home in England is not convincing, according to the American idea of what English life is like" (*MPW,* 19 August 1922).

Other magazines shared similar assumptions about American technical superiority: *Variety,* reporting the Berlin showing of Lubitsch's *Anna Boleyn* (released in America as *Deception*), offered a generally favorable assessment, but attacked the "amateur" lighting effects (21 January 1921). When it reviewed the film a few months later on its American release (22 April 1921), however, it was less concerned with this aspect of the film, deeming the photography to be perfectly adequate after all, than with the reservation that it was unlikely to do well outside the larger cities. For many reviewers the general unsuitability of foreign films for American audiences, whatever their "artistic" merits, became the prime consideration, resulting in the kind of schizophrenia evident in *Variety*'s review of Christensen's *Heksen* (titled *Witchcraft* on its initial U.S. release): "Swedish and Danish pictures easily hold the palm for morbid realism, and in many cases for brilliant acting and production. 'Witchcraft,' made by Benjamin Christensen, leaves all the others beaten. . . . Wonderful though this picture is, it is absolutely unfit for public exhibition" (30 August 1923). The serene confidence displayed in these and many similar comments as to instantly recognizable and all-embracing national (and even Continental) characteristics was not necessarily new: Henrik Ibsen's plays provided a ready-made stereotype of Scandinavian despair that *Variety*'s reviewer had already reached for in offering a guarded welcome to Victor Sjöström's *The Stroke of Midnight* (better known by its alternative English title, *The Phantom Chariot*): "The picture is murky with Scandinavian gloom. It is as depressing as Ibsen at his very worst and then some" (9 June 1922). (It comes as something of a surprise to discover that the reviewer actually admires Ibsen for being relentlessly and uncompromisingly depressing, and objects to Sjöström's departing from stereotype by introducing a happy ending; optimism of any kind is obviously inappropriate where a Swedish film is concerned.) By the mid-1920s, however, this kind of response had become completely automatic, even when the immediate danger of foreign imports swamping the American market had long since receded, leaving a legacy that was easily drawn on when the next major surge of interest in foreign films occurred some forty years later, as seen in the endless clichés about "gloomy," "morbid," "depressing" Ingmar Bergman.

Some reviewers were remarkably explicit in assigning particular national traits to each country's pictures. *Motion Picture Magazine* initially offered an enthusiastic welcome to foreign films, praising *Passion* as "a bolt from the blue—and a few more bolts of a similar nature will cause the American producers to realize that they no longer have a monopoly"

(February 1921), while remaining remarkably levelheaded about the alleged effects on American morale of a surfeit of German "propaganda": "We may take their art and let their propaganda go. . . . The Germans have given us productions that are artistic. The German producer has not been afraid of facts—he has not gilded everything till there is a deadly monotony of all things." (August 1921) By February 1925, however, the magazine had adopted entirely the opposite opinion, and a vehement editorial headed "We Want What We Want So There" criticized foreign directors for "wasting their considerable talent in an effort to sophisticate the American motion picture public." American audiences were no longer expected to learn anything new from imported films, nor were they advised to adjust their tastes and expectations to accommodate unfamiliar ideas or techniques. The public wanted simple, uncomplicated stories with happy endings in which virtue emerged triumphant ("gilding everything to a deadly monotony," as the magazine's own reviewer had contemptuously phrased it four years earlier), and foreign producers would have to learn to adapt to this if they wished to survive in the American market. It would be difficult for "gloomy" Swedes, "cynical" Germans, and Russians wallowing in "black despair" to achieve this, but they would have to make the effort nevertheless, or else accept defeat.

By the end of 1925 a writer for *Variety,* in an extraordinarily slackly written review of Fritz Lang's *Siegfried* on 23 December, seemed to feel that it was enough to repeat endlessly that the film was "artistic" in order to condemn it for American audiences:

> The picture is purely artistic and holds but few things to interest the average picturegoer of today.
>
> It's an artistic but not a commercial film. . . . The rave about these German pictures is that the directors are artists to their fingertips (so forth). But after looking at "Siegfried" the only conclusion is that their artistry consists in playing the film story before settings of a very stagey nature and in playing the various scenes in a slow and stodgy pace, not only tiresome to an American audience, but ruinous to the picture. . . . Just an "artistic success," which doesn't mean 10 cents in Mexican money.

One of the most remarkable and vituperative of such attacks, which brings together all the assumptions and prejudices scattered through the criticisms already quoted, came from *Photoplay* in June 1922. The article begins with the triumphant claim that "the 'tidal wave' of German pictures moved hardly

a pebble on the beach." As a result "of an output of seven years' intensive productivity . . . the entire German industry has produced so far as America is concerned, one 100 percent financially successful picture—'Passion'— three or four mediocrely successful pictures—'The Golem,' 'Gypsy Blood,' 'One Arabian Night'—and several failures, such as 'Hamlet' and 'Deception.'"[12]

The magazine is quite explicit about the reasons for this "failure": one is the inappropriate subject matter ("all the Germans have given us since ['Passion'] is a lot of Kings and Queens"), but more important are the differences in national character that make German films unfit for American audiences. The Germans want a hierarchical society based on class distinctions, with the kaiser on top, while Americans are staunchly egalitarian. "There are no two countries so widely separated in their aspirations, ambitions, and manifestations as Germany and America." The Germans are class-ridden, racially prejudiced, patriarchal, sexually immoral, and non–philanthropic; they have a taste for obscenity, enjoy "horror and suffering on the screen," are cynical, sadistic, and pessimistic. Admirably non–racially prejudiced Americans, on the other hand, believe in "the eternal destiny of splendid youth, in the glory of motherhood, in the square deal, in the equality of sexes, in equal opportunities for all . . . and in laughter." Finally, the Germans enjoy "eating, drinking and ordering people—especially your women—about" and revel in watching "other people's emotions put in a test tube . . . with a residue of nastiness left in the bottom."

Two additional statements, one from the implacable *Photoplay* and one from *Screenland,* further emphasize this perspective. James R. Quirk, writing in the former in November 1927, speaks for what was certainly the majority opinion by that time when he writes that "all foreign pictures are art. . . . All German directors are geniuses" is merely "the credo of [a] group of pseudo-intellectuals." In truth, most foreign films (like impressionist paintings and free verse) were simply mediocre. In "An Open Letter to Erich von Stroheim" in *Screenland* for March 1925, Myron Zobel advises the director that *Greed* was a total failure because "you got away from the continental sort of thing in which you are supreme. You know the foreign run of mind. You don't know ours. We don't think and we don't act the same way over here that they do abroad."[13]

Just as, on the wider national scene, Americans reached the decision between 1921 and 1924 to keep their country more or less they way it was by restricting disruptive alien influences, so the critics, representing a popular rather than a highbrow mentality, after an initial period of

disorientation, denounced European films as essentially un-American because of their lack of commercial appeal, their "morbid and depressing" themes, and their refusal to view the world through healthy and optimistic American eyes. The moral was clear: If foreign films (or foreign directors) were to survive in the American marketplace, they would have to adapt themselves to American tastes and values, rather than expecting their audiences to adjust to alien concepts that were both unwanted and unnecessary. Even if the Hollywood studios had not quickly reached the conclusion that the easiest way to meet the foreign challenge was to appropriate the services of the major talents responsible for it, it is unlikely that the vogue for European, and especially German, films would have lasted much beyond the mid-1920s.

Further confirmation of this are the lukewarm receptions given to such works as F. W. Murnau's *Nosferatu* (Germany, 1922) and Mauritz Stiller's *The Legend of Gosta Berling* (Sweden, 1924) when they made belated appearances on the American scene in 1929 and 1928, shortly after each director had achieved considerable critical success with an American-made film (*Sunrise* and *Hotel Imperial* respectively). The *New York Times* (NYT)(4 June 1929) was scornfully dismissive of *Nosferatu* as "a would-be spine chiller," while both it and *Variety* found the only attraction of Stiller's (no doubt severely truncated) film to be the chance to see a youthful Greta Garbo in an unfamiliar role. *Variety* seized the opportunity to make some uncomplimentary remarks about Swedish films in general: "About par for the average Swedish picture in costume, . . . a picture only for the sure-seat circle, . . . another case of a great literary effort lost between the scenario and the cutting room. . . . Photography is never good, a very general commentary on Swedish film product" (31 October 1928).[14]

These comments were made in sharp contrast to the widespread enthusiasm with which even the trade papers and popular magazines had greeted the earliest imported films. Then the emphasis had been on the difference between these and the American product and on what American filmmakers could, and should, learn from their European rivals. Summing up the first year (1921) in which foreign films made an impact on American screens, Frederick James Smith, writing for *Motion Picture Classic*, had no doubt whatever about their beneficial effect:

> At the outset of our comments upon the past twelve months
> we are going to venture a broad and sweeping prediction. The
> film season of 1920–21 will stand in the history of the American

cinema as representing the end of the glucose era of the photo-play. This breaking of old barriers was not due to native progres-siveness, we regret to report. Four or five productions of the stu-dios of our late enemies, the Germans, succeeded in toppling the film god of banality to the ground. Month by month, and year by year, we have commented upon the way American producers have avoided the actualities of life in gilding and sugarcoating actualities. The adolescent Pollyanna photoplay went on, how-ever. Producers kept on giving the public what they declared it wanted. They sought stories with a fine lack of literary discern-ment. They beheaded literary merit wherever it revealed itself. The result has been the erection of a stereotyped screen standard by which celluloid stories were ground out in routine fashion. True, certain directors broke away here and there, but, in the main, they sought the path of least resistance.

Then came the German photoplays. Violating almost all the carefully erected "laws" of our screen, they, nevertheless, succeeded in sweeping fashion. Suddenly American audiences discovered that they had been getting technical perfection in their native pictures, and an adroit skill of direction and lighting, all masking a platitudinous tale in which the breath of life was lacking. Moreover, they discovered that our vaunted standards of film acting were not so lofty, after all. The docile fan found that personality had too often been parading as histrionic merit, for the oncoming German photoplays revealed vivid and varied dra-matic skill.

We do not look upon these German invaders as perfect, by any means. But we believe they are going to break the way and lift the photoplay out of its rut. We look forward to a silent drama, which will possess, not only technical dexterity but literary and dramatic merit, good acting, a respect for the observer's intelli-gence, imagination in handling and a distinct style as various new personalities in direction assert themselves. We regret that the rending force had to come from abroad—but we are glad that it is here.[15]

Smith went on to list five German films (*Passion, The Cabinet of Dr. Caligari, Deception, The Golem,* and *Gypsy Blood*) among his ten best films of the year, with *Passion* at number one.

POLA NEGRI IN "PASSION"   FN 13-29

*L*ubitsch's epics attracted attention in America for their extravagant production values and their depiction of sex and sin in high places. Emil Jannings and Pola Negri in *Passion* and a typically lavish set from *Deception*.

L 316

As this list makes clear, despite the isolated success of such films as *Caligari* and *The Golem*, Murnau's *The Last Laugh*, and E. A. Dupont's *Variety* a few years later, it was Lubitsch's films that made the initial, and most consistent, impact on the American scene. Rather oddly (in view of the later development of his career), American taste proved to be almost exclusively for his epics and historical spectaculars, and not at all for the (often excellent) German-made comedies, and a brief survey of some of the early reviews of his films should convey something of the initial enthusiasm with which foreign films were greeted before the mood turned sour in the mid-1920s.

For the *NYT* (13 December 1920) *Passion* was "one of the pre-eminent motion pictures of the present cinematographic age," while the more pragmatic *Variety* (17 December 1920) greeted it as "100 per cent, good market stuff," praising acting, directing, photography, and editing. "This is great direction," it concluded, though inadvertently spoiling the effect of this acclaim by crediting the direction to one "Emil Subitch." For *Motion Picture Magazine* (February 1921) the film came as "a bolt from the blue" and its (unnamed) director was worthy of being called the "European Griffith."

With *Deception* a few months later, the *NYT* emphasized the virtues attributed to German films in general by Frederick James Smith in *Motion Picture Classic:* though technically the film was no better than many American productions, what distinguished it was that it offered "a real story told so that intelligent people can enjoy it." The review continued: "Rich, colorful, dramatic, 'Deception' is a photoplay for those who want genuine realism and can do without simpering heroines, pretty heroes, mechanical plots, and sentimental happy endings" (18 April 1921). *Variety* (22 April 1921) also welcomed the film, though it added the reservation that it was unlikely to do well outside the larger towns. *Moving Picture World* (30 April 1921) called it "powerful drama masterly handled" and ranked it high "as a work of art. It has color, form and the onward march of real drama." In its advice to distributors on "exploitation angles," the magazine recommended: "Drive on the fact that this is a story of Henry VIII made by the master hand which drew the story of du Barry in 'Passion.' That's the big selling point: not another 'Passion,' but another play by the same master of stagecraft; which is something else again."

Carmen (retitled *Gypsy Blood* for American release) was cut for U.S. distribution, and the *NYT* complained that once again the original name of an imported film had been changed "to suit a supposed domestic demand for a peppy title." Once more, however, "Mr. Lubitsch has made a motion picture that can hold the interest and excite the discriminating admiration of intelligent people." After lavishing praise on Pola Negri's performance, the review concluded: "But the director still remains the most important person connected with the production of a photoplay, so it is to Mr. Lubitsch that first and last praise must go. . . . His production as a whole is a vigorous, glowing, living thing that never lets the spectator's interest slacken for a moment" (9 May 1921). Though other reviews were not quite as ecstatic, *Variety* (13 May 1921) commended the raw sexuality of Negri's acting, and *Motion Picture Magazine* (August 1921), still in its initial phase of approval for foreign films, found it "extremely worth seeing."

As with European films overall, however, the virtual unanimity of praise did not last for very long.[16] *Sumurun (One Arabian Night)* attracted attention for Lubitsch's acting as much as for his direction. The *NYT* (3 October 1921), while acknowledging that Lubitsch was "the superior of most directors anywhere," found "the intensity of his acting" more effective in this particular case than his direction, which "compared with Mr. Lubitsch's other works . . . has serious shortcomings." *Variety* (7 October 1921) also singled out Lubitsch's acting as displaying "the fact that he is just as great an actor as he is a director," even going so far as to claim that "It is impossible to recall a screen performance that equals his in this picture." It felt, however, that the film was not being marketed aggressively enough, for, if properly exploited, "it would more than top the business 'Passion' attracted." An additional comment, that the film had been "titled and cut by Leslie Mason of the First National forces," is left without further embellishment, prompting speculation as to how many foreign films were shown in America in versions adapted, to a greater or lesser extent, to suit American tastes. Neither *Motion Picture Magazine* nor *Moving Picture World* had much to say in favor of the film, however, and the latter (1 October 1921) felt that Lubitsch "seriously overacted his own part."

Lubitsch's first feature *Eyes of the Mummy* attracted little attention when it opened in New York in August 1922. Neither *Moving Picture World* nor *Variety* so much as mentioned Lubitsch's name in connection with the film, and *Variety* (18 August 1922) was particularly scathing: "Another of those labored dime novel dramatic stories from the U.F.A. Plant. The situations are an affront to adult intelligence, but might make a thriller for juvenile audiences. The release of so many films of this quality is a sure index of the poverty of current release material."

Both *The Loves of Pharaoh* and *Montmartre* (originally *Die Flamme*), the last two films made by Lubitsch in Germany, were tampered with on their American release and given happy endings, an ominous and significant reversal of the very reason for which Lubitsch's films had originally been praised: their departure from the convention of "sentimental happy endings." As much as anything else, this confirms the overall trend already noticed by which European films, welcomed in 1921 and 1922 because of their difference from the native product, were very quickly being called upon to toe the line and adapt themselves to the expectations of an unsophisticated mass audience if they wanted to survive. *Variety*'s review of *The Loves of Pharaoh* (3 March 1922), besides suggesting that the film had been extensively cut, spent most of its space describing the production values and decided that, like most of "the elaborate foreign pictures brought to this side," the film was destined to be "a quick flash and a prompt die away at high box office admission." *Moving Picture World* (4 March 1921), on the other hand, was wildly enthusiastic, calling the film "a masterpiece of the spectacular in moving pictures," and claiming that "the gorgeousness, stupendousness and sheer artistry in direction baffle description." Unlike *Variety* it lavished praise on the "expert editing" of Randolph Bartlett and Julian Johnson, once again prompting the suspicion that many European films must have been shown to American audiences in a form significantly different from that in which they left their country of origin.[17]

In all but a few cases (such as *Eyes of the Mummy*) reviewers almost always emphasized the fact that each new film was a "Lubitsch" picture and that this guaranteed a certain standard of excellent direction, fine acting, elaborate production values, and superb entertainment. Given the widespread assumption that, until the implications of the auteur theory became generally accepted in the early 1960s, American audiences were blissfully ignorant of the very existence of film directors (with a few exceptions such as Griffith, von Stroheim, Orson Welles, and Alfred Hitchcock), it is surprising to find newspapers, trade papers, and magazines directed toward a popular and nonspecialist audience consistently drawing attention to the work of the director and very often discussing each new film in terms of an overall career with which the reader was expected to have at least a nodding acquaintance. Attributions such as "King Vidor's latest picture" or "the new film by Maurice Tourneur" were commonplace at the beginnings of reviews throughout the 1920s; and these two directors, along with James Cruze, Henry King, John Ford, Clarence Brown, Cecil B. De Mille, Rex Ingram, and William K. Howard (along with the more obvious Griffith, Chaplin, and

von Stroheim, and Lubitsch, Sjöström, and Murnau after their arrival in the United States) were clearly assumed to be recognizable names to the majority of readers. It seems very likely, in fact, that the 1920s saw a much higher awareness of the role and importance of the director, and of particular directorial identities, than any other time before the 1960s, and this too has its importance when considering the careers of those directors—most notably Lubitsch, Sjöström and Murnau—whose work in the United States received the most sustained attention from critics.

Maurice Tourneur, who was one of the earliest and most articulate spokesmen for the concept of the director as the true "creator" of a film, was quoted in an issue of *Moving Picture World* (vol. 36, p. 1689) for 1918 (the same issue, incidentally, that reported the death of the young—and recently "rediscovered"—director John Collins) as saying:

> The charge is made that to substitute the prominence of the director in place of the player is but to shift stars, and is therefore no cure for the star system evil. This is obviously not true. The director is the man who paints the dramatic picture. Give him a bigger canvas and recognition and he will do bigger things; but make him paint around the limitations of a certain player and you curb him, stunt his growth and prevent his development. Let us not forget that the director and the scenario writer must be the big factor of the photoplay's future.

In a letter to *Variety* (28 June 1923; 20), headed by the magazine "Tourneur Defends Director Control: Producer Against Pruning of One-Man Authority as Obstacle to Progress," Tourneur gave a detailed statement of his position:

> Dear Sir:—Under the heading "Inside Stuff on Pictures" in your June 7th issue you carry a story to the effect that the director—in the eyes of some big producers—is becoming of minor importance in the production of pictures. Here you have hit upon something that represents one of the greatest obstacles in the progress of the motion picture. Show me where a director has nothing to say about the story, the cast and the building of sets and I'll show you where a low average of quality is the result.
>
> As indicated by you, there have been instances where the story was purchased, the scenario prepared, and the players engaged and the sets built before the director was engaged. This is like buying the finest broadcloth obtainable, the best silks and

buttons money can purchase, designing and cutting the cloth and then calling in a tailor to make you up a suit of evening clothes.

In some instances, after huge sums were spent on story, players and sets, a director of doubtful talents has been entrusted with the fate of valuable property. This surely indicates that in the eyes of some, the direction of the picture is of the least importance.

Again it is like buying the finest goods, cutting the cloth and then turning it over to a cheap East Side tailor to make into a suit. No director of reputation and self-respect should allow someone to do the most essential part of his work for him before he is engaged. He must be allowed to carry the full responsibility of the direction of a picture. This responsibility includes a say in the selection and adaptation of the story, the selection of the cast and the building of the sets.

Wonderful pictures from large organizations are very much the exception. Big organizations can maintain a certain average quality of production, but they cannot create the real master-pieces that mark progress in the march of the photoplay. A review of the big successes of the industry clearly indicates these achievements have been the work of one man, the realization of ideals of an individual, the unmolested production in charge of a single person. The works of D. W. Griffith, the late George Loane Tucker, Marshall Neilan, Rex Ingram and others of prominence in the producing field which represent the leading factors in the advancement of pictures, are embodied in the execution of the creative ideas of an individual and not the dictatorial conglomeration of an organization.

Pictures by organizations such as you mention in your story are of average merit and will always be of average merit. Pictures of individuals will in the future, as in the past, prove the only productions that will attain the really big successes.

Organizations that consider the director last will never attain that success in productions that has marked "The Birth of a Nation," "The Miracle Man," "The Four Horsemen," and other similar achievements. The practice such as outlined in your story will keep the standard of product where it is today. It will never be conducive to progress. The business cannot stay where it is today. If it does not progress it will stagnate.

The director is to the motion picture what the artist is to the painting. You cannot tell the artist what to paint, what colors to use and what size the painting should be, and expect a masterpiece. The story, the players, the sets are to the director what the brush, palette and colors are to the artist. To dictate to the director what story, what players and what sets to use without giving him a voice in the matter is as silly as attempting to make similar demands of the artist and expect to achieve success.

Confirmation of this viewpoint from the critical side can be found in an important series of articles written for *Motion Picture Classic* in 1926 by Matthew Josephson, a young critic who proved particularly sympathetic to such foreign directors as Lubitsch and Murnau both before and after their arrival in the United States. One of these articles, discussing Lubitsch, Chaplin, von Stroheim, Vidor, Cruze and Murnau, was headed with the confident—if ungrammatical—claim that these directors "have developed a complete character of their own as an art," and his individual assessment of each of them displayed considerable sensitivity to the stylistic and thematic concerns that distinguished them. The magazine's overall heading to the article aptly summarizes its standpoint: "There is a Handful of Directors Who Have Developed a Complete Character of Their Own as an Art. The Discerning Eye has Caught the Quality of Their Work. They Have Created for Us the Illusion of Absolute Understanding and Sympathy with the Moods Expressed Thru Their Celluloid Figures." (Josephson's discussions of Lubitsch and Murnau can be found in Appendix A.)

By the time that the directors with whom this book is concerned had arrived in the United States, several factors were in operation that were to have a profound effect on the success or failure of their work there. Some of them—notably Lubitsch and Murnau and, to a lesser extent, Sjöström—were already well known through their European films and were confidently expected to make a considerable impact on the American scene. Others (like Christensen, Stiller, and Paul Leni) were virtually unknown and were brought over on the strength of a single film that had impressed an American studio, or even on the off chance that it would be safer to have them in America than as possible rivals abroad. They came into a cultural context which—though far from the director's paradise envisaged by Tourneur—had some critics at least who took the work of the director seriously and made a clear distinction between filmmakers with artistic aspirations and commercial hacks.

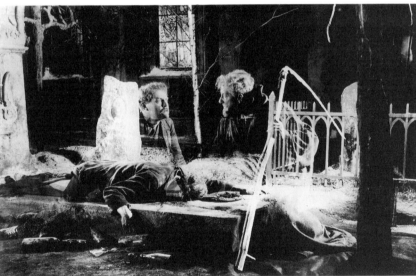

*O*ther directors intrigued audiences and (especially) critics with stylistic inno-
vation and experimentation. The superimposition from Murnau's *The Last Laugh* brings the viewer inside the old doorman's mind; the double exposure in Sjöström's *The Phantom Chariot* leads into the flashbacks that form the substance of the film.

Behind this, however, was an ominous tendency away from the initial welcome given to foreign films in the early 1920s toward a distinct hostility by the end of the decade. The racial and economic opposition of 1920 and 1922 had been counterbalanced by an awareness of the artistic values of the foreign films and a hope that they would offer a challenge to which American films would rise in terms of quality and imagination. By the late 1920s, however, those critics most in touch with the popular taste and mood had retreated into a complacent confidence in the overall superiority of American films and rejected the idea that imported works could offer anything of value either to filmmakers or audiences—with the very word "artistic" becoming a term of abuse for many of them. At almost exactly the time that the major influx of foreign directors took place, the popular mood had thus turned against the very qualities that had attracted interest to them to begin with and they were expected—if they wanted to survive—to adapt themselves to American norms rather than provide an alternative to them: one significant forerunner of this was the way in which Lubitsch's German films, after being initially praised for departing from the conventions of American popular entertainment, began to be fitted with happy endings in order to make them conform to popular taste after all. In much the same way as Americans as a whole decided that they would cope with alien influences simply by turning their backs on them and restricting further immigration, so American audiences and critics, after a brief flirtation lasting three or four years, moved to reject the seduction of imported films by returning to tried and tested American values: they had had enough of "those artistic German pieces" that weren't "worth a dime" either as entertainment or at the box office. The tragedy for many of the incoming directors was that they were caught up without warning in this unexpected switch of taste and had somehow to attempt to cope with it—along with all the other problems involved in working in an unfamiliar environment and with a production system totally different from that which they had been accustomed to at home. What is surprising, perhaps, is not that so many of them finally gave up in despair, but that they achieved the success they did and produced so many films of genuine and lasting quality.

Ernst Lubitsch

2

"In the Lubitsch Manner"

— o —

ommentators both at the time and since are in general agreement that, of all the foreign directors lured to America in the 1920s, Ernst Lubitsch was the most likely to adapt smoothly to his new environment and to the Hollywood system of filmmaking. He was already keenly interested in Hollywood techniques and production methods and had a shrewd commercial sense that enabled him to adapt his work to American tastes while retaining something exotic and daring in theme and style. He was also by far the best known in advance of his arrival, for several of his films had been widely seen and praised, even if, as with other German imports, their commercial success had not always matched the enthusiastic critical acclaim.[1]

His first visit to America, however, at the end of 1921 and at the invitation of Famous Players, which was interested in having him direct an epic spectacular along the lines of *Passion (Madame Dubarry)* and *Deception (Anna Boleyn)* coincided with one of the upsurges of American xenophobia, on both economic and irrationally nationalistic lines, as discussed in chapter 1, and Lubitsch sailed home after a few weeks, alleging that he had been subjected to constant harassment "by strange phone calls and other means."[2] In addition, Equity had officially objected to his presence and to his plans to film in Hollywood—despite the fact, as *Variety* plaintively pointed out, that a typical Lubitsch spectacle could have provided employment for thousands at a time of widespread economic hardship.

His return, less than a year later and at the specific invitation of Mary Pickford, had longer-lasting consequences and followed the move to the United States of Pola Negri, the actress with whom his earlier successes had been most closely associated. The project for which Pickford had selected him, *Dorothy Vernon of Haddon Hall,* proved unacceptable to Lubitsch and after considerable debate, *Rosita,* a story of the director's own choice, with a Spanish subject, was agreed upon. In much the same manner as F. W. Murnau's first American film, *Sunrise,* a few years later, the foreign—and, in this case, deliberately exotic—setting allowed Lubitsch breathing space in which to effect a transition between the characteristic aspects of his German films and the demands of Hollywood; his next American film, *The Marriage Circle* (1924), began the series of witty and cynically amoral comedies with which his name was to be almost exclusively associated for the remainder of his career. Until very recently, it was assumed by most film historians that these comedies were a radical new departure for the director, sparked by his professed admiration for Chaplin's *A Woman of Paris,* released the previous year. Recent scholarship, however, has drawn attention to the fact that Lubitsch had made a large number of comedies in Germany, many of them of considerable interest, and that there is a stronger overall continuity in the director's career than had been previously recognized; though there was definitely a change of direction with *The Marriage Circle,* it may have been due to Mauritz Stiller's 1920 *Erotikon* as much as *A Woman of Paris,* and many of Lubitsch's later comic techniques had already been developed in his German work.[3]

As it was the historical and Oriental films, however, that established Lubitsch's reputation in the United States, it is necessary to make some attempt to characterize them before concentrating, as I intend to do, on why Lubitsch the comedy director in Germany should still be relatively unknown, while Lubitsch the American comic director is almost universally admired. For the sake of convenience I will refer to the films by the American titles, and will categorize *Passion* and *Deception* as historical films, and *The Eyes of the Mummy, One Arabian Night,* and *The Loves of Pharaoh* as "Oriental" films; *Gypsy Blood,* which stands apart from both categories, will be treated separately.

Lubitsch's historical and Oriental films alike were rapturously acclaimed by American critics for qualities that were praised with almost ritualistic monotony in almost every review. They are history (or exotic fictions) "humanized" and "brought to life"; the handling of crowds and mass action is vivid, spectacular and masterly; the sets are overpoweringly gorgeous and authentic; the pictorial effects are sensational; the pacing and tempo are controlled with superb skill; the characters leap to life on the screen through the quality of the acting; and dramatic tension and tragic events are skillfully interwoven with comic relief. Some, like the *New York Times* reviewer of *Deception* (18 April 1921), were surprised to find films with such lightness of touch coming from Germany, which they associated with "methodical ponderosity"; others, like the *Moving Picture World*'s critic on the same film, welcomed it as "conclusive proof that humanity is on the mend, in spite of the political shortcomings of the present" (30 April 1921).

Not all the virtues claimed for these films by critics of the 1920s are immediately apparent to a viewer today. Certainly the crowd scenes, especially in *Passion* and *The Loves of Pharaoh*, are generally well handled, shot from a variety of angles and edited so as to integrate the actions of individuals into an irresistible surge of mass movement. (One shot near the beginning of *The Loves of Pharaoh*, in which a woman and her child advance up a flight of steps to plead for better treatment from Pharaoh, before being driven by soldiers down the steps in the midst of a confused crowd, anticipates—no doubt fortuitously—some of Eisenstein's methods in *Potemkin*.) In *One Arabian Night* elaborately formal groupings are used to comic effect, as when eunuchs standing in line move their heads in unison, or heads appear and disappear in choreographed motion above a row of battlements. Equally often, however, especially in the last-mentioned film, the crowd scenes are mechanical and contrived, while the battle in *The Loves of Pharaoh*, though intended to convey a sense of confusion, is simply meaninglessly chaotic.

The acting, especially when judged against the effects that Victor Sjöström and Stiller in Sweden, and Eric von Stroheim and Cecil B. DeMille in America were achieving at the same period, is rarely particularly subtle and gives little indication that Lubitsch was shortly to become a master of understatement and suggestive nuance. Putting aside Lubitsch's own atrociously overplayed role as the hunchback in *One Arabian Night*, the performance of Emil Jannings in both *Passion* and *Deception* can only be described as demonstrating "methodical ponderosity," while Negri in *Passion* is allowed to display a coy skittishness that even D. W. Griffith might have blanched at: on her first meeting with Louis XV, for example, she throws her arms around the monarch's neck, kisses him, and then jumps into his lap.

Contemporary praise for the authenticity of sets and costumes might charitably be attributed, as least in part, to North American vagueness as to the realities of life in societies distant from their own in space and time, and to a preference for simplified and familiar clichés when

presenting "exotic" settings and the activities of kings and queens. Some of the anachronisms may, like Mephisto's "cocktail-mixing" in Murnau's *Faust,* have been deliberately presented tongue-in-cheek: at a banquet near the beginning of *Deception* a young lady of decidedly 1920-ish appearance emerges from within a huge silver salver in the kind of image that was to become familiar in gangsters' reunions in the movies later in the decade; the women later in the film, however, whose loose shifts make them look like contemporary "flappers," are probably conforming to what was already a standard filmic convention that the clothes, hairstyle, and makeup of women in period films should not distance them too obviously from their counterparts in the audience.

In the Oriental films in particular, Lubitsch and his writers rely on a mass of visual and thematic clichés that make very little attempt to grapple with the sheer alienness of ninth-century Baghdad or Ancient Egypt. *One Arabian Night* offers deserts, camels, harems, slaves, eunuchs, sheiks, towers, arches, minarets, and dancing girls. *The Loves of Pharaoh* has decidedly eclectic costuming and a display of the all-purpose "Middle Eastern" architecture that became standard in costume films of this type in the wake of *Intolerance;* and *The Eyes of the Mummy,* though taking place in a contemporary setting, centers around the fulfillment of an age-old mummy's curse. In much the same way as these films appeal to standard literary and pictorial preconceptions about the nature of Oriental life and culture, they also proceed on the assumption "human nature is everywhere the same" and that the actions and motivations of characters in societies thousands of years distant from our own can be comfortably understood in terms of twentieth-century preoccupations (reduced, in their essentials, to romantic love and a vague popular sentiment that prefers a "just" ruler to a "tyrant").

Though these films are more important today for their impact at the time than for their intrinsic merits, they are interesting in that they confirm that Lubitsch was far more closely attuned to a Hollywood style and mentality, even before he set foot in the United States, than were Murnau or Sjöström. The formula of his historical epics is essentially that followed by Hollywood's "costume" films for the next half century; this goes beyond the superficial aspects of elaborate costumes and sets, high-powered acting, and eventful plots, to encompass a complete set of assumptions about the nature and causes of historical events. According to both Lubitsch and Hollywood, complex historical changes and upheavals are caused primarily by the actions of individuals, and these actions are motivated almost exclusively by sexual passion. Attention is focussed almost entirely on the ruling and upper classes, who are alone worthy of serious attention; the lower classes provide colorful background, and examples of picturesque poverty and discontent that often erupt into violence but can be handled by firm and/or appropriately compassionate action by the rulers. Apart from that, the main function of the lower classes (as in *Passion* and *The Loves of Pharaoh*) is to provide material for romances (invariably at first sight) across class barriers. A "democratic" perspective is maintained, however, by the revelation, either through the love theme or by carefully planted comedy "touches," that despite gorgeous costumes and awe-inspiring settings, these are essentially ordinary human beings just like ourselves, subject to the same joys and sorrows, the same strengths and weaknesses, the same follies and caprices, as we are. In fact, the characters, in the long run, are to be pitied rather than envied for their wealth and apparently limitless power: prisoners of their roles, they become either dehumanized monsters or are lonely, miserable, and dissatisfied, finding true happiness only in renouncing their privileges and choosing the single genuinely fulfilling experience that life can offer, a pure romantic love.

The attraction of the formula can be gauged from its sheer persistence across the decades and from the fact that it still exists—though often under a veneer of apparently sophisticated, no-nonsense realism—even today. It allows audience identification on several levels, particularly in the pattern that was to become characteristic of Hollywood cinema as a whole, whereby envy at the wealth, beauty, talent, and apparent freedom from conventional moral and social restraints of the people on the screen is interwoven with the realization that either they are no happier for all this than we in the audience are, or they find true happiness only in the simple basic pleasures and needs that are fundamental to "human nature" as a whole. Along with its emphasis on the universality of human experience, the historical epic in particular serves as a powerful reinforcement of the myth of progress, offering us, in the words of *Moving Picture World*'s review of *Deception*, "conclusive proof that humanity is on the mend": whatever the faults of the present, we have at least rid ourselves of the grosser defects presented, either comically (so that we can scorn them) or horrifically (so that we can congratulate ourselves on having escaped them) on the screen.

Though *Passion, Deception,* and *The Loves of Pharaoh* are set in eighteenth-century France, sixteenth-century England, and a vaguely "ancient" Egypt respectively, they share a common pattern and structure. In *Deception* the minor aristocrat Anne Boleyn deserts her true love Henry

Norris to flirt with, and then become the mistress of, Henry VIII, while the king's determination to marry her and make her his queen is the direct (and apparently sole) cause of the Reformation in England. The king's subjects take to the streets to protest against this action, but in vain. Anne soon suffers for her betrayal of Norris as she sees the king's attentions transferred to new favorites; a belated expression of remorse leads only to her own arrest on suspicion of infidelity. Norris attempts to help her but dies of wounds received in a tournament, and Anne is executed on the basis of false charges and trumped-up evidence.

Passion has a lower-class heroine who rises rapidly in society by exploiting her sexual attractiveness. She abandons her one true love, the student Armand, first for a Spanish envoy and then for the Comte Dubarry, before becoming the mistress of the king; but justifies this to herself on the grounds that her new status will allow her to assist Armand, which does in fact prove to be the case. After Jeanne's marriage to the Comte's brother, which acts as a facade for her involvement with the king, jealous rivals at court stir up popular unrest and the king's subjects take to the streets to protest against his scandalous behavior. The riots are suppressed, but resentment continues, merging with widespread popular discontent with social injustice and wretched living conditions. Further riots take place, with Armand now one of the leaders; Jeanne promises to use her influence with the king to help the suffering masses, but betrays Armand again. After the king's death and Jeanne's fall from favor, Armand leads an assault on the Bastille to release prisoners and Jeanne is arrested and sentenced to death. Armand relents and tries to save her life, but is himself shot as a traitor. Jeanne is dragged to the scaffold and executed on the guillotine. Though the cause-effect relationship is not as explicit as in *Deception*, the clear assumption is that the French Revolution, which is prefigured in the rioting at the end of the film, is the direct consequence of Jeanne's baleful influence over the weak-willed Louis XV.

In *The Loves of Pharaoh*, Ramphis, the son of an architect, is in love with the beautiful serving girl Theonis; but she attracts the attention of the Pharaoh who, in spite of his god-like status, is subject to human lusts and desires. She consents to marry him to save her true love's life, but the wedding leads to Pharaoh's breaking off a previously arranged marriage alliance with Ethiopia and causes war between the two countries. Pharaoh's subjects are reluctant to fight on such an arbitrary and personal motive, but are forced to obey. Pharaoh is apparently killed in battle and Theonis, as his

widow, is allowed to choose whom she will marry as his successor; naturally she opts for Ramphis, who has meanwhile helped bring about the victory of the Egyptian army. The population is overjoyed and enthusiastically approves her decision. Pharaoh is not dead, however, and returns to reclaim his throne; Ramphis offers to surrender the throne on condition that he and Theonis are allowed to live in humble happiness together, but the indignant crowd, incensed at being handed over to the tyrannical Pharaoh once more, stone the lovers to death. (The American version of the film provides a happy and more truly "democratic" ending by having the crowd refuse to acknowledge the claim of Pharaoh, who dies on the steps of his throne.)

In all three cases, "true love," which is associated with humble or moderately prosperous circumstances, is threatened either by female vanity and ambition or by the arbitrary exercise of kingly power. The ruler's lust leads directly to popular anger and resistance and a major political upheaval results, sometimes leading to the overthrow of the ruler or his dynasty. Though there is a possibility toward the end of the film that the original lovers might be reunited, this is always thwarted and, though both lovers die, it is the woman, whose beauty and/or ambition has set the whole chain of events in motion, who is most spectacularly punished. The audience, whether in the fledgling democracy of Germany immediately after the First World War or in the more self-confident United States, can take satisfaction in recognizing its freedom from the exercise of arbitrary and tyrannical power and in seeing the awesome consequences of the betrayal of a true, faithful, and modest love in pursuit of the vain chimera of riches and social status.[4]

Though it is hardly surprising that someone who had shown himself so fully attuned to what were becoming the standard formulas of American popular cinema should have moved so smoothly and surefootedly into the mainstream of Hollywood filmmaking, it may seem strange at first that Lubitsch's American successes were in comedy rather than in the genre of historical epic with which he was almost exclusively associated in American eyes. Only *Die Puppe (The Doll)* of his German comedies seems to have been publicly shown in America during the 1920s and at a time (1928) when the director was identified with a supposedly superior type of film-making: "[It] reminds one hardly at all of Lubitsch's later work," as one reviewer commented.[5] Yet, while these films are in many ways very different from the sophisticated comedies of manners that Lubitsch specialized in for the remainder of his career, they are not without their own interest, and they have closer links with his later work than has often been assumed.

○

A useful framework within which to look at Lubitsch's German and American comedies and the development from one to the other can be constructed from some suggestive remarks made by Russian formalist critic A. Piotrovskij in "Toward a Theory of Cine-Genres."[6] Writing in the 1920s, and thus concerned exclusively with silent comedy, Piotrovskij distinguishes between what he calls "cine-comedy" and "society comedy." Cine-comedy, which he associates primarily with Charles Chaplin, Harold Lloyd, and Buster Keaton, is a completely original form "alien to the higher genres of both literature and the theatre, but similar to the compositional elements of the oral folk tale and the show-booth slap-stick comedy. Furthermore, terminology borrowed from literature can only obscure the intrinsic originality of this extraordinary genre. It demands its own independent terminology."[7] Characteristics of this form of comedy include "semantic circularity (a reverse ordering of puns which end up at their starting points), gag-refrains, which sometimes are emphasized by an intertitle; the special, graduated build-up of gags." The central principle, however, is the combination of "comical actor-masks" and "the eccentric play of objects": "Here, perhaps more than anywhere else, the semantic identity of object and person on the screen is absolutely evident. The comical actor is automatized by the personification of objects; and the object-label, which monopolistically characterizes the comical mask (Chaplin's bowler hat, Lloyd's eyeglasses) emphasizes this identity." After arguing briefly that "the discovery of the laws of montage and photogeny" have led to the replacement of the earlier "external dynamics of movement (racing around, the chase)" by "the internal dynamics of juxtaposed pieces and the bold and unexpected alternation of shots," Piotrovskij concludes, giving Keaton as his main example, that "it is quite possible to produce cine-comedies using objects exclusively, or using an actor who plays the role of an indifferent and passive guide through a wax museum full of surprises."[8]

Society-comedy by contrast, is more literary and theatrical, "burdened with 'character' and psychology" and hindered by "knots of intrigue."[9] Though this is in complete contrast to the spirit of cine-comedy, Piotrovskij perceptively notes that a "hybrid genre" is emerging in which "American comedy of the pure type may sometimes, through compromise, be combined with forms of the traditional theatrical comedy which are fundamentally alien to it," and, interestingly enough, he uses an example of this hybrid Lubitsch's *Die Austernprinzessin (The Oyster Princess)*, claiming that "in terms of the treatment of the secondary characters and the use of details, this is a cine comedy; however, in terms of the basic love intrigue, it is a society comedy" (and thus suffers from certain flaws).[10]

Looking at Lubitsch's comedies from this perspective it is possible to see a clear movement from pure cine-comedy in the early German films to a "hybrid" form in the later ones and then, in the American silent comedies, a development of the society-comedy in a direction that resulted in making it entirely "cinematic." Lubitsch thus provided an essential bridge between silent comedy and early sound comedy that Keaton, Chaplin, and Lloyd, more firmly rooted in pure cine-comedy, were unable, for all their genius, to create for themselves without a major transformation (and even abandonment) of the typical elements of their earlier work. In other words, and although I will not be examining Lubitsch's sound films, Lubitsch, together with such still neglected directors of the period as Harry D'Abbadie D'Arrast and Mal St. Clair, had developed by the end of the 1920s a form of film comedy that could easily incorporate the inclusion of sound and yet was not stagily "theatrical," thus contradicting the assumption of critics like Piotrovskij that a radical move away from a reliance on "the comical actor-mask" and "the extravagant world of objects" would totally destroy comedy as a cinematic form.

Though not all of Lubitsch's German comedies are known to survive today,[11] it is possible to follow the main outline of this development quite easily. He began his film career as an actor, working in music halls and then undergoing seven crucial and formative years as a member of Max Reinhardt's theater company. After acting in films directed by others, he began both to direct and act in his own comedies, often working from scripts by Hans Kraly, who was to become a regular collaborator and who accompanied him to America, where their association ended as a result of Kraly's affair with Lubitsch's wife. One of the earliest of these films, *Schuhpalast Pinkus* (*Shoe Salon Pinkus*, 1916), works primarily in terms of "gag-refrains" and "the comical actor-mask," though both are employed in a relatively unsubtle fashion. One running gag involves the young hero, Sally Pinkus (played by Lubitsch), being rebuked by his father or his boss for flirting with an attractive woman, after which the older man immediately starts to force his own attentions on her. Though most of the acting and the settings are relatively naturalistic, Lubitsch's own performance, full of excessive winking, grimacing, and doubling up with laughter at the success of one of his ruses, and showing a constant awareness of and playing to the camera (at one stage he holds an object directly in front of the camera so that we can fully understand its significance, then winks at us), seems at first merely grotesque. It could be, however, that, aware that he lacked the sort of clearly defined screen personality that was being developed by the great American comedians, Lubitsch was clumsily attempting to single out Sally as the center of attention and thus provide the equivalent of Piotrovskij's "mask." A slightly later film, *Das Fidele Gefängnis* (1918), though this time without Lubitsch's own presence on the screen, displays the same uncertainties, with characters sometimes playing directly to camera and signaling the desired response from the audience, and with a similar mixture of obviously grotesque characters (a Chester Conklin–like prison guard) and relatively normal ones.

By this time, however, Lubitsch had begun to construct some of his comedies around a particular and constantly recurring screen character, the actress Ossi Oswalda, usually identified simply as "Ossi" on the screen. She appeared in more than a dozen of his films, including three of his most interesting comedies, *Die Austernprinzessin* (*The Oyster Princess*, 1919), *Die Puppe* (*The Doll*, 1919) and *Ich Möchte Kein Mann Sein!* (*I Wouldn't Want to Be a Man!* 1920), all three of them displaying the "hybrid" qualities identified by Piotrovskij. Much of *Die Austernprinzessin* is built around the comedy of masks, objects, and repetition: the heroine's capitalist father with his huge, ever-present cigar and heavily made-up, at times almost ape-like features, is sheer caricature, while the heroine consistently expresses her feelings by means of violent physical action, throwing a tantrum and wrecking her room until her father agrees to provide an aristocratic husband for her, and later engaging in a boxing match with her friends to decide who is most worthy of the prince's favors. A recurrent visual gag in the film, which is linked to the fondness for both visual and thematic symmetry that Lubitsch displayed throughout his career, centers around visual anticlimax or disproportion: in the oversized, elaborate decor of his home, the father dictates a letter that is taken down, not by one typist, but by a whole bevy of them, clattering away in unison; when the prince's servant, standing in for his master, arrives at the mansion, we see an apparently endless procession of horses and then finally the tiny carriage that they are drawing along; the wedding dinner is staffed by an army of servants, each of whom performs only one trivial function before yielding to the next; the prince and his friends, exhausted after a night's drinking, flop down in choreographed sequence on to a series of park benches. In a similar vein, scenes of the heroine taking a bath, with the assistance of dozens of servants, are intercut with shots of the prince's servant following out the designs on the floor of the

$\mathcal{T}$*he Oyster Princess* offers an early example of Lubitsch's mockery of social forms and conventions, as in this highly formalized dinner scene.

huge anteroom and jumping from one point to another as if playing hop-scotch; and when the daughter attempts to secure her father's attention by snatching the newspaper out of his hand, he proceeds imperturbably to pro-duce a replacement from an apparently endless source behind him.

Though there is little of the conscious playing to the camera of the earlier comedies, Lubitsch occasionally reminds us of its presence, either by changing the screen shape, as in the sequence of the "fox-trot epidemic" where three layers of dancing feet are presented in horizontal strips, or by having the prince dispose of the clutter in his room by the simple expedient of throwing everything just out of camera range. These too can be seen as characteristic devices of cine-comedy (most notably in Keaton's work), but, as Piotrovskij observes, they are combined with a love intrigue that is based on the traditional theatrical premises of father-daughter conflict,

mistaken identity, and marriage of lovers from different social backgrounds. The film also offers an early example of the "Ruritanian" setting
that Lubitsch was to make characteristically his own, with its blending of
the costumes, ritual, and social hierarchy of Central Europe at the turn of
the century, and the fads and paraphernalia of the contemporary world (in
this instance, the fox-trot).

   Die Puppe, in many respects the strangest of all Lubitsch's extant
comedies, is built around an interaction of the theatrical and the real, the
artificial and the lifelike, that the director was to explore, from a different
perspective, over twenty years later in *To Be or Not to Be.* Despite its theatrical origins in an operetta, it can be seen primarily as a cine-comedy in
its emphasis on the artificiality of its own devices and use of objects. It
begins with Lubitsch himself setting up a small-scale set, after which the
characters enter into a larger, but still obviously artificial, version of this:
the scene then changes to an apparently "realistic" movie set, yet even here
cardboard clouds can be drawn aside to reveal a painted sun. The wealthy
hero, ordered by his uncle to marry and attempting (like Keaton in *Seven
Chances*) to escape the attentions of a horde of fortune-hunting women, first
tries to conceal himself among the scenery of the set, then takes refuge in a
monastery where the worldly monks advise him to conciliate his uncle and
obtain his inheritance by "marrying" a life-sized doll. Fortunately a nearby
toy maker happens to specialize in creating these, though, as the result of an
accident whereby the owner's son has broken the arm of one of the dolls, his
older sister has offered to stand in for it to conceal the damage for the time
being. The hero of course buys this "doll" and sets off home in a carriage
drawn by pantomime horses; meanwhile his uncle has fallen ill and his relatives are squabbling about his inheritance at the bedside: an elaborate
split-screen effect shows sixteen different images here, each of a circle with
a pair of rapidly moving lips inside.

   When the toy maker discovers the substitution, his hair first stands
on end then instantly turns grey; he pursues his son in a typical silent-
comedy chase full of hair's breadth escapes and the destruction of objects,
until the child (who has earlier shown himself prone to bouts of formally
phrased existential despair) evades him by pretending to commit suicide.
The hero marries the "doll" at a ceremony at which she snatches food and
drink while his attention is elsewhere, receives his inheritance, and returns
to the monastery, where more celebrations take place. That night the girl
tries to reveal her true identity to him, but he refuses to believe her until she
shows the genuinely "feminine" response of being frightened by a mouse.

Later the lovers are in a park complete with painted moon when the toy maker, who has been carried off into the air by balloon, is shot down by his son, and falls at their feet; explanations and reconciliation follow and the father's hair returns to its normal condition. In addition to the interplay between appearance and reality, from the viewpoint both of the characters and of the audience, the film makes a few gestures towards exploiting the obvious potentials of the situation for sexual innuendo, as when the hero attempts to undress the "doll" after purchasing her, and she has to devise a credible means of deterring him.

Ich Möchte Kein Mann Sein! is the most interesting of the three "Ossi" films, partly for its "hybrid" character and partly for its increasingly bold exploration of sexual themes. Ossi, who plays a role rather similar to that of the heroine of Die Austernprinzessin, rich, spoiled, pert, and bad tempered (she too hurls her belongings around the room when her wishes are thwarted), is both a comic mask and an example of rudimentary psychological development: like Chaplin and Lloyd, she has both physical and temperamental characteristics that seem to have been associated with her from film to film, but, unlike them, she changes significantly as a result of the action of the film.[12] There are some now familiar Lubitsch gags, as when Ossi's governess tries to combat her unladylike tendencies by taking her cigarettes away from her, then tries a puff herself—and then another and another; but most of the humor centers around the confusions and ambiguities that result from Ossi's disguising herself as a man in order to evade the restrictions that limit her behavior as a woman. When she buys a man's evening suit, the shop assistants compete with each other to measure her and end by dividing the task between them; then, like Catherine in Jules and Jim, she tests the effectiveness of her costume by asking a man in the street for a light. Her disguise, however, causes her unexpected problems: she is made to give up her seat to a woman on the Metro, and at a dance hall she is jostled around and elbowed aside in the rush for partners and is then herself mobbed by a crowd of eager women. Here she encounters the tutor who had earlier been appointed by her uncle in a vain attempt to teach her manners, though of course he fails to recognize her; they drink and smoke cigars together and when Ossi begins to feel sick, she has to resolve the dilemma of which toilet she should take refuge in. After a few more drinks the two begin to embrace and kiss drunkenly in a curiously ambiguous fashion which is intensified when they enter a cab and start to kiss each other on the mouth rather than simply on the cheek. Both then fall asleep and the cab driver mistakenly delivers them to the wrong addresses, where the tutor

collapses into Ossi's bed; in the morning, Ossi, still in her male costume, returns home and meets the tutor in the hallway. He discovers her true identity only when he follows her to her room and finds her half undressed, and the film ends with a more conventional embrace than those of the previous night.

Though the film makes no attempt to challenge conventional sexual roles and offers no particularly profound comment on their nature and effect, it is a breezy, cheerful, and good-humored work which suggests that Ossi Oswalda may well have merited the title "the German Mary Pickford" applied to her at the time. It remains essentially a "gag" comedy, working multiple variations on the same basic theme and presenting these according to the methods of "the show booth slap-stick comedy," and combines these with a clear plot structure that brings the character to a better understanding of herself and her real needs and potentials. Yet a non-"Ossi" comedy made immediately after this, *Kohlhiessels Töchter* (*Kohlhiessel's Daughters,* 1920) returns to the crude overemphasis, overacting, and nudging of the audience that Lubitsch seemed by this period to have left behind him for good. Though Henny Porten's performance in the dual role of the "good" daughter Gretel and her loutish older sister Liesel is generally quite effective and creates two genuinely different characters, both physically and temperamentally, the handling of the "Taming of the Shrew" theme at the center of the film suggests, as most treatments of the subject do, that it is the responsibility of the woman to change and become the perfect housewife (servile, devoted, and submissive), after which the husband (previously shown to be gross and insensitive) will condescend to accept her. Lubitsch's next comedy, *Romeo und Julia im Schnee* (*Romeo and Juliet in the Snow,* 1920) is an updated version of Shakespeare that manages to parody most of the highlights of the play—the masked ball, the balcony scene, and the lovers' suicide—in an appropriately slapstick form. The feuding families take their case to court, each offering the judge a sausage as a bribe, but as the sausages are the same weight he decides in favor of neither of them. The duels and combats between the families take the form of snowball fights, and Romeo signals his interest in Julia by throwing a snowball at her. Julia's family are determined that she should marry the local idiot; Romeo succeeds in making him drunk, then takes his place in disguise at the village's fancy dress ball; his rival returns at an inopportune moment, however, forcing Romeo to jump off the balcony on which he had been wooing Julia. Later, after some unsuccessful attempts, Romeo manages to climb into Julia's bedroom by means of a ladder, but is nearly discovered there and has

*T*he often bizarre décor of *Die Bergkatze* allows Lubitsch to give physical expression to the metaphor of the sexual chase that dominates both his German and American comedies.

to hide under the bed. Finally, driven to despair by the parents' intransigence, the lovers ask the local chemist for "poison for two"; unknown to them, he supplies them with sugared water and adds kindly that they can pay him later. They retreat to a barn to drink the poison, which Romeo finds so tasty that he scarcely leaves enough for Julia; the distraught parents, finding their suicide note, rush to the barn and the lovers wait until the mutual recriminations and remorse have ended in reconciliation before demonstrating that they are not dead after all. The grotesque and parodic elements in the film are handled imaginatively and with considerable visual flair, successfully mediating between an explicitly theatrical subject and the forms and techniques appropriate to visual comedy, and the rapturous reception accorded the film at the 1999 Bologna *Il Cinema Ritrovato* festival

suggests that, even if it lacks the sophistication and refinement typical of Lubitsch's later work, it remains thoroughly entertaining and enjoyable.

The last of Lubitsch's German comedies, *Die Bergkatze* (*The Mountain Cat,* 1921), is, like *Die Puppe,* a bizarre and unexpected work that pushes to an extreme the interest that Lubitsch had shown in some earlier films in experimenting with screen shapes and sizes. In fact the film is virtually a compendium of these devices, many of them interestingly adapted to the composition and nature of the action on the screen. Action that is primarily horizontal or vertical in nature is often isolated by means of blacking out all but the relevant portion of the image, while diagonal and circular effects are similarly emphasized. Besides this, however, the image on the screen can be that of an arch, an oval, a hexagon, or a whole variety of shapes that resemble fragments of a jigsaw puzzle; at times too the corners or the top and bottom of the screen are blacked out in jagged, saw-like shapes. A couple of the more daring effects simply isolate the main characters, in almost abstract geometric patterns, and leave the remainder of the screen black. One example of this has the hero, Lieutenant Alexis, flanked by soldiers in this fashion:

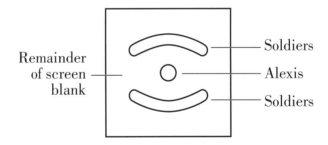

In addition, the sets of the film, especially those of the fort, are dominated by elaborate, often bizarre geometric shapes that have no function, apparently, other than to call attention to themselves.

The characters and events of the film both derive from some of the earlier comedies and interestingly anticipate some of Lubitsch's American work. The comic-opera military setting was one that he was to find particularly congenial in his early sound films, and the opening of this film, both in the nature of its hero and in its exuberant sexual innuendo, looks forward to the roles played a decade later by Maurice Chevalier. Lieutenant Alexis, summoned to a new posting, leaves behind him a town full of sorrowing

women, who mob him in an attempt to make him stay. With the clear implication that he has been to bed with all of them, Alexis explains apologeti-
cally, "I did what I could," but now it is time to obey orders and move on. In
a variation of a joke from *Die Puppe*, the women disperse only when a horde
of mice are released among them and Alexis is able to escape, passing, as
he leaves, a group of little girls who wave and call out, "Goodbye, Papa!"

Once the main story of the film gets under way, however, Lubitsch
reverts to the primarily physical comedy that characterized his previous
films. On his way to the fort, Alexis is ambushed by a band of robbers and
stripped of all his clothes except his shirt and long underwear; on a later
journey he is waylaid again, and this time the robber chief wants to take the
underwear too, though he is dissuaded by his daughter Rischka (played by
Negri). She makes her interest in Alexis clear when she returns to their
hideout and uses his trousers to frame a photo of him obtained during the
earlier robbery. Various farcical encounters between the soldiers in the fort
and the robbers take place, and during one of the robbers' attacks Rischka
discovers that Alexis is engaged to the commandant's daughter; she
expresses her displeasure by wrecking the bridal suite and throwing even
the bed out of the room, then douses herself in her rival's perfume. Alexis
discovers her and pursues her through the fort; though he is attracted to her,
he is forced to put her under arrest and she escapes after overpowering the
commandant's daughter. After this, the plot moves in a rather unexpected
direction, separating rather than uniting Alexis and Rischka; the latter
(after an extraordinary dream sequence in which Alexis literally gives her
his heart and she begins to eat it, to the accompaniment of music played by
dancing snowmen) is forced by her father to marry the weakest and most
pathetic of the robber band. Her husband, following the example of Liesel's
husband in *Kohlhiessels Töchter* "tames" her by dragging her through the
snow; but she has a final encounter with Alexis who, on his way to his wedding, gets so drunk that he falls out of his carriage into Rischka's arms and
they roll down a snowbank together into a nearby inn. Despite this, Alexis
goes back to his bride and Rischka to her husband who, in a grotesque
scene rather reminiscent of an episode in Chaplin's contemporaneous
A Dog's Life, has been weeping so copiously that his tears have melted the
snow outside and formed the beginnings of a river.

The grotesqueness of much of this humor, though a far cry from a
film like *Trouble in Paradise*, is perfectly in the spirit of the mainstream of
cine-comedy of the pre-1920 period; significantly, however, when put in the
context of Lubitsch's surviving German comedies, it shows the director

experimenting with a wide variety of techniques and comic devices and thus giving himself, by the time he came to America, a flexibility and adaptability that allowed him to establish himself very quickly as one of the leading directors of comedy in Hollywood. Some of these experiments proved to be virtually dead ends: split-screen effects and variable screen shapes, though used intermittently by directors like Keaton and Griffith, never became part of the mainstream of Hollywood film language, and Lubitsch made little attempt to persist with these after *Die Bergkatze.* On the other hand, his integration of the visual and physical humor of silent comedy with the conventions of plot and characterization associated primarily with theater (in contrast to Chaplin, Keaton, and Lloyd, who rarely used stage dramas as a source for their own work, and, when they did, altered them radically to suit their own comic methods) enabled him to develop in America a new style of comedy that was instantly recognized as distinctive and proved itself capable of adjusting to sound with little disruption of its basic appeal. The clearest pointers to this style of comedy are in the increasingly bold sexual innuendoes, both visual and verbal, of the later German comedies, which were soon to manifest themselves as central to what critics came to call—endlessly—the Lubitsch "touch."[13]

Film historians, taking their cue both from Pickford's supposed vehement dislike of *Rosita* and from the difficulty of seeing the film itself (which Pickford, who owned the rights, withheld from public showing for several decades), have taken it for granted that the film was both an artistic and a commercial failure and that it is therefore of little interest. It is surprising, then, in view of the widely held belief in Pickford's hostility to Lubitsch, to discover *Variety* reporting, as late as 6 August 1924, that Lubitsch had been signed to direct her next film, though the project never actually materialized. At any rate, *Rosita* is interesting both for itself and as an opportunity for Lubitsch to accustom himself to American production methods while handling familiar and tractable material: the film is virtually a compendium of themes from his German work, bringing together aspects of both the epics and the comedies, and having particularly close affinities to one of his earlier successes with Negri, *Gypsy Blood* (German title *Carmen,* 1918).

Like *Gypsy Blood, Rosita* is a costume film set in Spain, with a lower-class heroine whose sexual attractiveness brings her into potentially destructive contact with those in a higher rank of society. A major difference, however, is that Negri's Carmen revels in her exploitation of the susceptible males around her, taunting, humiliating, and betraying them, while

*M*ary Pickford's role in *Rosita* is probably intended to recall Pola Negri in
Lubitsch's earlier *Carmen*.

Pickford's *Rosita*, in conformity with the star's established screen image, is embarrassed by the king's interest in her, resists his advances, and ends reunited with her one true love—a move which involves a considerable rise in social status but which is "merited" by her faithfulness. In both cases, however, the overall moral is consistent with that of the larger-scale historical epics: Carmen's betrayal of the staunchly faithful Don José in favor of richer and more powerful lovers is punished by her death at his hands and his own subsequent suicide; while the violence constantly threatened throughout *Rosita* is averted by the heroine's unswerving loyalty (together with the shrewd worldliness of the queen, a figure who anticipates some of Lubitsch's later women in the patient scheming by which she contrives to thwart her husband's attempts at infidelity and win him back).

Both heroines sing and dance for their living, but for different reasons and with different results: Carmen's dancing is deliberately sexually provocative and attains its desired effects; while Rosita's performances are intended to earn a living for herself and her family, and her songs express her personal feelings and emotions—anger at the king, in one case, for distracting her audience before they have handed over their money, and later an overt song of defiance and revolt when she believes that the king has double-crossed her and has caused her lover's death. In both films sexual interest is presented in a blatantly physical manner, with Carmen (like Jeanne in *Passion*) jumping into a prison guard's lap in order to distract him from noticing Don José's escape, and an excited male in each film chasing the heroine around a room in an attempt to embrace her. *Rosita* also incorporates some of the spectacular visual effects and elaborate sets for which Lubitsch's historical films had been noted, as well as looking both backward and forward in terms of his comic methods: the heroine's unsophisticated family misuse the expensive gifts offered her by her royal admirer, while the upper classes display a worldly tolerance of infidelity and adultery and the film as a whole appears to endorse, in tongue-in-cheek manner, their acceptance of hypocrisy and corruption as ineradicable facts of life.

Whatever Pickford may have come to think of the film later on, it was greeted with virtually unanimous ecstasy by the leading reviewers of the time. For *Variety*, *Rosita* presented "a Mary Pickford different and greater than at any time in her screen career," to such an extent that she even surpassed her work in *Stella Maris*, "the greatest picture she ever made until the current feature." The *New York Times* found it "one of the most charming productions in which Miss Pickford has appeared"; while *Moving Picture World* agreed that "it certainly will take rank as among her best" and later, when covering the West Coast opening, quoted the *Los Angeles Times* as noting that "Miss Pickford herself really has outdone anything she has previously achieved." Lubitsch came in for his share of the general approbation: for *Moving Picture World* he "fully lives up to his reputation as being one of the world's leading directors" and had transferred the virtues of his German films—handling of actors, control of mass action, artistic composition, spectacular sets and striking photography—fully intact to an American production. *Variety* ended its rave review with the assurance that "to Lubitsch full credit must be given. He seemingly inspired his cast and compelled them to give greater performances most people thought beyond them *[sic]*, and his work in this production is a revelation as to what the picture industry may expect from foreign directors when they are given the material to work with that American directors have."[14]

Even though *Variety* reported a few months later (14 February 1924) that the film (like the subsequent *The Marriage Circle*) was performing less well than had been expected at the box office, and though the three-year, three picture contract with Pickford that was announced by Motion Picture World on 8 September 1923 to coincide with the opening of *Rosita* was never fulfilled, there is no reason to accept a purely retrospective adverse judgment on the film. To all intents and purposes it achieved its aim of establishing Lubitsch as a credible force on the American film scene and did this in a manner that provided a recognizable link with his past successes while introducing the tone of tolerant, amused, idly cynical acceptance of human sexual foibles and self-deceptions that was soon to become his trademark.[15]

It might once again appear paradoxical that, while Lubitsch was to make his reputation in America as a chronicler, and perhaps even open advocate, of unconventional sexual behavior, the German costume films that had brought him to public acceptance espouse, for all their surface titillation and apparent daring, a rigidly conventional moralism that was already perfectly in accordance with the guidelines to be established by the Production Code in the 1930s—guidelines which the Lubitsch of that later period delighted in circumventing and subverting. The costume films recommend sexual fidelity, both before and within marriage, and modest financial and social aspirations; those characters, especially women, who are promiscuous, unfaithful, greedy, and ambitious, are severely punished, usually by death, and generally drag an innocent and loyal male victim to destruction with them. It was only in such comedies as *Ich Möchte Kein Mann Sein!* and *Die Bergkatze* (unknown, of course, in America) that he

began the tentative exploration of the themes of sexual ambiguity and sexual role-playing that came to be associated indelibly with his work, and hinted at a more tolerant attitude toward unconventional and "immoral" lifestyles.

Critics who see the costume films as central to Lubitsch's career in Germany are understandably struck by the apparent "change" in his work from *The Marriage Circle* onward and, searching around to account for it, they generally seize on his acknowledged admiration for Chaplin's *A Woman of Paris* (released in 1923) to explain both his "new" themes and the style of visual implication and suggestion that conveyed them. Without denying that Chaplin's film certainly had some influence on Lubitsch, a search for "outside" sources should also take into account Mauritz Stiller's 1920 *Erotikon* (discussed more fully in chapter 5), which impressed and influenced both Chaplin and Lubitsch. *Erotikon* is witty, stylish, elegant and, for its period, sexually daring; it handles the subject of marital infidelity in a tolerant and totally uncondemnatory manner, leaving us with a doubly adulterous ménage at the end, and it presents its sexual themes by means of visual ellipsis and implication in a style that Lubitsch was to develop and build on. Along with this, however, it should be recognized that Lubitsch already had been proceeding in much the same direction in his German comedies; Chaplin's and Stiller's films may have made clearer to him exactly what it was that he wanted to do, but they did not cause the radical shift from "epic" to "intimate" and from "dramatic" to "comic" films that too many film historians have assumed.

Lubitsch is also conventionally credited with introducing a European sophistication into American cinema, providing a tolerant and worldly alternative to what Robert Carringer and Barry Sabath call "the more absolutist moral strictures of the American tradition, which typically hold that marriage is inviolate, sex outside of marriage is sinful, adultery is reprehensible regardless of the circumstances, and transgressors ought to suffer proper punishment for their misdeeds."[16] (Amusingly enough, as has just been noted, this could serve as a perfect summary of the moral outlook of Lubitsch's German epics.) However true it may be that American cinema has always paid lipservice to these values (while gaining, of course, its mass popularity by allowing them to be enticingly threatened or defied in the course of the film, before the ending re-establishes them), it is misleading to see Lubitsch's 1920s comedies as being to any great extent outside the mainstream of acceptable thinking, or even practice, where sexual behavior was concerned—in the larger cities at any rate; the rural audience, still a major factor at the box office, remained more easily shocked by, and antagonistic to, the "New Morality," which perhaps accounts for the fact that the financial returns for Lubitsch's silent comedies rarely matched up to the ecstatic critical response. Whereas a Cecil B. DeMille knew exactly just how far to exploit the fashionable themes of the day before discarding them at the end of the film and retreating to a conventional moral standpoint, Lubitsch's challenge to traditional sexual mores was pushed much closer to its logical conclusion and was thus more genuinely subversive.[17] At the same time, the lightness of touch on the surface of the films prevented them from being perceived as directly threatening to established values and allowed them a measure of commercial success denied to the more intractable Murnau or Sjöström.

Historians of the 1920s such as William E. Leuchtenberg in *The Perils of Prosperity, 1914–32* and Lary May in *Screening Out the Past* stress the sexual and moral "revolution" that followed the achievement of women's suffrage in 1920 and the growth of a strong feminist movement in the period. The increased freedom and independence of women, socially, sexually, and financially, combined with the growing interest, among intellectuals at least, in Freudian psychology and behaviorism to challenge traditional concepts of "human nature" and the moral, social, and political conclusions to be drawn from these. One immediate and much remarked-upon consequence was a sharp increase in the divorce rate and a questioning of accepted ideas about the importance of marriage and the family as the central pillars of the social structure. The demand for increased sexual freedom formed part of a much more widespread attack—often openly contemptuous and scornful—on "bourgeois" values as a whole, and a rejection of the Puritan, capitalist heritage that provided the basis for these. The materialistic outlook of the period, fostered by growing industrial prosperity, advertising, and mass production of consumer goods, was constantly, in a favorite word of the period, "debunked" by intellectuals, while patriotism, conformity, and religion came to be used as terms of opprobrium by them.

In due course, after an initial period of disorientation, the defenders of traditional morality fought back strongly, securing some revenge in the imposition of prohibition and increased control over those elements in the media, and especially in the cinema, that were perceived as doing most to popularize and make attractive the new, allegedly nihilistic, ideas. Some apparent justification for this was given by the way in which popular magazines and tabloids, together with a stream of films with such provocative titles as *Why Change Your Wife? Is Matrimony a Failure? Is Divorce a Failure? Why Get Married?* and *Why Men Leave Home*, had trivialized and

sensationalized what had begun as a serious and intellectually honest inves-
tigation, thus giving moralists an opportunity to avoid facing up to the real
challenge that these ideas presented to their beliefs. Suppression of their
more lurid and debased manifestations could be used to discourage subversive thinking of any kind and so bring about the restoration of a slightly
modified version of the status quo.

Before this reaction had fully run its course, however, Lubitsch had
been able to lay the groundwork for the style of filmmaking that was to be
his trademark for the remainder of his career: elliptical, allusive, suggestive, subversive of conventional concepts of chastity and sexual fidelity, yet
challenging these by implication rather than head-on, and in such a toler-
antly good-humored manner that audiences were as much inclined to laugh
as to feel shocked. The tone established by *The Marriage Circle* in 1924,
and carried over, in its essence, into all his most successful films thereafter,
is Lubitsch's own, yet his work is very close in its substance to the intense
and deliberately provocative essays in the symposium *Our Changing
Morality* (1930) in which Bertand Russell and others argued in favor of
moral relativity rather than moral absolutism and claimed that current sexual mores were outmoded, and marriage and the family obsolete.

The subjects covered by these essays include marriage, divorce,
sexual freedom, the status of women, the validity of moral absolutes, the
double standard, prostitution, female genius, the intellectual ability of
women, and sexual stereotyping in which women are defined primarily in
their relationship to men; not only do they all strike a resoundingly contemporary note, even today, but almost all of them are topics touched on in
Lubitsch's work. Though he avoided the kind of directness found in
Beatrice M. Hinkle's "Women and the New Morality," it is probably fair to
say that his genius lay in making subversive ideas of this kind accessible,
and even acceptable, to a mass audience that would almost certainly reject
them in their blunter form, and in doing so without compromising utterly
the essence of the challenge that they presented. Hinkle states that
"women are demanding a reality in their relations with men that heretofore
has been lacking, and they refuse longer to cater to the traditional notions
of them created by men, in which their true feelings and personalities were
disregarded and denied. This is the first result of the New Morality."[18] The
heroines of Lubitsch's films, in their various ways, make much the same
demand.

Lubitsch had been officially under contract to Famous Players
when he made *Rosita*, but the contract was cancelled by mutual agreement

in June 1923. He then signed a four-year agreement with Warner Brothers that gave him (as was also to happen with Murnau for *Sunrise*) an unusual degree of creative autonomy, including the right to select his own stories, to work with writers and technicians of his own choice, and to control both shooting and editing without studio interference. On these terms he made five films for Warners over the next three years, as well as one, *Forbidden Paradise*, on loan to Paramount. *The Marriage Circle*, the first of these films, shows Lubitsch bringing together all the elements, both in theme and in visual style, that were to characterize, not just his silent comedies, but his sound films as well.

More than any of his German comedies, the film provides a near-perfect synthesis between the methods of cine-comedy and those of society-comedy. The plot (which is actually based on a stage play) is explicitly theatrical and moves through a series of formal permutations and regroupings of actual and potential sexual partners. The pattern can be summarized as follows: Joseph Stock (Adolphe Menjou) is married to Mizzi (Marie Prevost) and wants out of the marriage; Mizzi wants Dr. Franz Braun (Monte Blue) who has recently married her friend Charlotte (Florence Vidor); Franz is tempted by Mizzi but really wants Charlotte, who in turn wants him but is desired by her husband's partner Gustav who, at the end of the film, sets up with Mizzi. Joseph is allowed to exit contentedly from the circle, and Franz and Charlotte stay happily married.

The film performs a skillful balancing act between the "old" and "new" moralities, endorsing the claims for sexual freedom of the worldly Mizzi while leaving the more naive newlyweds in a state of somewhat ambiguous marital bliss (ambiguous in the sense that both have compromised themselves, wittingly or otherwise, with other parties, and their reconciliation is only made possible because Franz refuses to believe his wife's truthful admission that she had had a rendezvous with Gustav. As Leland Poague suggests, there is every reason to assume that similar misunderstandings and reprisals will continue to dog their marriage in the future.)

The visual style of the film demonstrates Lubitsch's complete mastery of the refined form of cine-comedy that is to be found in sound films like *Trouble in Paradise* and *The Merry Widow* as much as in a silent film like this one. One major device centers around the use of objects to suggest or imply relationships or actions between the characters: though contemporary reviewers were quick to notice the link with Chaplin's *A Woman of Paris*, most of them did so in obvious ignorance of the fact that Lubitsch had been experimenting along similar lines for years in his German comedies.[19]

The other pervasive technique is what might be called "misreading of visual evidence," whereby either a character misinterprets what he or she is seeing, or, more rarely, the audience is led to draw mistaken conclusions from ambiguous visual evidence. Both are favorite devices of Keaton and Lloyd, as well as of an essentially visual comedian like Jacques Tati. Films like *M. Hulot's Holiday* and *Playtime* make extensive use of both types of misreading; Harold Lloyd's films often open with a carefully framed shot that persuades the audience to make a particular assumption about the character's situation or actions, before changing the angle to reveal that this assumption is incorrect;[20] and the first half of Keaton's *Seven Chances* is a virtual compendium of these devices.

Examples of the use of objects, gestures, or body movement to reveal states of mind or personal relationships abound in *The Marriage Circle*. The famous opening sequence of the film summarizes the emotional deadness, even hostility, of Joseph and Mizzi's marriage in a series of brief vignettes: Joseph's foot is seen in close-up as he attempts to put on a sock and finds that there is a hole in the toe; Mizzi shrugs off his protests and he tries vainly to find a replacement in a drawer crammed with celluloid collars and a heap of socks also in need of mending. Elaborate gestures of mutual insult and neglect follow, culminating in a shot of Mizzi attempting to talk to him as he does his exercises, bobbing up and down with his back turned to her and his rear thrusting rudely towards her at each movement.

The contrasting affection between Franz and Charlotte is also demonstrated in a kind of visual shorthand: we see a close-up of boiled eggs, coffee cups, and two hands holding spoons; Franz's hand abandons his spoon and vanishes off screen; Charlotte's hand drops her spoon and likewise disappears from view; a hand reappears to push aside the unwanted eggs and coffee.

Later in the film, Mizzi lures Franz to her home and threatens to kill herself with what she knows to be an empty pistol; he discovers the deception and leaves angrily, opening and slamming no fewer than four doors[21] behind him. The unperturbed Mizzi calmly starts to file her nails and, when Joseph arrives home unexpectedly, feigns an embrace in order to distract him while she kicks the gun out of sight under the sofa.

In all these cases information about the feelings and relationships of the characters is being presented to the audience; a more elaborate effect is achieved when these devices are employed in scenes where characters misinterpret the actions of others on the basis of the visual clues provided. After her first encounter and attempted flirtation with Franz, Mizzi pretends to be ill in order to have him visit her at home (he is a doctor). She sets herself up for the visit by perfuming and powdering herself and maneuvers him into embarrassingly close proximity to her; he tries to leave and she seizes his wrist to detain him; at this point Joseph arrives unexpectedly and a close-up shows Franz hurriedly shifting his hand to take Mizzi's pulse. This shot is primarily for the audience; what Joseph delightedly notices is the two wineglasses on the table, which are evidence to him of a prearranged tryst.

Shortly after this, and after the breakfast scene that establishes for the audience Charlotte and Franz's mutual affection, Gustav comes to visit Charlotte, who is seen on the balcony of her home holding a rose. She accidentally drops this as she greets him and he takes this as an invitation to begin a flirtation with her; in her innocence, she is merely amused by this and plays along with it, allowing him to wave the rose gaily at her as he says goodbye. Next, Mizzi imposes herself upon the reluctant Franz in his office and attempts to seduce him; Gustav enters and sees Franz standing with his back to him and a pair of female arms clasped around his neck. Assuming that the arms belong to Charlotte, he is surprised to encounter her in the waiting room, though encouraged at the same time to believe that he might profit from the potential tensions in her marriage. When Charlotte becomes angry at Franz's apparent dalliance with Mizzi, he asks Gustav to calm her down; the scene fades on a shot of the office door closing as Gustav enters the office to fulfill the request.

Preparing for a dinner party at the Brauns', the repentant Franz switches the place cards around so that he will not have to sit beside Mizzi; Charlotte notices that he has done this, but misinterprets the reason, thinking that he wishes to place himself beside an attractive and unattached young woman; she therefore returns the card to its original position. In a mirroring of Franz's unwise confiding in Gustav (the film is full of such parallels, with virtually every scene between one couple having its counterpart with another couple), she reveals her suspicions to Mizzi and asks her to keep an eye on Franz and the dangerous Miss Hofer. Like Gustav, Mizzi seizes on the opportunity to disrupt the marriage and reseats Franz beside Miss Hofer. Charlotte, of course, assumes that the change is once again Franz's doing, and responds by flirting openly with Gustav.

Charlotte quarrels with Franz as a result and he goes off to seek consolation with Mizzi. Too late, Charlotte repents and tries to call him back: seeing a man outside the house who looks like her departing husband, she assumes that it is Franz and beckons to him to come inside, then seats herself with her back to the door and her eyes closed. The man, not surprisingly, turns out to be Gustav, and a companion scene to the embrace between Mizzi and Franz follows: hearing someone enter, Charlotte says, without looking, that she loves him and, still with her eyes closed, puts her arms round his neck. When he enthusiastically cooperates, she becomes aware of her mistake and orders him to leave, yet she smiles enigmatically as the scene closes, aware that she now has a weapon to use against her straying husband.

The film ends with two parallel scenes in which truthful information about one of the marriage partners is revealed but is ignored or deliberately misused, paving the way for Joseph to obtain his divorce, Franz and Charlotte to stay together, and Mizzi to be free to work her enticements on Gustav, which she is seen doing in the last shot of the film. Joseph has been having Mizzi followed by a detective in the hope of finding some evidence that he can use against her; the detective's report provides apparent confirmation of his suspicions and, though he accepts Franz's assertion that nothing in fact happened between him and Mizzi, he says that he will use the report in any case to secure a divorce from her. More misunderstandings between Franz and Mizzi follow until Charlotte is shown a letter from Mizzi that establishes that Franz had spurned her advances; in a somewhat ambiguous gesture that can be read either as a reprisal or an attempt at consolation by admitting that she too has been tempted, she admits to the encounter and embrace with Gustav. Franz smugly refuses to believe her and, when Gustav is called on to confirm her story, Franz signals to him that he should pretend to "confess" in order to satisfy Charlotte.

Relationships which are resolved or held together in this manner, on a basis of self-deception, deliberate deceit, or a refusal to acknowledge facts, cannot be said to be particularly healthy and, though Lubitsch manages to give all the main characters at least a veneer of charm or attractiveness, their motives are primarily self-regarding, opportunistic, and treacherous. Most contemporary reviewers, however, seemed happy to accept the glittering surface and were unwilling to probe too deeply beneath this, though Matthew Josephson (see Appendix A), despite his professed admiration for Lubitsch, was warning as early as August 1926 against the cynicism and emotional shallowness that he detected even in his best work. *Motion Picture Classic* (May 1924) had fewer qualms: "We are presented with a quadrangle which never becomes sordid; we are offered mild flirtations entertained by young married trespassers who believe in having their fling. These very human beings have a gay time of it in scenes which are so delicately handled, so skillfully suggested—that it is bound to appeal to anyone with imagination and a sense of humor." *Moving Picture World* (16 February 1924) considered that Lubitsch had "handled a rather daring and sensational theme with simplicity and directness," but warned:

> So different is this picture that its box office appeal is difficult to gauge. With its distinctly continental flavor and atmosphere and with the code which surrounds married couples weighing lightly on the conscience of several of the characters, although there is no great moral transgression, the theme is snappy and skims on thin ice and will not appeal to the conventionally minded, its subtlety and wit may also be over the heads of certain classes of patrons.

Some of these forebodings seem to be confirmed by a report in *Variety* two days previous to this that both *Rosita* and *The Marriage Circle* were performing relatively poorly at the box office, despite excellent reviews.

Although sophisticated opinion of the time seemed to welcome the apparently frivolous tone of the film and to find nothing out of the ordinary in its tolerant acceptance of "young married trespassers . . . having their fling," the more serious-minded contributors to *Our Changing Morality*, together with their modern equivalents, might have considered that Lubitsch had skillfully hedged his bets in order to stay abreast of "advanced" opinion while being careful not to advocate anything genuinely shocking or disruptive. Though Mizzi succeeds in establishing her sexual independence and freedom of choice, she is presented as shallow, opportunistic, and disloyal rather than a battler for sexual equality; it is possible, therefore, for audiences to see her behavior as frivolously promiscuous, in a long-established theatrical tradition, rather than as a challenge to conventional sexual morality. Her neglect of her duties as a housewife, emphasized by her refusal to darn her husband's sock, can likewise be interpreted ambiguously, and seems to be presented more as a justification for Joseph's dissatisfaction with his marriage than as a legitimate refusal "to cater to the traditional notions of [women] created by men." (It is interesting, incidentally, that Joseph, alone of the major characters, is not shown as having an alternative sexual interest; all he seems to want is to be rid of Mizzi.) A subtle, and perfectly traditional, distinction is also made between the degree, and nature, of marital transgression performed by Charlotte and Franz: the woman is genuinely "innocent" (her embrace of Gustav is performed with her eyes closed, not knowing who he really is), whereas the man is permitted rather more whole-hearted cooperation with his would-be seductress.

*L*ubitsch's *The Marriage Circle* presents the "New Woman" of the 1920s as an overt sexual aggressor. Mizzi (Marie Prevost) makes her intentions unmistakably clear to Franz (Monte Blue).

Lubitsch, in short, seems to have learned very early on one of the basic rules of survival in a Hollywood context: to cover his tracks and make sure either that his probings into controversial territory were susceptible to multiple interpretations, some of which at least could provide reassurance to more conventional minds, or that they could be laughed off as essentially frivolous and lighthearted.

Though his next film, *Three Women,* begins in an apparently comic mode with the middle-aged heroine Mabel Wilton (Pauline Frederick) trying to resist the advance of age by changing the weight recorded on her bathroom scales, it gradually takes on a more somber tone and here the sexual betrayals and deceits cause genuine emotional pain, at least to the two main female characters. Attempting to compete with the youthful beauty of her college-age daughter Jeanne (Mary McAvoy), Mabel becomes involved with a fortune-seeking man about town, Edmund Lamont (Lew Cody), who later becomes attracted to Jeanne and begins a simultaneous affair with her. When Mabel discovers this, Lamont offers to marry Jeanne and does so, to the distress of her would-be fiancé Fred. Soon, however, Lamont starts yet another affair, with the equally amoral Harriet (Marie Prevost). Jeanne learns about this, informs her mother, and then confronts Harriet, who taunts her with the revelation of her mother's previous involvement with Lamont. Jeanne returns to her mother's, but finds that she has gone to see Lamont and arrives just as Mabel, infuriated by Lamont's lack of remorse for his behavior, shoots him. Mother and daughter are reconciled and, at her trial, Mabel is acquitted by an understanding jury.

Mabel's initially comic concern over her appearance becomes almost obsessive as the film proceeds: she anxiously studies and preens herself before mirrors, wears elaborate clothing and jewelry, and attempts to compete with the younger generation in dancing and party-going. Typical Lubitsch devices present information visually or in scenes that parallel each other: Lamont, after his first meeting with Jeanne at her mother's home, waves goodbye from the street as each woman, watching from a different window, takes the gesture as intended for her alone. Mabel, expecting Lamont to join her for dinner at her home, receives a phone call saying he can't come; she begins disconsolately to eat the meal on her own and a cut shows Lamont dining in a fashionable restaurant with Jeanne. Later, as Lamont is preparing to receive Jeanne for an intimate dinner in his home, Mabel arrives unexpectedly just before Jeanne does; Lamont tries to prevent the two women from meeting, but Mabel recognizes Jeanne's shawl as he tries to smuggle her out unnoticed and forces an explanation. Her killing of

Lamont is made less explicit—and perhaps also more "forgivable"—by being presented as a struggle between shadows cast on a wall. And on two occasions, Mabel's sexual involvement with Lamont is—somewhat masochistically—hinted at by her examining, with obvious pleasure, a bruise on her arm.

Much play is made of photographs to suggest the changing relationships among the characters. Fred, not knowing that Jeanne has taken up with Lamont, cuts out her picture from a group photo at college and sticks it on his mirror; the shot dissolves to Jeanne in front of a mirror preparing for an assignation with Lamont. Lamont guiltily hides a photo of Mabel as he prepares to welcome Jeanne to his rooms. And photographs of Mabel, Lamont, and Jeanne, displayed on Mabel's sideboard, are several times rearranged in ways that suggest the hidden connections between them, with Jeanne, after her encounter with Harriet, finally tearing up her own photo and leaving those of her mother and Lamont facing each other. As the mother-daughter rivalry reflected in these readjustments, has not, however, been deliberately created by either of them, a final reconciliation is possible and the film's conclusion (it is, unusually for Lubitsch, set in America rather than Paris or Central Europe and may therefore have been expected to conform to more conventional moral codes) offers a departure from the genial cynicism that marks his more typical works.

The film was well received by most critics, with *Moving Picture World* praising Lubitsch's "masterful" direction and the film's "excellent dramatic construction" (27 September 1924, 334). The direction was "marked by the same subtle touches, the same unerring ability to portray human nature, its fine points and its frailties; the delightful touches of comedy, the power to register his points by short and constantly changing scenes and shots focused on exceedingly limited areas, all the while preserving excellent continuity." Commenting on the plot, it noted "some daring scenes and sensational inferences in the development, but they have been cleverly and discreetly handled. Obviously this is not a Sunday school story and it may mildly shock the unsophisticated, but it is a production that should register heavily with a large majority of spectators." The *New York Times* (6 October 1924), which also praised the film, remarked on what were already seen as typical Lubitsch "touches," especially the opening shot showing first "the registering bar of a weighing machine, which is followed by the appearance of Mrs. Mabel Wilton (Pauline Frederick) consuming a lemon as she gazes dejectedly at her weight," or that showing "close-ups of diamonds and pearls worn by different women" to reveal that "the insidious

Edmund Lamont (Lew Cody) is mentally weighing the earthly possessions of these members of the fair sex before asking one of them to dance." The *Times* also commented on the very sparing use of subtitles throughout: "it has fewer captions than any other film we have seen which had subtitles at all."

Forbidden Paradise (1924), for which Lubitsch was loaned out to Paramount, both reunited him with Pola Negri and returned him to the "Ruritanian" type of setting of some of his German comedies.[22] It also provides some interesting thematic links between aspects of his costume films and later Hollywood treatments of sex and royal politics such as *Queen Christina* and *The Scarlet Empress* in the 1930s. Lubitsch's historical epics showed kings and pharaohs whose sexual weakness aroused the indignation and hostility of their subjects and led to the loss, or threatened loss, of their autocratic power; the 1930s treatments of a similar theme focus on a female ruler whose sexual choices threaten the stability and continuity of her kingdom and must be thwarted or somehow held in check. In the case of the male rulers, the main force of popular rage is directed less against them than against the women who have led them astray; the female rulers, however, cannot separate sex from politics so easily: though Christina is presented as a good and popular ruler, she cannot enjoy both her sexual freedom and her privileges as a monarch and must give up one in favor of the other. And though Von Sternberg's Catherine II of Russia is able to impose her will on her rebellious subjects, the film is concerned almost exclusively with her sexuality and presents her political ability primarily in terms of her convincing her courtiers that her sexual freedom is in fact compatible with the stability of the empire.

Like Von Sternberg, though in an explicitly comic context, Lubitsch handles the political aspects of *Forbidden Paradise* in an extremely perfunctory way, and little effort is made even to provide reasons for the various rebellions and conspiracies against the czarina's rule that punctuate the story, These seem to have nothing whatever to do with whether or not the czarina (Negri) is a good ruler, but exist solely to provide motivation for the young officer hero, Alexei. At the beginning of the film he gains her attention by warning her of a planned rebellion and is rewarded with promotion and her sexual favors. Later, when she appears to lose interest in him, he becomes involved in a plot against her.

The deliberate frivolity of the treatment ensures that the czarina is not required to make any serious choice between love and duty: Alexei ends up with his neglected and loyal sweetheart, Anna, and the ruler continues happily with her life of promiscuous sexual pleasure. The inversion of the values of a film like *Passion* is striking: where Louis XV's descendants are punished for his sexual looseness by the overthrow of their dynasty, and both Jeanne and Armand die as a consequence of her lust and ambition, here sexual infidelity is cheerfully condoned—at least where the main characters are concerned. Doubtless the unreality of the setting and the deliberate theatricality of the plot helped to prevent American audiences from taking the implications too seriously or from considering them within the context of their own society; there was always, moreover, the figure of the pure and long-suffering Anna to set against the contentedly amoral czarina.

Once again, as *Moving Picture World* shrewdly noted, Lubitsch had "demonstrated that he has grasped the American psychology of entertainment and has made a picture that is a delight. He has taken a plot that is daring and sophisticated and in which sex is always uppermost . . . and presented it as a romantic comedy, handling it with such skill and deftness and with such a pleasing lightness of touch . . . that it should not offend anyone, but prove decidedly pleasing" (29 May 1924, 448). As with *The Marriage Circle*, the film is full of devices associated with cine-comedy. There are several gag-refrains, most notably in the use of the decoration, or Star, that signals, both to the audience and to the courtiers, that the wearer is, or has been, one of the czarina's lovers. When Alexei is awarded his Star, he naively assumes that only he has the right to wear it; when he sees several other officers at a banquet also wearing Stars, his response is both confused and irrational. First he tries to defend his ruler's honor against the sexual looseness implied by the collection of Stars and then, when the czarina makes it clear to him that her scandalous reputation is fully justified and that she glories in it, he reacts violently against her promiscuity, rips off his own Star, and hurls it at her feet. At the very end of the film, the fact that the czarina is less than completely heartbroken at losing Alexei is signaled by the fact that the French Ambassador leaves her audience chamber wearing a Star.

Other visual gags include the drawing of a curtain to signal, to the audience and to a character watching, that sexual activity of some kind is taking place: the chamberlain, peering through the keyhole at Alexei's first audience with the czarina, is thwarted by a curtain being drawn across it and later Anna, waiting outside the palace while the czarina completes her seduction of Alexei within, realizes that she has lost her lover when the curtains are drawn. The seduction itself is presented in typical Lubitsch fashion by means of objects and props: the czarina deliberately drops a champagne glass at her feet, pretends to be frightened, and grabs hold of Alexei, meanwhile skillfully nudging a stool into place with her foot so that she will have something to stand on when the moment comes to embrace the tall, handsome officer. Alexei tries to resist, walks toward the door, hesitates, turns at the door and comes back; his movements are intercut with shots of the czarina's eager, pleading face, and the whole scene is framed by shots of the deserted Anna waiting mournfully outside.

The chamberlain's bargaining with the leader of the second rebellion is also wittily presented through gestures and visual implications: the general's hand is seen in close-up holding the handle of his sword; the chamberlain's hand fondles the wallet in his pocket; the general's fingers clasp and unclasp as he calculates how much he should ask for. Near the beginning of the film, the chamberlain suggests to the ambassador that he should curl his moustaches upwards if he wishes to make a favorable impression on the czarina; the visitor obeys, but grows impatient at being kept waiting, smooths them down again and leaves. At the end, after the chamberlain has ushered him into the czarina's presence, the ambassador remembers to curl up his moustache, thus ensuring that he will receive an enthusiastic reception.

Adolphe Menjou's performance as the chamberlain is particularly subtle throughout, conveying information and meaning through a raised eyebrow, a shrug, the faintest flicker of a smile. In this, as in the other films he made with Lubitsch, he is the perfect interpreter of the Lubitsch style, smooth, refined, worldly, elegant, with every gesture and movement precise and exact and, more often than not, hinting at meanings other than those evident on the surface. Though these qualities can also be seen in his work with Chaplin in *A Woman of Paris* and with Harry D'Abbadie D'Arrast in *A Gentleman of Paris,* they represent the kind of refinement in acting technique that reviewers quickly came to associate with Lubitsch's American work in particular—a refinement that can be tested by comparing Negri's exaggeratedly physical performance in *Passion* or *Gypsy Blood* with the coolness and restraint of her work in *Forbidden Paradise.*

Kiss Me Again (1925) is unfortunately a "lost" film at present, with no print known to exist. Though it is credited as an original story by Hans Kraly, it works within an explicitly theatrical tradition of French farce and Carringer and Sabath give Sardou's *Let's Get a Divorce* as the basic source of the material. Once again the film was enthusiastically welcomed by reviewers, with *Motion Picture World* even complaining that "praising the directorial genius of Ernst Lubitsch has gotten to be an old story"—yet praise was the only possible response (15 August 1925, 736). The French setting once again allowed this and other critics to welcome the "suggestive" nature of the material, as well as "one or two situations [that] border on the risque but . . . have been handled discreetly so that they amuse and do not offend." *Variety* remarked on a bedroom scene near the end "that will cause audiences to gasp when they get the suggestion of the two disrobing," before adding, somewhat delphically: "It is cleverly done, and at the finish there is a touch that takes away the suggestiveness."[23] The central situation, involving a husband and wife who decide to divorce but have to find an acceptable legal excuse first, allows each of them to experiment with other partners before they finally decide to stay together after all. In contrast to the Franz and Charlotte situation in *The Marriage Circle*, however, here the wife is allowed to become quite seriously involved with another man, while the husband's affair is deliberately contrived so that the wife can claim adultery as grounds for their divorce. The "continental touch" apparently sufficed to keep moralists at bay once more, though the *New York Times* (3 August 1925) grumbled that, despite the "ease and charm" of the film, "it is high time that this director put forth a more serious dramatic subject, something with tense and gripping situations." The *Times* review, despite its reservations about the film, conceded that one scene at least was worthy of comparison with Oscar Wilde's *The Importance of Being Earnest*, though it did so secure in the knowledge that Lubitsch had already announced that his next film would be *Lady Windermere's Fan*. The paradox of attempting to make a silent film based on the work of a playwright renowned for his verbal wit was not lost on contemporary reviewers or on Lubitsch himself, and most of the former agreed that he had risen triumphantly to the challenge. In essence his method was simply to substitute his own characteristic visual wit for Wilde's epigrammatic dialogue, and the fact that the complicated plot relied on devices of mistaken or concealed identity, and misunderstanding, jealousy and retaliation between lovers and married couples, allowed him to do this in a perfectly natural way by employing the methods of *The Marriage Circle* and *Forbidden Paradise*.

The film opens with a scene reminiscent of *The Marriage Circle* as Lady Windermere plans the seating arrangements for her dinner party and toys with the idea of placing herself next to the attractive Lord Darlington. When he actually arrives to visit her, he begins to make his interest in her evident and, though she resists him, she does so in an ambiguous enough manner not to discourage him completely. It is only later, however, after a series of misunderstandings of her husband's behavior, that she is prepared to compromise herself more openly with him and to consider leaving her husband and going off with Darlington. These misunderstandings are to some extent deliberately fostered by Lord Darlington, who assumes in the opening scene that a letter which Lord Windermere is trying to conceal from his wife is from a mistress: close-ups show Windermere with his hands behind his back, fumbling to reach the letter and push it out of sight into a drawer; Darlington helpfully edges it within his reach and then, as soon as Windermere has gone, he tells Lady Windermere that he loves her. The letter is in fact from someone unknown to Windermere, the notorious Mrs. Erlynne, who wishes to re-establish herself in English society with Windermere's help; she is in reality his wife's mother and will accept discreet financial payments in order to keep this fact a secret.

Darlington later discovers that Windermere has been giving money to Mrs. Erlynne and once again tries to use this information to his own advantage. He encourages Lady Windermere's suspicions when they see her husband dismiss his own car and take a taxi to an unknown rendezvous; he then mentions that Windermere has given Mrs. Erlynne a check. Lady Windermere finds the check, confronts her husband with it, and refuses to believe his (truthful) protestations that his relations with Mrs. Erlynne are innocent. At her birthday party that evening she is upset by evidence of Mrs. Erlynne's social acceptance and popularity and allows Darlington to meet her privately in the garden; though they agree to part, Lady Windermere changes her mind after seeing Mrs. Erlynne obviously flirting with a man on the terrace. As in similar scenes in *The Marriage Circle*, the man's features are hidden from view, but Lady Windermere assumes (wrongly) that he is her husband and agrees in retaliation to go off with Lord Darlington.

Another pattern of misunderstanding evolves round Mrs. Erlynne and especially her relationship with her elderly admirer Lord Augustus. It is he, of course, who is really with her in the garden, and in an earlier scene it had taken a good deal of effort on her part to convince him that a cigar butt in an ashtray in her home was really his own and not a relic left by an earlier lover. The multiple misunderstandings are resolved at the end of the film in a manner that, once again like *The Marriage Circle*, involves concealment as much as revelation of the true facts. Mrs. Erlynne saves Lady Windermere from social disgrace by pretending that the fan found in Lord Darlington's room was brought there, by mistake, by herself. The result is that she loses her own newly acquired social respectability in order to save her daughter (who never learns her true identity) from the consequences of her own folly; she steadfastly refuses to let Lady Windermere admit to the truth later, telling her that this would negate the effect of the only good action she has ever done. At the very end of the film, however, she is able to turn the tables on Lord Augustus (who had joined the other men in spurning her after her "confession") by telling him that his shameful behavior has

convinced her she no longer wants to marry him; he is so impressed by her self-possession that he is seen trailing after her once more in the final shot.

Lubitsch uses this structure based on misreading of visual evidence very effectively as a means of keeping the complex relations between the characters clearly understandable without undue recourse to lengthy verbal explanations in the subtitles. In the details of the film he provides numerous examples of visual wit that fully compensate for the absence of Wilde's own language. When Lord Windermere writes a check for Mrs. Erlynne, the writing of each figure of the sum is intercut with a shot of her impassive face as she waits for the total to reach a satisfactory amount: first a five, then a zero, then another zero, and another. As even this fails to elicit a sign of approval, Windermere cunningly adds an initial number one rather than continue the series of zeroes indefinitely. When Mrs. Erlynne arrives for Lady Windermere's party, the heads of three ladies bob into view on the screen in succession as they rise to greet her, each head having as a backdrop a large biblical tapestry. The most obviously flamboyant visual effects in the film come during a sequence at the Royal Ascot races, and here Lubitsch employs some of the experimentation with screen shape that characterized his German comedies. As the other women exchange gossip about Mrs. Erlynne, we see her framed in a screen blacked off round the edges to signify the binoculars trained on her; the scene culminates in a succession of dissolves showing her from all angles and ending in an extreme close-up as one woman remarks that she is "getting gray." When Mrs. Erlynne leaves the racecourse, the camera tracks with her as she walks in front of a row of hoardings plastered with advertisements; Lord Augustus follows her and the sides of the screen close in to isolate them as he catches up with her.

Perhaps because Wilde's play itself is heavily moralistic underneath its elegant surface, the film conforms more strongly to conventional, even clichéd, moral standards than the preceding ones do. Mrs. Erlynne's scandalous behavior masks a heart of gold in a well-worn theatrical fashion; her character is altruistic and self-sacrificing in a way that women like Mizzi or the czarina could scarcely have begun to understand, much less imitate. And though Lady Windermere attempts to revenge herself on her husband by flirting with another man, his actions are genuinely innocent throughout and her heart is never seriously engaged elsewhere. Once again the film was greeted warmly by the critics, though there was less emphasis than usual on the presumed appeal to a sophisticated audience; perhaps in recognition of its more conventional nature it was felt that it could be more popular "in provincial communities" and with "the average patron" than

A "fallen woman" still risks social disgrace and ostracism even in the worldly and sophisticated society of *Lady Windermere's Fan.*

Lubitsch's films usually were. The initial box-office receipts seemed to confirm the film's popular appeal, with *Moving Picture World* (9 January 1926, 161) reporting that it had smashed all attendance records at the Warners Theatre on Broadway during the first week of its run.

So This is Paris (1926) follows the pattern of relationships in *The Marriage Circle* remarkably closely.[24] Once again there are two couples: Paul and Suzanne Giraud (with the husband a doctor, as in the earlier film), who are genuinely in love yet susceptible to involvements with others; and Maurice and Georgette Lallé, who are bored and antagonistic towards each other. A connection between the two couples is provided by the fact that Paul and Georgette had once been lovers. The denouement of the film leaves them virtually in the same state as the parties in *The Marriage Circle:* Paul flirts with Georgette, and Suzanne with Maurice, but, after various quarrels and misunderstandings Paul and Suzanne come together again. The husband has

been the more tempted of the two, but is forgiven by his wife; like Franz in the earlier film he refuses to believe evidence of his wife's entanglement with someone else. Meanwhile Georgette is in the process of moving on to an affair with a stranger she met at a masked ball, while Maurice, who is spending three days in jail, is temporarily out of the reckoning.

Despite the clear similarities in plot and the reliance on what are now familiar stylistic devices, Lubitsch manages to give the material a fresh and original quality. The motif of misperception is given a new twist at the opening of the film in a manner that recalls the opening of some of Harold Lloyd's comedies:[25] the audience sees a man in Oriental costume stabbing a slave girl and embracing her as she expires in his arms. The camera then pans to the left where a pianist gives the performers the cue for their next routine and a written title then explains who the characters are. Our own readiness to jump to mistaken conclusions on the basis of a partial understanding of a scene is then matched by Suzanne, who has been languorously reading an exotic Oriental romance; closing the book in a state of ecstasy she looks out of the window and sees what appears to be the sheik of her dreams in a room across the street. At this point Maurice is still wearing the turban needed for his performance, but, after Paul has come home and greeted his wife with little of the ardor that she obviously requires, Suzanne looks out of the window again and sees that Maurice is now apparently naked. She insists on Paul going over to "punish" the stranger for his indecent behavior and, after some resistance, Paul reluctantly picks up his cane and sets off. The matching staleness of Maurice and Georgette's marriage has meanwhile been suggested by a point in their routine where he is supposed to lift her up, can't manage it, and has to be picked up by her instead; the parallel with his sexual performance is clearly implied. Maurice is out of the way when Paul arrives and recognizes who Georgette is; a flurry of arm waving as they excitedly embrace is interpreted by the watching Suzanne as evidence of a fight between her gallant husband and Maurice. Belatedly remembering his mission Paul changes his gestures to make it look as if he is beating someone, then moves out of Suzanne's visual range to talk to Georgette. He tells her that he is married and, with a limp, bored flap of the wrist she confirms not only her own marital status, but the essence of its inadequacy. Maurice returns to the room and Paul maneuvers him out of Suzanne's sight, then draws the curtains. Returning home to report on his triumph he realizes that he has forgotten his cane, but claims that he broke it to pieces while chastising the offender. As Paul is having a rest, Maurice appears, to return the cane; he is immediately attracted to Suzanne and

*L*ubitsch also took care not to discard conventional moral restraints entirely. The married bliss of Paul (Monte Blue) and Suzanne (Patsy Ruth Miller) may be fragile and shallow, but the couple remains together at the end of *So This is Paris*.

starts to make advances which, angered at her husband's lying, she does little to discourage. Paul overhears some of Maurice's flattering words but assumes that they refer to himself; and when Maurice leaves Suzanne gives him the cane in an attempt to conceal his visit from Paul. The cane then becomes one of the main gag-motifs in the film as Maurice continues to use it as an excuse for visiting Suzanne while her husband is out. There is also a strange dream sequence, rare in Lubitsch's films after *Die Bergkatze*, in which Paul guiltily dreams of being continually prodded by the cane until finally it appears to be forced right down his throat.

      Though Lubitsch keeps the subsequent intrigues, deceptions and misunderstandings among the four characters lighthearted and apparently inconsequential, the implications of their behavior are often both disturbing and unpleasant. When Paul discovers that he can pretend to be obeying a summons to spend three days in jail for speeding, while in reality he slips off to attend a masked ball with Georgette, he performs a dance of joy in the bedroom (he accounts for his wearing a tuxedo to set off for prison by explaining that he wants to impress the other prisoners). As he takes a farewell embrace from Suzanne he signals over her head to Georgette across the street, and his subsequent dancing the Charleston with her at the ball conveys a strong sense of mutual sexual attraction. Meanwhile, although Suzanne is responsive to Maurice's advances, she compromises herself with him (like Charlotte with Gustav) more by accident than by intention. A policeman arrives to escort Paul to prison during one of Maurice's visits to Suzanne; to spare her embarrassment, Maurice pretends to be Paul and allows himself to be led off, but not before he has taken a touching and lingering farewell from his "wife"—so heartbroken is he at having to part from her that he returns from the doorway five times to embrace her. Suzanne indignantly sets off in disguise for the ball to track Paul down and meets him as he is leaving, very drunk, to serve his prison term. As Georgette has found a new partner, he starts to flirt with this stranger, though some palliation of his sexual opportunism is provided by the suggestion that this masked woman reminds him of his wife. In the course of the argument and mutual recrimination which follow when they return home Suzanne seems at first to have the upper hand, though she is momentarily silenced when she discovers the incriminating cane that Maurice had left behind on his previous visit. The conclusion, as in *The Marriage Circle*, leaves a relatively innocent wife in full knowledge of her husband's transgressions, and a smugly complacent and rather shallow husband refusing to believe that his wife could contemplate the sexual freedom that he takes for granted himself: seeing a newspaper report of his supposed arrest and tender leave-taking from his wife he dismisses the whole thing as an absurdity without attempting even to investigate it.

As with *Lady Windermere's Fan*, Lubitsch makes use of a far greater amount of technical trickery and elaborate cinematic effects than had been customary in his American films. The visual set piece is the scene of the masked ball, which is somewhat reminiscent of the smaller-scale "foxtrot epidemic" in *Die Austernprinzessin*. A complex, kaleidoscopic montage of wild dancing, excited crowds, and frenzied saxophone players is built up from a variety of camera angles, rapid editing, and superimpositions, all backed by a bizarre and outsized set constructed round a motif of gigantic female legs, and culminating in the energetic dancing of Paul and Georgette that both serves as a metaphor for their sexual excitement and wins them the prize that reveals their whereabouts to Suzanne as she listens to the dance contest on the radio. Later, when Suzanne has finished reproaching Paul for his behavior and has announced that she will be the boss of the household in future, he seems literally to shrink as the camera tracks back from him; the setting retains the same proportions, but his figure becomes progressively smaller, until finally he walks out through a huge door several sizes too large for him.

"Once more Ernst Lubitsch turns to the pleasure loving set in a European capital who do not let the mere fact of being married stand in their way of flirtations, as the personages for a clever and scintillating light comedy" (*Motion Picture World*, 4 September 1926, 41). Lubitsch now had a string of critical successes behind him and a by no means negligible record at the box office; he was receiving lucrative offers from other companies and, though his contract with Warner Brothers had still some time to run, he began negotiations with both United Artists and Paramount.[26] The outcome was that Paramount and MGM agreed to buy him out of his contract with Warners; he would then make one film for MGM (which had already asked to have him on loan from Warners) and then start a three-year contract with Paramount.

The film for MGM was, like *Lady Windermere's Fan*, an obvious paradox: a silent version of Sigmund Romberg's operetta *The Student Prince*, (1927). With the exception of *Variety* (28 September 1927), which felt that the film as a whole totally misfired, reviewers seemed not to feel that the lack of the original music was any great disadvantage; most agreed, however, that either Ramon Novarro or Norma Shearer, or both, were miscast in the leading roles and, though the film contained many of the expected "touches," there was an almost subliminal awareness that the material was not really the kind that Lubitsch could work with satisfactorily. One of the warmest reviews, in *Moving Picture World* (24 September 1927, 250), makes this almost embarrassingly clear in its attempts to praise the film: "a play in which exuberant youth has its fling amid ideal surroundings and goes to take up the burden of regal responsibility and a loveless marriage of diplomacy, sustained by the memory of a clean and sincere love." A conflict between love and duty, in which duty finally wins out, was not the right material for the director of *Forbidden Paradise* or *So This is Paris* and, despite some incidental felicitous touches, the film as a whole is labored and stilted. *Variety*'s forebodings of box-office disaster seem to have been fulfilled as well, according to the figures supplied by Carringer and Sabath (92), which show the film making a substantial loss on its world-wide earnings.[27]

The Student Prince was a much more elaborate production than the small-scale, intimate works that Lubitsch had made for Warner Brothers. At times the scale and the formality are used effectively for dramatic purposes, as in the opening scene where King Karl rides through the streets in his carriage and a collection of top hats are removed in unison to acknowledge him; at the end of the film, when his nephew has accepted his fate as a ruler and abandoned his dreams of personal happiness, a similar shot emphasizes his destiny. The young prince's isolation is shown by shots of him watching other children play from behind a barred gate and then being allowed to play with a group of solemn footmen as they decorously toss him a huge ball to catch. These scenes are intended to contrast with the spontaneity of his student life in Heidelberg and his innocent love affair with the innkeeper's daughter Kathi, but the ultimate effect is insipid rather than refreshing. Deprived by his material of the opportunity for genuine sexual innuendo, Lubitsch resorts to some halfhearted and ultimately contradictory devices: as Kathi is showing the prince his bedroom, she bounces up and down on the bed to test the springs and later she spends some time smoothing down the pillows. Neither gesture, however, is intended to suggest that her mind is wandering to other uses that could be made of the bed. And love scenes in a flower-covered meadow under a sky sprinkled with stars, though pleasantly enough handled, are cliché-ridden by comparison with the effects that Lubitsch normally achieved—as is the use made of springtime as the season of young love, with rain accompanying the prince's return to the capital, and the deserted Kathi visiting a meadow where the flowers no longer bloom.

    Lubitsch's first film under his Paramount contract, *The Patriot*, is another "lost" film, but the synopsis and contemporary reviews suggest that it was an unexpected return to some at least of the methods of the German epics. Emil Jannings appears to have been given the opportunity to act his head off as the mad Czar Paul I of Russia, with Lewis Stone turning in a more restrained performance as Count Pahlen, the conspirator torn between his duty to his emperor and his love of his country: "Mr. Stone gives a balanced and polished performance. Pahlen is pictured as a suave man of the world rather than the paragon of virtue as legendary heroes are usually presented. Character comes on the screen without heroics. Until the end you are left to guess whether his motives are noble or selfish" (*Variety*, 22 August 1928, 14). The film departs from the formula of using a woman as the catalyst for the action, though Pahlen is a worldly enough figure to be shown having an adulterous affair at the beginning of the film, and he is later willing to use his mistress as a lure to trap the czar into calling off a journey that would disrupt an assassination attempt. Generally the film (which was released both as a silent and in a version with some dialogue scenes and sound effects) was well received, with praise being given to the acting, the handling of action, the composition and pictorial effects, and the elaborate sets—very much in the manner in which *Passion* and *Deception* had been welcomed.[28]

Eternal Love (1929), Lubitsch's last silent film,[29] was made on loan to United Artists and is in some respects a throwback to German films such as *Gypsy Blood* or a version of *Die Bergkatze* played seriously rather than as comedy. It boasts a highly over-the-top performance by John Barrymore, much obviously fake mountain scenery, sexual rivalry and jealousy, with a wild mountain girl competing with the virtuous heroine for the affections of the hero and a disappointed rival attempting to murder him, numerous snow-storms and a concluding avalanche. Set in Switzerland, it begins in 1806 with the invading French army of Napoleon confiscating the guns of the lib-erty-loving mountain villagers; Marcus (Barrymore), out hunting at the time, at first refuses to surrender his treasured weapon but is finally persuaded to do so by his sweetheart, Ciglia (Camilla Horn). Meanwhile he is preoccupied with fighting off the far from subtle advances of Pia, the wild mountain girl (Mona Rico), while the faithful Ciglia tries to deter his jealous rival Lorenz.

The French army leaves and, during the masked carnival that cele-brates the villagers' restored freedom, Marcus drinks too much and makes overenthusiastic advances to Ciglia, who resists him. Pia seizes her oppor-tunity and seduces him. The next day, though Ciglia is willing to forgive the repentant Marcus for his behavior to her, Pia and her unscrupulous mother tell the local pastor what has happened and he forces Marcus to marry Pia. Shortly afterwards Ciglia enters into an unhappy marriage with Lorenz and the miserable and reckless Marcus prowls the mountains alone. When Marcus appears to have been trapped in a severe snowstorm, Pia appeals to Lorenz to help rescue him; when he refuses, Ciglia goes out to help but meets Marcus returning safely after all. Lorenz now tries to bribe Marcus to leave town; to Pia's disgust, he rejects the money and Lorenz then follows him into the mountains and threatens to kill him. Shots are heard and Marcus returns to the village alone, saying that Lorenz has been injured in a fall; the villagers set off to find him and, when they bring him home, he accuses Marcus of trying to murder him and Pia claims that Ciglia incited him to do it. The villagers turn on Marcus and Ciglia, who flee into the mountains; but, knowing that their love is hopeless, they choose to die together by walking into the path of an avalanche.

Such a story clearly gives little scope for Lubitsch's brand of sub-tlety and ambiguity. Ciglia is uncomplicatedly virtuous; Marcus is weak and led astray rather than consciously deceptive or unfaithful; and Pia's sexuality

is almost ridiculously overt and blatant. Marcus and Ciglia tamely accept the "stern code" of morality[30] displayed by the pastor and the villagers rather than defying or manipulating and subverting it as the characters in Lubitsch's comedies might have done, and the film seems to approve of their acceptance by surrounding their fate with a plethora of religious imagery: Ciglia begs God for forgiveness and crosses herself; Marcus looks at her awestruck and kneels in prayer beside her; and, after they have been swept away by the avalanche, the snow slackens to reveal a fiery sun that seems to promise redemption.

Reviewers were less than complimentary about the film as a whole. *Variety* (15 May 1929, 27) commented that "the tragic ending, for all its sentimentality, is not the least of the flicker's shortcomings," and the *New York Times* was equally disappointed: "Although it is capably acted and intelligently directed, with excellent scenic effects and settings, the story is not especially moving" (13 May 1929). It also condemned the "extravagant grimaces" of Barrymore's acting and the contrivances and implausibilities of the plot. *Eternal Love* and its two predecessors make a rather odd and unsatisfying ending to Lubitsch's silent career, especially when he had such a distinctive and successful body of work as the Warner Brothers comedies behind him. Perhaps he was concerned about being trapped into a formula and repeating himself too easily, or perhaps he wished to show that he could still produce the kind of dramatic or historical spectacle that had initially brought him fame in America.[31] On the other hand, the reasons may have been more prosaic and mundane and have simply involved the fulfilling of contract obligations. At any rate, his first three sound films took him back, and very successfully, to the vein of light comedy that was to occupy him, with very few exceptions, for the remainder of his life.

Though this study is not concerned with examining Lubitsch's career once the silent era had ended, it should be clear from the foregoing account that he was able to move into making sound films with remarkably little disruption of his characteristic style or themes. The key to this is to be found in the way in which, over a period of some fifteen years, he had evolved a comic style that was, in the best possible sense, a genuine hybrid of the virtues of cine-comedy and society-comedy. From the former came the use of objects, gestures, facial expressions, gag-refrains, and a structure based on misperception and misreading of visual evidence; from the latter came plot patterns based on complex sexual and social relationships and the rapid switching of emotional and sexual allegiance. The two aspects are blended so skillfully in films like *The Marriage Circle* and *So This is Paris* that, though sound acted an extra dimension to them, it involved no fundamental alteration of "the Lubitsch manner."

Lubitsch's virtually unbroken run of critical and relatively popular success in America during the 1920s stands in stark contrast to the tribulations experienced by Murnau, Sjöström, Stiller, and Christensen; yet his career contains many paradoxes. His reputation in the United States was achieved through his German costume films, which were praised at the time for their exotic themes, extravagant production values, and skillful direction, though much of the true, almost subliminal source of their appeal, must have lain in their impeccable correspondence to a central code of Hollywood cinema that allowed audiences tantalizing glimpses of sinful goings-on in high life for most of the film's length, before duly punishing this behavior at the conclusion. Lubitsch's American comedies are—for the most part correctly—credited with rejecting or evading this code, yet the films were not quite as far out of line with contemporary moral values, or as completely uncompromising, as they are sometimes thought to be. Reviewers of the period constantly stressed their appeal to "sophisticated" audiences (among whom, of course, the reviewers themselves were included) while noting that they were never "offensive" or "tasteless." Though Lubitsch, especially in the behavior of his heroines, touched on many important issues of the day, in particular the sexual and social freedom of women, the question of the double standard, the need for sexual fidelity within marriage, and the value of marriage itself as a central pillar of the social structure, he was always careful to allow his audiences to draw their own conclusions from what they saw on the screen. A sexually free woman like Mizzi or Georgette is balanced against a woman like Charlotte or Suzanne who may have her (relatively innocent) fling, but opts for remaining with her husband at the end; and for every couple which agrees to split up there is one which stays together (even if the basis on which their marriage is built has been implied to be extremely shaky). And the fact that all of this is taking place in some "Continental" environment in any case, permits the viewer to assume, if he or she wishes, that none of it has any relevance to respectable American society. Without accusing Lubitsch of opportunism, for his best films from this period retain their sparkle and their charm even seventy or more years later, it is fair to say that, in contrast to the more intransigent Murnau or Sjöström, he knew exactly when and how to compromise in order to suit "the American psychology of entertainment."[32]

F. W. Murnau

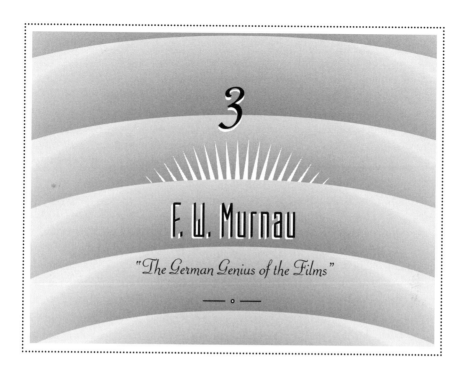

3

F. W. Murnau

"The German Genius of the Films"

——— o ———

hile Lubitsch had arrived in Hollywood with a strong interest in American production methods and with an already established reputation for films that were both "artistic" and reasonably successful commercially, Murnau, by contrast, was virtually unknown to the American public on his arrival in July 1926 to work for the Fox Film Corporation. Only *The Last Laugh (Der Letzte Mann)* of the seventeen films he had made up to then had received any commercial exposure in the United States, though it had aroused widespread critical admiration for its innovative use of the moving camera and its almost complete avoidance of explanatory titles. *Faust,* which had just been completed, was to open in New York in December 1926, and, although most reviewers agreed that it did not quite reach the level of *The Last Laugh,* it was given a generally favorable reception and was seen as confirming the reputation both of Murnau himself and of Emil Jannings.[1] *Tartuffe,* however, made in between these two, but not released in America until July 1927, was greeted with considerable contempt by reviewers, who confessed themselves both baffled and bored by it (many of them were clearly unfamiliar with the Molière play). *Variety* saw only "an impression of sordid buffoonery," situations "beyond the realm of understanding of the present generation," and "a total loss as far as the box office is concerned," though it did concede that "Murnau's fine directorial touch is very much in evidence." *Moving Picture World* agreed that it was not "a type of story that appeals to the average patron in this country," and concluded that it "does not begin to measure up to the

usual work of either Jannings or Director Murnau." The *New York Times*, though suggesting that the film might be more favorably rated by others, found it heavy-handed, naive, and obvious: "Whatever else may be said about it, the picture is heavy and primitive."[2] Finally, *Nosferatu*, though its critical reputation has flourished since, arrived very late on the American scene (June 1929) and was given little serious attention.

The relative lack of advance knowledge about Murnau's work was not the only problem he was to face in the United States, for his films, despite their common origin in post-war Germany, were the product of a rather different aesthetic sensibility and background from those of Lubitsch. While Murnau, like Lubitsch, had worked with Max Reinhardt, as an actor and assistant director, he had also studied art history at university, and had shown in his German-made films particular interest in set design, lighting, framing and composition, and pictorial beauty in general, sometimes at the expense of narrative clarity. While his connection with the expressionist movement of the early 1920s is debatable,[3] it seems clear, as Janet Bergstrom has suggested, that he associated himself with the more self-consciously "artistic" elements of Weimar cinema, with their tendency to abstraction and an appeal to an educated audience that could recognize references to "particular genres and styles of painting."[4] Though this was to cause him considerable problems in an industry that valued strong narratives and clearly defined characters and motivation above all else, he was initially hired by William Fox specifically for his artistry, as exemplified above all in *The Last Laugh,* and for the cultural prestige that his work and reputation would bring to the studio.

Unfamiliarity with Murnau's earlier work in Germany is not, unfortunately, restricted to American audiences and critics of the 1920s; even today the four films mentioned above remain virtually the only ones discussed by English-language critics, even in surveys of Murnau's career as a whole. Once again the reasons for this are partly circumstantial: eight of the German films (together with the American-made *Four Devils*) are currently considered "lost," while most of the others are available only in isolated archive copies. Even as late as 1965, when the English translation of Lotte Eisner's influential *Murnau* was published, *Der Brennende Acker* (which has since been discovered) was thought to be lost, and Eisner admits to having seen *Phantom* and *Die Finanzen des Grossherzogs* in incomplete and very poor-quality prints that distorted much of their original visual beauty. Far better prints of both these films now exist in the Munich Film Museum, and these, together with the renewed accessibility of *Der Brennende Acker,* make it possible to see the overall continuity of Murnau's career in a much clearer light. *Der Brennende*

Acker, besides being a masterly film in its own right, is an important forerun-ner of both *Sunrise* and *City Girl*, and *Phantom* certainly deserves to rank with the best of Murnau's work as a whole.[5] I intend, therefore, to center my com-ments on the German films around the lesser-known ones, in an attempt to redress the largely fortuitous balance of interest that has prevailed up to now.

Although Murnau was reported as saying in an interview for *Theatre Magazine* (January 1928): "I will not do a picture that is based on a theme not to my liking or conviction," there seems at first sight little consistency in the subject matter even of those of his German films that survive. There is the often stilted melodrama of the earliest of these, *Der Gang in die Nacht* (1920); an early treatment of the "Old Dark House" theme in *Schloss Vogelöd* (1921); the classic horror of *Nosferatu* (1922); the close-to-the-soil values of *Der Brennende Acker* (1922) and the city themes of *Phantom* (1922) and *The Last Laugh* (1924); the idyllic island setting and aristocratic characters of *Die Finanzen des Grossherzogs* (1923); and the adaptations of classic theatre in *Faust* (1926) and *Tartuffe* (1925). The scripts for almost all these films were written either by Carl Mayer *(Der Gang in die Nacht, Schloss Vogelöd, The Last Laugh,* and *Tartuffe)* or by Thea von Harbou, sometimes in collaboration with others (the four successive films *Der Brennende Acker, Phantom,* the lost *Die Austreibung,* and *Die Finanzen des Grossherzogs*), but there seems no obvious continuity in theme or treatment that would point to the overriding influence of one writer or the other.

The visual style of the films shows a similar combination of recur-ring names and divergence of effects: from 1922 onward Murnau used either Rochus Gliese or the team of Robert Herlth and Walter Röhrig as his set designers, while Karl Freund and Fritz Arno Wagner were the cameramen most often employed (sometimes together, as in *Der Brennende Acker*). Yet the visuals of the last-named film—dark, brooding, introspective, and full of "Rembrandt lighting" effects—are in complete contrast to the location shooting of *Die Finanzen des Grossherzogs*, where sunlight sparkling on water, the open air, physical sensuality, and natural beauty are emphasized. Rochus Gliese designed both films, nevertheless, and Freund photographed them. Lotte Eisner has discussed at some length (in chapter 4 of her *Murnau*) the director's involvement in creating the overall visual effect of his films, and there can be little doubt that, despite the fact that (like Hitchcock) Murnau rarely even glanced through the viewfinder, he had a very clear idea of how he wanted his films to look and was constantly offer-ing suggestions and advice as to how to achieve this; it can be assumed, then, that these differing effects are intentional rather than fortuitous.

The fact that his early films at least seem to offer no instantly recognizable thematic or visual "signature" may derive from Murnau's concern to take each film as it came along and find the correct visual solution to the problems that it presented, rather than to adapt varying types of material to suit the requirements of an overriding visual style (in contrast to a Jancsó or a Fellini). By the time he came to America his watchword—if we are to judge from the interviews that he gave there—had become "simplicity," but it was to be a simplicity achieved through the fullest possible acceptance and utilization of the camera's technical resources. "Real art is simple, but simplicity requires the greatest art," as he put it in the interview for *Theatre Magazine* already mentioned.[6] For *McCall's Magazine* he outlined a "dream" scenario that anticipates with startling exactness the ideal film project of the Italian neorealists twenty years later: "One of my dreams is to make a motion picture of six reels, with a single room for setting and a table and chair for furniture. The wall at the back would be blank, there would be nothing to distract from the drama that was unfolding between a few human beings in that room. Some day I shall make that picture."[7] Yet two paragraphs later he is talking enthusiastically about the filming of *Four Devils* and the elaborate equipment devised to suit the particular requirements of that film:

> The picture I am working on now is a circus story and naturally the camera must not stand stock still in such a gay place as a circus! It must gallop after the equestrienne, it must pick out the painted tears of the clown and jump from him to a high box to show the face of the rich lady thinking about the clown.
>
> So I have had them build me a sort of travelling crane with a platform swung at one end for the camera. My staff has nicknamed it the "Go-Devil." The studios will all have Go-Devils some day, to make the camera mobile.

In the fullest and most interesting of these interviews, conducted two years earlier by Matthew Josephson for *Motion Picture Classic* (October 1926), Murnau had already stressed the same ideas:

> "Simplicity! Greater and greater simplicity—that will be the keynote of the new films." Murnau was speaking with ardor, gesticulating with his long limbs, whenever his English, altho correct and without foreign accent, failed him.
>
> "Our whole effort," he went on, "must be bent toward ridding motion pictures of *all that does not belong to them*, of all that

is unnecessary and trivial and drawn from other sources—all the tricks, gags, "business" not of the cinema, but of the stage and the written book. That is what has been accomplished when certain films reached the level of great art. That is what I tried to do in "The Last Laugh." We must try for more and more simplicity and devotion to pure motion picture technique and material.[8]

Interestingly, Murnau went on to suggest later in the interview that Lubitsch had not yet "entirely cast off the influence of the stage" and that "many of his films give you the feeling of watching action on a stage."

Though Murnau's ambition to "photograph thought" is probably most fully realized in *The Last Laugh* and *Sunrise,* all the other surviving films contain sequences in which either special photographic effects or the use of landscape and setting are intended to convey states of mind, emotions or ideas. In most cases, however, there is little attempt at "simplicity," at least on the level of plot: melodramatic contrivances, mechanical changes of heart, deceptions, disguises, misunderstandings, convoluted and often incomprehensible schemings and maneuverings, combine to make any attempt at coherent plot summary a thankless and ultimately useless task, for it is not on that level that the films' lasting interest is to be found.[9] Equally, though Murnau's declared aim from *The Last Laugh* onward was to eliminate the use of subtitles[10] as completely as possible, the earlier films are often bogged down in elaborate verbal explanations and descriptions.

The most systematic use of special effects in the German films (other than *The Last Laugh,* which I will discuss separately) is to be found in *Nosferatu, Phantom,* and *Faust.* The various devices used in *Nosferatu* are all intended to create a sense of awe and fear in the audience and to set Nosferatu himself—physically at least—apart from ordinary human experience. Some of these no longer work for a modern audience: speeded-up and stop-motion photography, as applied to the phantom coach and the stacking of the coffins, is (and perhaps always was) too indelibly associated with comic effect to create the shudder of fear that Murnau was seeking. Nosferatu rising bolt upright from his coffin on the ship, fading from sight, or dissolving through the wall of the house he has rented in Wismar, are rather more successful; but the most authentically eerie effects are achieved through less obvious camera trickery. Most of these involve a slight rather than a blatant distortion of the familiar: removing an expected element from a scene in order to turn it into something strange, or setting a character and his environment into unanticipated juxtaposition.

Such images would include the shots of the doomed ship, all sails set and its crew already dead, making its way ominously across the ocean and later gliding impeccably into place into the harbor as Nosferatu's assistant, the insane Knock, watches from his prison cell. Or Ellen standing on a bleak seashore studded with crosses, searching for some sign of Hutter's arrival, while her friends enjoy a leisurely game of croquet. (Many of Murnau's most memorable images, throughout his career, are linked in some way with water: all the most striking scenes in *Der Gang in die Nacht* take place on the seashore, especially the shot of the blind pianist standing erect in the prow of a rowing boat, hands in the pocket of his overcoat, silhouetted against a bleak expanse of empty water, with a thin horizon of land near the top of the frame separating sea and sky.)

Architecture too is used to accentuate the sense of strangeness and weirdness, though without the deliberate visual distortions of an expressionist work like *Caligari*.[11] Murnau's buildings are real enough; it is the way in which they are filmed, and, especially, the positions in which the characters are framed within them, that create a sense of omnipresent oppressiveness throughout the film. Nosferatu's castle is full of arches: low, wide ones which seem ready to crush Hutter as he stands beneath them; high, pointed ones that make him look small and vulnerable; arches hardly bigger than a human being that both match and accentuate the angular figure of Nosferatu huddled inside them; archways, even, within archways, so that we see the characters in a series of multiple framings and confinements. Then, too, there is the decayed building into which Nosferatu moves to complete the last stage of his quest, its facade riddled with empty window sockets so that it is almost more emptiness than brickwork, and has an uncannily anthropomorphic quality as if it had somehow lost all its teeth, or its eyes.[12]

Judicious and restrained use of high- and low-angle shots accentuates moments of particular importance: high for the raft full of coffins making its way down the river, or the procession of coffins through the streets of the stricken town; and low from within the hold of the ship as Nosferatu prowls around the deck, silhouetted against the sails and the sky. Shadows, elongated and distorted, haunt the film—mostly, of course, of Nosferatu himself, his lean body and claw-like hands pulled even further out of shape as he moves stealthily up stairways and along corridors.

Though Murnau is conventionally classified as a mise-en-scène director, the most striking thematic patterns in the film are created by editing, in particular those that link Ellen and Nosferatu together and draw him inexorably toward her. When Nosferatu makes his first night visit to the terrified Hutter, the cutting sequence is as follows: Hutter hides under the sheets; the ominously static vampire is seen in the arched doorway; Ellen, in bed at home, wakes suddenly, then gets up and goes on to the balcony; she is perched on the balustrade, as if sleepwalking, and is rescued by Harding at the last moment; the shadow of Nosferatu, and of his long fingernails, creeps across Hutter's bed; Ellen calls Hutter's name; as if hearing this, Nosferatu turns his head, pauses, then leaves the room.[13] Later, when the ship bearing Nosferatu is on its way to Heligoland and Hutter is meanwhile hastening back home by coach, an editing pattern is established by which Ellen appears to be expecting and encouraging Nosferatu's arrival as much as that of her husband: we see the ship, for example; then Ellen standing in a doorway; then Hutter's coach; Ellen standing on a balcony, her arms stretched out as if in welcome; a shot of the ship; Ellen saying, ambiguously, "I must go to him!"; Hutter's coach; then the ship gliding into the harbor. Hutter's arrival home and his meeting with Ellen are intercut with shots of Nosferatu making his way through the streets of the town, with a coffin under his arm. When a variation of this pattern appears at the end of the film, it is, of course, used ironically, in that Ellen, while appearing to respond to Nosferatu's enticements, is in reality luring him to his destruction; yet the previous scenes create a sense of ambiguity in the Nosferatu-Ellen-Hutter triangle: the hints of a submerged attraction between the pure woman and the vampire enrich the erotic motifs of the film and make her choice much more interesting than the simple rejection of unmitigated evil in favor of the vapidly hearty goodness represented by Hutter than it might at first appear. The pattern here, reduced to its essentials, is: Nosferatu in close-up at a barred window, claws clutching the bars; Ellen moves to open her own window, then hesitates; she flings the window open; Nosferatu, framed in an arched doorway, raises both hands shoulder-high and moves away; Ellen sends Hutter to fetch the doctor; Nosferatu's shadow is seen on the stairs, making his way toward her.

Phantom, in contrast to the deliberately dark tones of *Nosferatu,* is clearly and evenly lit throughout its more realistic sequences; the dream and fantasy sequences, however, are filmed in a style which anticipates their more famous counterparts in *The Last Laugh.* Like *Sunrise* and many of Murnau's other films, it is a story of sexual obsession, with Lorenz, a failed poet, frenetically pursuing the "wrong" woman while neglecting the "right" one who waits patiently for him to see the light and return to her. Lorenz, in fact, is doubly obsessed: first by a mysterious and beautiful blonde, whose carriage knocks him over in the town square, and then, when his pursuit of her is thwarted by the disparities of their social and financial positions, he is diverted into a

$\mathcal{M}$urnau's image of the vampire in *Nosferatu* has become the classic one.

relationship with a woman who vaguely resembles his ideal and who, in alliance with her mother, ruthlessly and methodically exploits him. His need for money to satisfy his mistress leads him to deceive his wealthy aunt and his mother, and involves him in a plot to rob his aunt that ends in disgrace and a brief period of imprisonment before he is released and forgiven.

The theme of delusion is central to the film, with Lorenz trying to live up to the double roles of great poet and vivacious, free-spending lover, to both of which he is pathetically unsuited. Many of the finest sequences in the film convey the sense of distortion and unreality appropriate to a mentality that lives in a dreamworld of its own creation and totters increasingly out of rational control, and the best of these are comparable to Murnau's later creation of a purely subjective reality in parts of *The Last Laugh*. After his first encounter with Veronika, his ideal woman, Lorenz returns home (literally) in a daze, his mind full of visions of himself vainly pursuing her carriage; he then fantasizes himself as a famous poet worthy of Veronika's admiration and respect. Reality and delusion increasingly diverge: he shows his poems to a well-known critic, who says that they are worthless; nevertheless he tells his aunt that his fame and fortune have been assured by the critic's approval, borrows money from her on the strength of his future prospects, and neglects his job to such an extent that he is dismissed. As he plunges deeper into financial dependence on his new mistress and resorts to increasingly desperate schemes of finding money, he justifies his actions to himself by his hopes that his poetry will earn him enough to pay everything back; reality forces itself upon him, however, and his unbalanced and desperate state of mind is mirrored in an astonishing scene in which the solid facades of the houses seem to collapse upon him as he hurries along the street, and then even their shadows pursue him. In the middle of an empty square he thinks he sees Veronika's carriage drive right over him and vainly chases its image to her house. Later, as he revels with his mistress in a restaurant, the camera, watching him from a high angle, rapidly recedes, after which the whole room appears to whirl and sway around Lorenz, reflecting his total loss of control and the final abandonment of his remaining moral scruples, before the movement ends in a sickening plunge or "fall."[14] An additional, bizarre touch in these scene is the superimposed image of what appears to be a monkey riding a bicycle above Lorenz's table.

    The special effects in *Faust* are more obviously related to the theme and influence of the supernatural and, impressive though many of them still are, they are rarely used to represent psychological reality, as in the earlier films. Most often, they suggest the power and manipulation of Mephistopheles who, especially in the first half of the film, is seen looming menacingly over the other characters—as in the shot where a preacher, appealing to his flock during the plague, is dwarfed by a huge blow-up of Mephisto's face emerging behind him, with the steeples and pointed roofs of the town outlined against the Devil's features. More interesting is the use of forced perspective, which Murnau mentioned as one of his main stylistic interests in the *McCall's Magazine* interview some years later, especially in the shot of Faust's room as he is being rejuvenated, where a foreshortened table in the foreground, a large pile of books, and a curving wall cutting off almost a third of the screen, serve to accentuate the vast bulk of Mephisto himself.

    Trick photography of magical flights through the air, horsemen galloping across the sky, supernatural transformations, and letters that appear to write themselves on parchment are standard and obligatory devices for a subject of this kind; in the scenes of Gretchen's madness, however, Murnau occasionally uses superimpositions to take us inside the character's mind.

As she calls out from her prison cell for Faust to help her, a close-up of her face is superimposed on a fast tracking-shot across a stretch of countryside; Faust, like Nosferatu responding to Ellen, "hears" her and hurries to her rescue. Shortly before this we have seen her own belief that she is rocking her child to sleep in her arms merge into the reality that she has unwittingly buried it in the snow, and, as she awaits her execution for murder, her memories of earlier happiness are intercut with shots of her present situation in which the angle and posture of her body remain constant throughout, suggesting that she no longer distinguishes between actual and mental reality.

Though one side of Murnau's visual imagination is clearly fascinated by the potential of the camera to take us into a character's thoughts, he is equally interested in using landscape and settings to convey emotions and states of mind. The scene in which Faust first invokes Mephisto at the crossroads is appropriately ominous and foreboding: a full moon gleams balefully in the darkness and two dead trees frame the meeting place. *Der Brennende Acker* begins with a death-bed scene while a storm rages outside, producing dramatic lighting effects that foreshadow the fierce personal and moral conflicts contained in this film and also establishing a mood of apprehension as the curse imposed on the land begins to work itself out once again, destroying those who seek to take unscrupulous profit from it. When Johannes and Gerda, whose affair is to end in mutual hatred, first meet, they appear as dark figures against a snow-covered landscape, with bare trees surrounding them. When Helga, Johannes's wife, discovers that she has, with the best of intentions, sold the land from which he planned to make a fortune by developing it for oil, she is seen trudging through the snow beside a river, collapsing and hauling herself to her feet again; shortly afterward her body is recovered from the river. Almost all the exteriors, in fact, are shot in winter, conveying an atmosphere of bleakness and barrenness that emphasizes that disaster comes to those who attempt to *misuse* the land; in contrast the interiors of the peasant farmhouse are bathed in "Rembrandt" lighting effects that stress the spiritual serenity and harmony of the family. These interiors also employ some remarkable deep-focus effects, deriving partly from the lighting and partly from careful grouping of the characters and arrangement of the props to emphasize perspective.

Schloss Vogelöd, often mistakenly thought of as a horror film along the lines of *Nosferatu*, is a precursor, both in setting and theme, of the "Old Dark House" motif that enjoyed a considerable vogue in America in the late 1920s and early 1930s: a house party assembles in an isolated castle, in an atmospherically bleak and stormy setting, where a series of mysterious events, both frightening and comic, occur. Disguises, flashbacks, and complicated plot revelations lead to the discovery of the truth about a crime committed in the castle several years previous. Stylistically, the most effective contrasts are between the "present" setting, dark, ominous, and highly formalized, and the flashbacks in which the Baroness recalls her happy life with her now dead husband, scenes in which nature is seen as fruitful and productive, with the young woman arranging flowers against a background of a lake and blossoming trees. Similar imagery, conventional enough in its associations, but handled with delicacy and visual tact, occurs at the end of *Phantom,* when the reformed and repentant Lorenz finally marries his long-suffering Marie and goes off to live in an idyllic country setting of spring, blossoms, and renewal.

The themes of most of Murnau's German films impose a "dark" visual treatment as the characters struggle against the mysterious and hostile forces, either external or internal, that threaten to destroy them. The main exception is *Die Finanzen des Grossherzogs,* a film full of a sensuous response to the physical beauty of both the natural landscape and the human body that, in this respect at least, resembles *Tabu* more than any of Murnau's other work. The island setting allows Murnau to indulge his love of water as a constant visual motif, but here the sea sparkles constantly in the ever-present sunlight and the threat to the characters comes from the machinations of other human beings rather than from natural forces. The film opens with an extraordinary homoerotic scene of naked youths swimming in the sun-dappled water and scrambling out on to the rocks to dive in once more to retrieve coins tossed in by the watching Grand Duke. (Lotte Eisner's dismissal of the erotic power of this scene may perhaps be attributed to the poor quality of the print in which she viewed it.) Here, and in the finest sequences elsewhere in the film, the screen is filled with light, movement, and a sense of spatial freedom; later in the film the camera appears to be set on a small boat as it approaches the shore, yet, as the boat docks at the harbor, the camera smoothly continues the forward movement and glides unexpectedly on to the land. Even the city, so often a source of temptation and corruption in Murnau's work, is here seen as visually attractive, particularly when it is viewed from the perspective of someone approaching it from the sea. Though the emphasis on natural beauty is important for the theme of the film, which concerns the duke's attempts to preserve the island from a group of unscrupulous businessmen who want to mine it to produce sulfur, the actual mechanics of the plot are both tedious and inane, and the realization of the theme in terms of character interactions is conspicuously unsuccessful.

Unsatisfactory as it is overall, however, the film embodies a major theme of both Murnau's German and American work: the conflict of values between the city and the country, or between modern and traditional moral codes. In this case, the values being defended are more aesthetic than moral, though the idea of preserving nature from indiscriminate exploitation is also found in *Der Brennende Acker,* where the search for oil, and the obsessive greed that accompanies this, brings disaster to several of the characters. The conflict of values is clearly embodied within the family itself here, with one brother, Peter, defending and trying to maintain the traditional values of the peasant family, and the other, Johannes, contemptuously rejecting these for the more immediate satisfactions—financial, social, and sexual—of the city. His attempt to import these back into the countryside, setting up the oil wells and (after rejecting the love of the faithful peasant girl Maria) playing off the affections of the married Helga against those of her stepdaughter Gerda, leads to death for both Helga and Gerda and financial ruin for himself. As with the similarly deluded Lorenz in *Phantom,* however, redemption is made possible though Maria's forgiveness and a return to acceptance of the unchanging values of his family. These values are both religious (the family is seen, in one particularly beautiful shot, grouped around the table at prayer) and ethical, with bread used throughout the film as a symbol of contact with the soil and a reminder that the truest human needs are very basic and straightforward: "Bread is a sacred thing," Peter reminds Johannes early in the film and, in the scene where the humbled and repentant Johannes is forgiven by his family and urged to return to them, a loaf of bread is prominently visible on the table.

Though there is a strong thematic parallel between this film and *Phantom,* where Lorenz, purged and chastened by his experiences in the city, finally recognizes the worth of the values that have been embodied in his mother, his aunt, and Marie throughout, the visual contrast between "city" and "country" is rather more bizarre in the latter film. It seems at first that Lorenz and his mother must live in a small village: she dresses like the peasant women of *Der Brennende Acker* and their home is lit and furnished in a style that elsewhere in Murnau's work denotes "rustic simplicity." Yet, once Lorenz goes out of doors, we realize that he lives in the suburbs of a modern city, complete with the nightclubs, fashionable shops, and high-class restaurants that will lure him to his downfall. Lorenz's sister too feels the need to escape from the restrictive monotony of her home life and leaves home near the beginning of the film; Lorenz encounters her at intervals afterward, always in the setting of sophisticated nightlife, surrounded by male admirers and obviously making her living by selling her sexual favors. Like Lorenz, she comes to see the error of her ways and returns to beg her mother for forgiveness, though she is not seen as sharing in the final reconciliation, after which Lorenz and Marie move firmly away from the city and retreat to a rural paradise. Despite the ambiguities of the setting, however, the contrast of moral values is virtually identical to that of *Der Brennende Acker* and prefigures both *Sunrise* and *City Girl* (originally called *Our Daily Bread*) in Murnau's American work.[15]

Linked to this theme is a typical structural pattern in which a character rejects or betrays the trust (or love) placed in him by another; succumbs to the temptations offered by the city, usually embodied in a destructive female figure; and finally, after undergoing a period of suffering and humiliation, returns, chastened and wiser for the experience, to his original starting point. In *Der Brennende Acker* Johannes even returns to the very room he had contemptuously abandoned at the beginning of the film to find that Maria has faithfully kept it in perfect order for him during his absence. Murnau's treatment of the Gretchen-Faust story shares the basic elements of this structure, though Faust's betrayal is manipulated by Mephisto (who exploits, nevertheless, his victim's weakness of will) and he retreats to the mountains rather than plunging into dissipation in the city (a theme explored earlier in the film). At the end Faust redeems himself by rejecting the illusory satisfactions of his bargain with Mephisto, accepting his condition as an old man rather than trying to hold on to eternal youth, and begging for forgiveness as Gretchen is led to the stake. Here, of course, the reconciliation ends in physical death and spiritual transfiguration rather than in the beginning of a new and happier life on earth, but the essential meaning is the same.

Dr. Boerne, of *Der Gang in die Nacht* rejects his fiancée Helene to marry Lily, a cabaret performer. Lily leaves him for a young painter whose blindness Boerne had earlier cured, and Helene refuses his attempts at reconciliation. By the end of the film Boerne has—unwittingly—been the cause of Lily's death and, in remorse, kills himself. Here self-knowledge is achieved, but too late to result in the usual forgiveness, and the city-country contrast is reversed, with Boerne retreating to a fishing village to live with Lily, and the deserted Helene continuing to live in the town.[16] A more interesting variation is found in *Nosferatu*, where the countryside is the source of evil and infects the city, while Hutter's responsibility for his bride's death is indirect and relatively innocent. Yet he does "abandon" her and he does act as the catalyst that brings Nosferatu to Wismar and to Ellen. If anything, it is the woman here who is intrigued by, and almost succumbs to, temptation; but she finally acts out her self-sacrificial role and redeems her husband through her death.

Neither *Die Finanzen des Grossherzogs* nor *Tartuffe* can easily be fitted into this framework, and *Tartuffe* in particular has always presented problems to critics attempting to find an overall unity of style and theme in Murnau's work. It is probably the least satisfactory of the films Murnau made between 1921 and 1925, partly because it removes most of the subtleties of the Molière play and transforms the characters into something very simplified and one-dimensional. There are some interesting visual and narrative effects, nevertheless: the Molière story is presented as a film shown by an old man's grandson to warn him against his scheming and hypocritical housekeeper; the young man also directly addresses the audience, warning us to be on our guard against similar behavior and asking rhetorically at the conclusion, "Do you know who is sitting beside you?" Within the framing story Murnau makes effective use of extreme close-ups, especially of the housekeeper's sly, unattractive features, and in the central story there are several moments where deliberate visual distortions help to remind us not to accept what we are seeing at face value. Objects such as candles are often placed disturbingly close to the camera so that they take on a disproportionate size and shape; shadows shift and move, apparently of their own volition, as servants carry lighted candles up and down the stairs. The disparity between Tartuffe's outward behavior and his true motives is usually signaled by close-ups of Emil Jannings's features, and especially his eyes: a typical pattern is to show Tartuffe's eyes, then what he is looking at (usually Elmire's bosom or ankles), then Tartuffe's leering expression, followed by a shot of Elmire's embarrassed face from his point of view. The process of flirtation will then be interrupted, as when Tartuffe catches sight of the distorted reflection of Orgon's features in the teapot and he quickly shifts to a display of virtuous self-denial. Deprived of the verbal dimension so necessary to Molière's play, however, this method inevitably makes Tartuffe's hypocrisy blatant and obvious throughout and the film soon becomes an insistent and strained harping on the one motif.

 Tartuffe (as American reviewers were quick to complain) isn't really particularly *funny*, and critics have always been rather uneasy about Murnau's sense of comedy, with Lotte Eisner being by no means alone in suggesting that he may have been "obliged to 'intermingle' the Luna Park gags in *Sunrise*" (p. 183). Many of the German films, however, contain comic sequences far more heavy-handed and arbitrarily motivated than anything in *Sunrise*. In *Die Finanzen des Grossherzogs* a would-be blackmailer is lured to a rendezvous where he is set upon by an ape and a man wearing a lion's-head mask; and *Schloss Vogelöd* contains two comic dream sequences, in one of which a guest sees himself being dragged from bed by the claw of

*I*n a parody of the youthful love interest in *Faust,* Mephisto (Emil Jannings)
flirts with Gretchen's mother.

a gigantic bird, and in the other a kitchen lad imagines himself being fed
endless spoonfuls of cream while his boss, the cook, is humiliated—neither
of them having much to do with the convoluted plot.

These sequences are perhaps merely bizarre; *Faust,* however, especially in the second half, contains many scenes of low comedy which,
though perfectly within the tradition established by earlier treatments of the
story, are generally rather embarrassingly broad and overdone. Faust's
courting of Gretchen is paralleled by a subplot in which Mephisto flirts with
the buxom Marthe: as Faust laughingly pursues Gretchen in an Edenic
garden, Mephisto and Marthe provide a grotesque and down-to-earth parody
of their innocent playfulness. One effect of this is to allow the older couple
to act out more blatantly the sexual desire that is sublimated in the young
lovers; Mephisto's costume at this point contains two clearly phallic

elements, a long curling feather and a sword that refuses to stay in place under his cloak, while the sexual imagery for the other pair is slightly more subtle, with Gretchen opening, closing, then opening her window again as Faust begs to be allowed inside her room; she tries once more to close it, but this time Faust pushes it open. Though reviewers at the time seemed to enjoy such deliberately anachronistic touches as Mephisto mixing up a love potion as though he were shaking a cocktail, these scenes as a whole introduce a jarring note and ensure that Murnau has to work very hard to create an appropriately solemn and intense tone for the ending of the film.

The Last Laugh contains many of the elements, both stylistic and thematic, outlined above, but, though it is almost certainly the best of Murnau's German films, it is by no means the most typical or representative. On the whole, the other films display a conservative philosophy, emphasizing tradition, continuity, the soil, the eternal values of the past, the family, and woman either as temptress or as self-sacrificing redeemer; these are combined, however, with a readiness to utilize every possible technical resource and to experiment freely—and often expensively—to secure unusual, but appropriate, visual effects. Shooting moves freely between studio and location, often combining scenes of deliberate artifice and extreme naturalism within the same film; great attention is paid to lighting, creating results, especially in *Faust,* that were enthusiastically compared at the time to Rembrandt, Leonardo, and El Greco; there is a conscious striving to achieve three-dimensional depth effects through lighting, sets, and camera angles, most noticeably in *Der Brennende Acker;* the camera is moved freely, and often elaborately, whenever necessary; and there are some remarkable experiments with the subjective camera, designed to take us inside a character's mind and "photograph thought."

The combination of simplicity of theme and elaborate technical innovation to present that theme in purely "cinematic" terms was certainly one major reason for the success of *The Last Laugh* in the United States. As *Moving Picture World* put it: "It is a simple theme, but well told, and wonderfully well acted. . . . The production keeps pace with the acting. . . . It presents many novelties in production."[17] Other reviewers said much the same thing, though generally with greater sophistication. Talking to Matthew Josephson, Murnau gave his own version of his intentions:

> I wanted to try a story that you could really tell in five
> words, an exceedingly simple idea or situation; but the range, the
> feeling of the film which gave this story was to be limitless in its

power of understanding and dramatizing ideas. You can tell the story of "The Last Laugh" in a sentence, but I wanted the emotions of the central character to become something beyond the power of words to express. I wanted the camera to picture shades of feeling that were totally new and unexpected; *in all of which there is a subconscious self* which in a crisis may break out in the strangest ways, and this picture at times reached the subconscious man under his hotel livery.

The whole action of the thing pointed, for instance, to the moment where Jannings takes off his hotel uniform, so that as he removed his coat with its brass buttons the highest point of the drama was reached, a drama that was purely *visual*. The type of lighting and architecture we used helped a great deal toward this effect; everything superfluous that did not help to carry on the main idea was suppressed and thrown out of the picture.[18]

The particular scenes in which these intentions are realized are now standard examples in textbooks of film history and theory, though it is worth remembering that several of them were prefigured in *Phantom* and thus were not quite as unprecedented as is still commonly assumed. The shot of buildings swaying over the doorman as he scuttles along the street clutching his stolen uniform clearly recalls the scene in which the houses and their shadows "pursue" the frantic Lorenz; and the elaborate wedding sequence where he drunkenly fantasizes his triumphant return to his former prestige can be compared to the restaurant scene in the earlier film. Though knowledge of *Phantom* might have modified some of the raptures with which the "novelty" of *The Last Laugh* was greeted, it remains true, nevertheless, that the later film sets about creating what Murnau called "the subconscious man" in a much more systematic and consistent manner.

At the beginning of the film we see the doorman primarily in his public role, parading his splendor in the hotel lobby and condescendingly accepting the admiring tribute of his family and neighbors. With his demotion, however, we begin to see events quite literally through his own eyes: as he tries to read the notice of dismissal, the image blurs and goes out of focus to suggest his inability to comprehend or accept what is happening to him. With the removal of his uniform he shrinks and ages almost instantly; his movements take on a dazed, puppet-like quality and his body becomes bowed and hunched over. The temporary restoration of his uniform allows him to maintain his public status during the wedding, but his inner doubts

*M*any aspects of *The Last Laugh* were foreshadowed in Murnau's earlier, German-made *Phantom*. In both examples the character's mental confusion is mirrored in the physical world that appears to collapse around and on top of him.

and fears are conveyed by the fantasy sequence which begins once the revels are over. Two shots—of the drunken doorman blowing his whistle in the
kitchen and a man playing a horn outside—persuade us that we are "hearing" what are purely visual effects and prepare us for the subjective images
that follow. The doorman attempts to dance, then flops down on a chair; we
see his face and the room through his eyes as it begins to sway and then
revolve more and more rapidly around him; there is another close-up of his
face on which is superimposed a smaller image of himself in uniform supervising the revolving doors of the hotel; this then takes over as the central
image and becomes a comic "revenge fantasy" in which, in a whirl of optical
distortions and hand-held camerawork, he "proves" that he has not lost his
strength and amazes his detractors by lifting a huge trunk with only one hand
and even juggling it above his head; the camera sweeps rapidly round the
foyer taking in the admiring faces and the clapping hands of the spectators.

When he wakes the next morning, however, he is once again nothing but a tired old man, pawing helplessly at his uniform as he tries to find
the button that had fallen off the previous day when the uniform itself was
taken from him. His mental confusion is emphasized by more optical distortions—faces seen in double image or stretched to unearthly proportions by
an anamorphic lens—and as he makes his way unsteadily to work we see
objects and people through his wavering eyes; when he reaches the corner
opposite the hotel the image blurs and then comes sharply into focus as
he—and we—remember that he is no longer the doorman; the camera
tracks rapidly across the street to close in on his successor, conveying the
old man's shock and bewilderment.

For most of the following sequences we observe the increasingly
pathetic figure of the doorman as he struggles to cope with his new job as
toilet attendant, unable even to perform that smartly enough for the satisfaction of the guests, with any unusual visual effects reserved for the reactions
of others to his degradation: the fast track in to the close-up of his neighbor's[19] horrified face as she brings him his lunch, and the series of pans from
one window of the tenement building to another as the news of his disgrace
spreads. When he returns at night, vainly attempting to maintain the facade
of his earlier prestige, the women flock out to jeer at him and we return to
sharing his experience of humiliation as we see the contemptuous faces
jumbled together in a mass of superimpositions.

This combination of objectivity and subjectivity allows us to see all
facets of the doorman: his initial pompous self-satisfaction, his deflation, his
pathetic attempts to delude others, his moments of joyful wish fulfillment,

$\mathcal{T}$he doorman (Emil Jannings) in *The Last Laugh* imagines himself restored to, and even surpassing, his former state of physical vigor.

and his ultimate humiliation and defeat; all of these are seen both from the perspective of others and from within the man himself, so that we are moved steadily toward understanding and sympathy for the human being originally concealed inside the uniform. The fact that none of his family, neighbors, or fellow workers (with the solitary exception of the night watchman) is able to make a similar adjustment, suggests that it is only by means of the privileged insights provided by the camera that the inner reality of the character can be exposed and understood. This aspect also removes the film from the normal pattern of the extant German films in that there is no sense of reconciliation, forgiveness, or self-transcendence at the end; the optimistic conclusion, added primarily for commercial reasons, in which the doorman inherits a fortune and becomes a millionaire, could be seen as a perfunctory gesture in that direction, but it is clearly out of key with the movement of the rest of the film and provides only an external rather than an internal change. The world of *The Last Laugh* is purely that of the city, with the characters either hardened or defeated by its values; there is no countryside to provide either an alternative or an escape, and even the women are totally imbued with the city's distorted moral values and are unable to see beyond these. The only young woman of any significance in the film is the doorman's daughter, and she too scorns her father when his deception is revealed. The redemptive act of imaginative sympathy, performed in most of the other films by the heroine, is thus transferred outside the structure of the film itself and has to be carried out—if it is to take place at all—within the audience.

Though the success of *The Last Laugh* in America was more on an artistic than a commercial level, with its techniques eagerly discussed and debated within the film community, it was enough to bring Murnau a contract from Fox to make at least one film in the United States; at a meeting with Winfield Sheehan, the general manager of the company, in Berlin in 1926, it was agreed that the film would be based on Herman Sudermann's story "A Trip to Tilsit." The terms of the contract appear to have been remarkably generous, with Murnau being given a completely free hand in the selection of the subject, encouraged to bring Carl Mayer with him as scriptwriter,[20] Rochus Gliese as art director, and Herman Bing as assistant director, and promised complete creative control over the production. According to an article in *Motion Picture Classic* for July 1927[21] William Fox adhered scrupulously to his pledge not to interfere in the filming and ensured that Murnau received every facility he asked for in creating the elaborate sets that the project required. If this is true, speculations such as Eisner's that some of the comedy sequences may have been inserted against Murnau's will could have no foundation. Apart from the fact that several of the German films contain similar scenes of broad comedy, Murnau (like Paul Fejös filming *Lonesome* at virtually the same time) seems to have become fascinated by certain aspects of American popular culture and everyday life; he had ended the interview with Matthew Josephson by mentioning that he was on his way to Coney Island and commented: "There are wonderful types here, wonderful faces. Tremendous energy. The whole tradition here suggests speed, lightness, wild rhythms. Everything is novel. Sensational. I was in Child's Restaurant last night. It was an amazing place to me. Tonight I am going to Coney Island. It must be barbarous there, I would like to do a wild picture about Alaska."[22]

Murnau's enthusiasm was matched by that of critics like Josephson who considered that he "arrives at exactly the psychological moment, as we are on the verge of an era of truly great motion pictures." Though the pre-diction was to prove true enough for 1927–28, which saw the production of some of the finest films in Hollywood's history, the vogue for foreign films and directors had in fact passed its peak, and the introduction of sound was to interrupt the smooth progress towards increasing artistic sophistication and perfection that Josephson (and Murnau himself) anticipated. *Sunrise* itself, however, triumphantly justified the hopes that had been placed in it—on the artistic if not necessarily the commercial level.

As contemporary critics observed, Murnau had made neither an "American" nor a "Continental" film, but something with a deliberately "universal" quality that mediated between the two: *A Song of Two Humans,* as the film's subtitle puts it. The village setting is clearly central or northern European and most closely resembles that of *Der Brennende Acker* among Murnau's German films; while the city, though furnished with shop signs in English, is not recognizably American in architecture. As a result the film looks exotic without being totally alien, while the presence of two familiar Hollywood stars gives the audience a central point of identification through-out. Interesting enough, one repeated complaint about the look of the film involved an outraged reaction to the wig worn by Janet Gaynor intended to suggest her sexually innocent—even repressed—personality in contrast to the dark-haired vamp played by Margaret Livingstone. Murnau felt obliged to defend himself in the interview for *McCall's Magazine:* "In *Sunrise* some of the critics were severe with me because of the ugly two-colored wig I allowed Janet Gaynor to wear. They complained that it extinguished her beauty and made her almost plain. They did not guess that that was exactly what I was trying to do! I wished Janet to play, not Janet Gaynor the screen beauty but a poor stupid little peasant girl. I had to submerge her physical beauty to emphasize the beauty of her heart."[23]

Though the structure of the film follows almost exactly the pattern of *Der Brennende Acker* and *Phantom,* it too mediates between the exotic and the familiar from the viewpoint of an American audience. The pattern of the man rejecting the pure love of his wife for the temptations of the woman from the city, then, after a period of humiliation and anguish, being redeemed by the wife's unflagging devotion, is varied to some extent from its earlier manifestations: the city provides the setting for the reconciliation; the husband's betrayal is taken to the extent of the attempted murder of his wife; and a happy ending is somewhat arbitrarily imposed on the film after the false alarm of the wife's death on the return journey. The moral absolutes embodied in this structure—the primacy of the monogamous couple, the preservation of traditional values, the superiority of a rural way of life to the corruption of the city, and the redemptive power of a pure asexual love were as acceptable to an American audience as to a German one[24] and would certainly not have required any great readjustment of habitual patterns of thought. The power of the film, as always with Murnau, came less from any originality in the subject matter than from the dramatic intensity and visual beauty with which it was presented.

In most respects, then, _Sunrise_ was the ideal subject for Murnau's American début: it had strong affinities with the themes and outlook of his earlier work and yet was close enough to the mentality of an American popular audience not to appear too strange or disconcerting. The change from the original ending of the Sudermann story, in which the husband drowns on the return journey but the wife survives to bear the child conceived during their reconciliation, may have been partly a concession to the American obsession with happy endings, yet it also fulfills the normal Murnau pattern in which, after a period of suffering and estrangement, the couple are reunited, with the husband in particular wiser and stronger for the experience. Meanwhile the artistic freedom permitted, and respected, by his contract with Fox allowed Murnau to push forward with the stylistic experimentation that had attracted Hollywood's attention to him in the first place. He was thus in a position to avoid the familiar traps for a foreign director in the United States: on the one hand, producing something too European, or alien, in its sensibility; and, on the other, trying too hard, and too soon, to assimilate himself to an outlook that he did not fully understand.

As Murnau's own comments on _The Last Laugh_ make clear, he was never particularly interested in exploring the economic or social contexts within which the human dramas of his stories took place. For him, the central issue of _The Last Laugh_ was the doorman's reaction to the loss of his uniform and the social status that it brought him; the question of whether it is right that society should be organized in such a way that an event of this kind can be so significant, is raised only obliquely and occasionally within the film itself. To put it another way: the doorman can be seen as both the exemplar and the victim of a petit bourgeois mentality; Murnau concentrates—powerfully and movingly—on his personal misery, but chooses not to analyze the ultimate reasons for it. Similarly, though both _Der Brennende Acker_ and _Die Finanzen des Grossherzogs_ mention industrialization as one of the causes of the characters' problems, this is left in the background while the films concentrate on personal conflicts and relationships. In _Sunrise_ too Murnau simply draws on a traditional body of assumptions about the virtues of the countryside and the

evils of the city as, first a starting point, and then a backdrop, for the personal drama of his characters; the film makes no attempt to examine whether these assumptions really retain any validity in the context of the 1920s, and they are in essence used as metaphors rather than clues, or tools, by means of which contemporary social realities can be more fully understood.

In *Sunrise,* as in *The Last Laugh,* Murnau was primarily concerned with devising methods to achieve what he had come to call "photographing thought":

> They say that I have a passion for "camera angles." But I do not take trick scenes from unusual positions just to get startling effects. To me the camera represents the eye of a person, through whose mind one is watching the events on the screen. It must follow characters at times into difficult places, as it crashed through the reeds and pools in *Sunrise* at the heels of the Boy, rushing to keep his tryst with the Woman of the City. It must whirl and peep and move as swiftly as thought itself, when it is necessary to exaggerate for the audience the idea or emotion that is uppermost in the mind of the character. I think the films of the future will use more and more of these "camera angles," or as I prefer to call them these "dramatic angles." They help to photograph thought.[25]

In an earlier interview, he had suggested some other ways in which this could be done and had stressed in particular the need to express ideas and states of mind visually: "One way of eliminating titles is by showing two antagonistic thoughts as parallels; for example, by wishing to convey the wealth of a certain person as being extreme, I would show alongside of him a greatly impoverished character. Symbolism would obviate titles. I like the reality of things, but not without fantasy; they must dovetail."[26] In many respects *Sunrise* goes beyond *The Last Laugh* in presenting thought and emotion visually, aided on occasion by an evocative musical score that, according to *Motion Picture Classic,* was based on motifs supplied by the director himself.[27]

The film opens with a visual contrast between city and country that reflects one of Murnau's major themes: the city is visually complex, crowded, full of motion and activity, with split-screen images showing fast moving trains, streets, ships, and beaches full of holidaymakers; the village, on the other hand, is static, timeless and peaceful. Next, the contrast is transmuted into human terms, with the Woman of the City (none of the characters is named) parading her alien values—her cigarette, her dark-hued fashionable clothing, her high heels, her newfangled dancing steps—before the disap-

proving eyes of the old peasant couple with whom she is lodging, as they stolidly sup their gruel with wooden spoons out of wooden bowls. The imagery is straight out of *Phantom* and employs exactly the same codes of lighting, furnishing, and clothing to set moral decadence against moral worth.

The Woman also imports movement into the village setting, the camera tracking with her as she sets out to lure the Husband (or Boy, as Murnau rather incongruously referred to him) from the loving arms of his wife. Another traditional visual contrast sets the dark-haired, stylishly dressed vamp against the fair-haired housewife and mother, the notorious wig drawn tightly back into a bun, and her prim and simple clothing given its ultimate significance by an apron. A flashback recalls the happiness of the earlier days of their marriage, but the temptation is too much for the Husband: the camera rushes with him across the marshes, brushing aside reeds and bushes, to discover the Woman, poised enticingly against the water's edge and silhouetted against the glare of a full moon. Their passionate embrace is intercut with a shot of the forlorn Wife cradling her baby.

The Woman suggests a means of disposing of the obstacle that the Wife presents to them: "Couldn't she get drowned?"—the written words trickling and dissolving to the bottom of the screen. The idea is visualized more successfully as a mental image of the Wife's body being thrown from the boat. The outraged Husband makes as if to strangle the temptress, but she turns the attack into an embrace and proceeds with her enticements: an image of the city appears as a background to the marshes, then takes over the screen completely in another complex montage of frenzied camera movement and multiple images, accompanied by vibrant jazz on the sound track. The vision of the delights of the city fades back to the marshes, with the Woman dancing frantically and seductively on the shore. She helps him pick rushes to keep him afloat after the "accident" and he walks slowly home past a row of fishing nets that serve to emphasize the mental and moral entanglements in which he finds himself. In bed that night he dreams of water, the superimposed image rising to overwhelm him until the camera tilts upwards to reveal the village church; waking in panic, he finds the dream replaced by a memory of the hidden bundle of rushes, the camera sweeping in toward them to convey his mental excitement and confusion. A superimposed image of the woman clinging round his neck completes the ambiguous cycle of sexual obsession, moral repugnance, and renewed sensual entrapment.

Though the attractions of the vamp inevitably appear dated to a modern audience, so that some of the imagery associated with her is now faintly ludicrous rather than alluring, this part of the film still succeeds remarkably in conveying emotions, ideas and moral conflicts in a purely visual manner. The attempted murder is presented more objectively, with the conflict between the Husband's conscience and his destructive obsession revealed through the sluggishness of his movements and gestures (Murnau made George O'Brien wear specially weighted boots for this sequence to impose a sense of strain and effort on every step he took). As he lurches zombie-like toward his shrinking, cowering wife, he hears the sound of the church bell (picking up the visual image from his dream in which the church also represented his conscience); he stops, rushes back to his place in the boat, snatches up the oars, and starts to row furiously to the shore.

The sequence in the streetcar which follows is probably the most beautiful and moving in the film, the most "natural" in human terms as the remorseful husband follows his wife, not daring to approach her but pleading mutely for forgiveness, and she huddles fearfully away from him in the furthest corner that she can find. Yet, as Lotte Eisner has shown in *Murnau*, this, like many other apparently realistic scenes in the film, was built up through a complex combination of natural locations and elaborate trick photography and special effects; out of it all, however, and assisted by the subtle rhythms of the cutting and the melodious harmonies of the music, we receive the impression of an unbroken movement that joins the country to the city and provides both a pause and a bridge between the destructive passion of the first half of the film and the constructive reconciliation which is to follow.

The mood of this sequence continues once they have reached the city: the wife still fearful and timorous, her body angled as far away from her husband as possible, while he attempts vainly to appease and reassure her. He persuades her to enter a restaurant and to eat what appears to be a piece of bread—the familiar Murnau symbol of family harmony and continuity. He buys her flowers and is allowed to touch her once again, stroking her shoulder protectively and holding her hand; a church bell rings, no longer the sign of an uneasy conscience, but an invitation to a new beginning. They follow a wedding party into the church and sit at the back watching; as the words of the service reach the admonition for the man to protect his wife "from all harm," the repentant Husband breaks down in tears, laying his head on her lap as she comforts him. Reunited once more, they leave the church together to the sound of bells and walk blissfully across the busy street, oblivious to the chaos of traffic around them and providentially immune to harm. As they reach the middle of the street, the image dissolves from the city to a peaceful country scene and, caught up in their own private

The couple in *Sunrise* set out on their journey to the city, the wife (Janet Gaynor) innocently happy and with no suspicion of the fate her husband (George O'Brien) plans for her. After the attempted murder she still shrinks from him as he tries remorsefully to console her. The contrast between the "primitive" village and the modern city is particularly striking.

world, they stop to embrace. Another dissolve returns us, and them, to reality as they find themselves at the center of a traffic jam.

The introduction of a comic note into this scene, tastefully and movingly handled as it is, signals a shift of tone within the film, and the remainder of the city scenes take the couple through a series of incidents in which their rustic naivete is contrasted—always to their advantage—with the superficiality and cynicism of city life. They are more at home at the fairground, a traditional meeting place for people of all types and backgrounds, as they use their country skills to recapture a pig that has escaped from one of the booths and later perform a peasant dance in front of an admiring audience. This section of the film ends with them dancing together, locked in a world of their own, as the camera tracks away and prepares for their return to their home environment.

Though the values of the city continue—in a relatively lighthearted way—to be presented unfavorably during these scenes, it is not incongruous that it should be the setting in which the reconciliation of husband and wife takes place: the stages through which their renewed understanding develops—bread, flowers, and then the church—are all "country" values and are not necessarily linked to a city context, and throughout their later adventures in the city they retain their native simplicity and openness. Though many viewers have found the comedy of these sequences jarring after the tenderness of the reconciliation scenes, they are generally well enough handled on their own terms and are not significantly out of key with the themes of the rest of the film: in some respects they are among its most "American" aspects, with their anticipations of Frank Capra's Mr. Deeds and Mr. Smith showing up the phoniness of the city slickers through the innocence and spontaneity of their actions.

The return home begins with the villagers dancing around bonfires on huge rafts in the middle of the lake; a storm suddenly bursts over them and the boat in which the couple are traveling is swamped. The disaster is unexpected and effectively handled, with the desperate husband searching, apparently in vain, for his wife and emphasizing his reformation by trying to strangle the Woman of the City when she incautiously attempts to approach him. With the rescue of the wife, Murnau shows that he has already learned one of the basic lessons of Hollywood narrative structure by signaling the release of tension and the imminence of a happy ending with a piece of comic "business": the peasant who has rescued the wife and is receiving her grateful thanks, is eyed with jealous hostility by his own partner, and the way is then clear for a scene of husband, wife, and child happily together and the final, inevitable, close-up of an embrace.

In theory, given its combination of "personal" themes with an acceptance of Hollywood narrative formulas, and its acknowledged visual power and technical ingenuity, _Sunrise_ should have been much more of a popular success than it in fact was. William Fox expressed himself satisfied enough with the film on completion to offer Murnau a five-year contract which the director, refusing competing offers from Famous Players and Metro-Goldwyn, was happy to accept.[28] Critical reaction was generally very favorable, with Welford Beaton in the _Film Spectator_ striking one of the few dissenting notes: "Murnau's direction reflects Germanic arrogance. His players are chessmen and he moves them as such. . . . Murnau is cold, too cold ever to give us a truly great picture. . . . A man who can make us cry is a greater director than one who only makes us think. . . . A combination of the Murnau mechanics and the Borzage humanity would have made _Sunrise_ the greatest picture of all time."[29] The reference to _Seventh Heaven_ here may suggest that the fuss over Gaynor's wig was not as trivial as it might appear today and that one major barrier in the way of the film's acceptance by a mass audience was that it tampered too much with a recognized star image. Another problem may well have been that the enthusiasm of the sophisticated big city critics for the artistic merits of the film may well not have been shared by the small-town and rural audiences who still made up a large proportion of the film-going public: if this was so, it would of course indicate that Murnau's paean to rural virtues had not struck home quite as forcefully as might have been expected.

Some of Murnau's recorded comments at this period suggest that—like von Stroheim several years previously—he was acutely aware of the problems of an "artistic" filmmaker who had to put his films into competition on the open market with works intended primarily as escapist entertainment. To _Theatre Magazine_ he declared:

> I believe that in the future various theatres will be known for special grades of production. Just as the different publishing houses are each identified with certain types of books, running from trash to the classics, so there will be cinema houses identified with specific grades of pictures. A time will come when the moving-picture patron will become addicted to one grade of picture and will not patronize a theatre that shows cheap comedies one week and classic productions another week.[30]

A few months later he said virtually the same thing to _McCall's Magazine:_ "I think that some day in the near future there will be many different kinds of movie theatres, just as there are many kinds of theatres of spoken plays. . . .

There will also be theatres, not very many perhaps, but a few in every city where the very highest type of films may be seen and where nothing else will be shown."[31]

Meanwhile, he had agreed with Fox that his next film would be *4 Devils*,[32] based on a novel by Hermann Bang—a rather surprising choice of subject in view of the mild scorn with which Murnau had referred to "circus films" when discussing E.A. Dupont's *Variety* with Matthew Josephson: "When an interesting experiment turns out to be a hit, as 'Caligari' did over there, they [German directors] all imitate it. Or 'Variety.' They are all doing circus pictures now."[33] Unfortunately, no print of the film is known to have survived at present, though the negative is rumored still to be in existence; an English translation of the script, however, is owned by the George Eastman House in Rochester and this has been summarized by Eisner on pages 187–94 of her *Murnau*.[34] Once again the ending was changed to suit an American audience and then, when a sound version of the film was released in September 1929, the last two reels of the film were altered still further to permit the hero and heroine (who had died in the silent version) to survive.

Though the film starred Gaynor (minus wig), most reviewers reserved their highest praise for the performance of Mary Duncan as the vamp; overall, whether the finished film fully reflected Murnau's intentions or not, it received considerable, and sometimes even ecstatic, acclaim. The *New York Times* began its review:

> It is a tale of the circus, of love and passion, that F. W. Murnau, the German producer, unfolds in "4 Devils," which was presented with dignity by William Fox last night at the Gaiety Theatre. This new pictorial effort from the director who gave to the screen "The Last Laugh," "Sunrise" and other distinguished photoplays held the audience from the moment the face of a painted clown appeared to the final fadeout. It sent one away feeling that the characters were real, that the humor was natural and that the pathetic events occur in everyday life. And not only are the players handled with unrivalled skill, but the photography is soft and seductive, calling attention subtly to the realism and art that pass in turn before the onlooker.[35]

Variety and *Motion Picture Classic*, while acknowledging that *Sunrise*, despite its artistic merits, had not been a huge box-office success, predicted that things might well be different with this film. As *Variety* put it:

> Murnau made "Sunrise" and it was not box-office in the
> sense a picture of its production cost should have been. Murnau,
> German, in the common way would have been thought too artistic
> for another try with an expensive big picture. Perhaps Winnie
> Sheehan did the unusual then and followed his belief that
> Murnau could be made box-office. Mr. Sheehan assigned him to
> "The 4 Devils" and Murnau has come through. Winnie appears
> to be right. It looks as though there is a big picture in Murnau.
> Maybe it will be his next and if one then more. For he classes
> among the big directors.[36]

Unfortunately, however, things were not to work out so smoothly. The pattern
of studio interference which had already affected *4 Devils* was to have an
even greater impact on Murnau's next film, a project suggested by himself
called *Our Daily Bread* that was shortened, re-edited, and partially reshot
by the studio before being released under the new title *City Girl*. Within
three years, then, Murnau had moved from being given virtually carte
blanche on *Sunrise* to being treated like any other contract director—a fate
very similar to that of Orson Welles a decade later after *Citizen Kane*.
Though Matthew Josephson may have been correct in suggesting that
Murnau had arrived in Hollywood at the right "psychological moment," it
was almost exactly the wrong time, from a business point of view, for a director of his type to attempt to establish himself. Audience resistance to "artistic" movies, whether homegrown or imported, was on the rise and, as
Murnau himself had recognized, the films that he really wanted to make
could not hope to compete in a system that "shows cheap comedies one
week and classical productions another week." To make this situation much
worse, Hollywood was in a state of upheaval, and often near panic, between
1927 and 1929 as a result of the introduction of sound. Films of all kinds,
and not just "classic productions," were constantly being tampered with,
both during and after production, in an attempt to keep them up to date with
the latest technological developments and to steal a march on rivals. The
same film could be released in a variety of competing versions: as a silent;
or with a synchronized music score; or as a part-talkie, with dialogue added
to a couple of reels in a purely arbitrary way and usually shot, as a result of
the limitations of the sound-recording mechanisms, in a painfully static
manner that could provide a grotesque contrast with the visual style of the
rest of the film.[37] Murnau was by no means alone at this period in having *4
Devils* and *City Girl* altered during and after production, though the results

in both cases were complicated by involving other than purely technological factors. A director of his acknowledged artistic stature, but with a problematic box-office record, could not have hoped to emerge from this particularly unsettling period totally unscathed.

Murnau's outline of the subject of *Our Daily Bread,* as quoted by Lotte Eisner (197), provides a strong link with *Der Brennende Acker* in particular among his earlier films, even going so far as to use the phrase "the sacredness of bread." Once again the subject was to involve a city-country contrast, showing the "estrangement of the modern city dwellers" from the permanence and continuity of Nature as found in the countryside. Much more of this survives even in the film as it now stands[38] than Eisner is prepared to allow, and on the personal level too some of Murnau's familiar concerns are re-examined. The estrangement between the young couple is here less the result of external temptation than of the young man's spinelessness and his total subordination to his autocratic father (a reworking perhaps of the Faust-Gretchen-Mephisto situation), while the heroine is rather more forceful and independent than usual and (like Ellen in *Nosferatu*) almost yields to the seductions of an intrusive and alien male. Their reconciliation, though acceptable enough in terms of their own private relationship, appears forced and arbitrary in that it has also to involve an unconvincing change of heart by the old patriarch, who turns suddenly from a rigid, unbending tyrant into a humble penitent and becomes a model employer into the bargain.

The presentation of the father, in fact, suggests a rather less wholeheartedly positive picture of rural life than in Murnau's earlier films. Previously the harmony and unity of the rural family, and of the village community to which it belonged, were emphasized; here the father is little more than a bully, tyrannizing over his grown son as if he were a child and finding fault with all his actions; threatening his small daughter (twice) with punishment for daring to play games with stalks of wheat; and being openly rude and aggressive toward his son's bride from the moment of her arrival. In addition he is a harsh and unsympathetic employer whose men welcome an opportunity to defy him and leave him in the lurch in the middle of harvesting and have to be kept on the job at the point of a gun. Much of this could in fact be seen as a recognition on Murnau's part that the old equation of the country with virtue and the city with vice and frivolity is no longer very satisfactory: rigid and unthinking adherence to the old ways may turn out to have a destructive effect, and modern large-scale farming involves an acceptance, not just of new machinery, but of the realization that farmworkers may well develop a "city" mentality and be just as concerned with their wage packets and conditions of employment as with any kind of mystical attachment to the soil. The emphasis, in other words, is now on compromise rather than on the outright rejection of one set of values in favor of another: the two extremes of the rural patriarch and Mac, the archetypal city slicker, are rejected, but the new generation unites a spirited "city girl" and a transformed country lad rather than bringing together rural childhood sweethearts who have been temporarily separated—though the couple finally choose the country as their home.

Once again Murnau presents the relationship between his characters and the conflict between competing value systems in as purely visual a manner as possible. Lem, the young farmer, is as out of place in the city as the couple in *Sunrise* were and is potentially the prey of those like the woman sitting near him on the train, who spots his roll of banknotes and immediately primps herself and begins a "friendly" conversation. Meanwhile the father, at home, says grace and reverently cuts a loaf of bread; the next shot is of bread being cut by an automatic slicer in the restaurant in which Kate, working as a waitress, is surprised to see Lem saying grace before eating. Kate's alienation in the city is suggested by the dingy room in which she lives, with elevated trains roaring constantly past the window; inside she waters a drooping plant (after blowing the dust off it) and keeps a mechanical bird in a cage; we see her pensive face in close-up next to this. (She later transports this cage with her to the countryside and shows it off proudly to her new in-laws.) In standard Hollywood fashion[39] the attraction between Lem and Kate is instantaneous, and only Lem's shyness prevents him from proposing to her on their next meeting; in an anticipation of his later decisive thwarting of Mac's attempted seduction, however, he intervenes to protect her from the leering advances of two city males. A series of mishaps almost prevents them from meeting again, but these are quickly overcome and Lem sends a telegram to his outraged father to inform him that he has married a "WAITRESS"—the old man's horror being signaled by size of the title.

The two walk together from the station to the farm, running through the fields as the camera tracks with them: it is clear that spiritually Kate belongs here rather than in the city. But she is left in the background, squeezed into the left-hand corner of the frame as Lem greets his mother; only after family obligations have been performed is she brought forward and presented. When the father returns, Lem reverts to his habitual state of apologetic dependence, trembling like a child as the old man (who has steadfastly ignored Kate) rages at him for not obtaining a higher price for the wheat he has sold. The father then orders Kate to leave and slaps her when

she defies him; she is shielded, not by Lem, but by the mother, and openly displays her contempt for her husband.

From being a waitress in the city, pawed at by her customers, she takes on a virtually identical role on the farm, carrying food out to the men working in the fields, where they leer at her legs in a shot intended to recall her customers in the diner. One of them, Mac, aware of the tensions between herself and Lem, attempts to take advantage of these; though she resists him, the father misinterprets her actions and Lem becomes the butt of the farmhands' mockery. In what is visually the most impressive sequence in the film, as they work through the night to harvest the grain in advance of an approaching storm, Mac stirs up discontent among the workers and then tries to blackmail Kate into leaving with him; she pretends to go along with his plan, but prepares to sneak away secretly on her own instead, leaving a note for Lem to inform him of this. Lem belatedly displays his forcefulness by assaulting Mac and subduing a team of bolting horses; he is then reconciled with his father after the latter has taken a shot at him in the belief that he is one of the rebellious workers. Lem then catches up with Kate on her way to the station and offers to drive her to the train if she still wants to leave; of course she doesn't and a triple reconciliation takes place before the mellowed patriarch drives them all back "home."

Even in its altered state, *City Girl* still contains much of interest and much that is characteristic of Murnau's visual style, especially in lighting, composition, and the creation of ideas and states of mind through visual juxtaposition. There are clear signs too, among the contrivances of the plot, that some of his familiar themes were being treated in a rather more complex and skeptical manner than before. Nevertheless, the interference by the studio had this time been on a scale that Murnau was unable to tolerate; he broke his contract with Fox and began to look around for a production arrangement that would allow him the kind of independence that he required.

The outcome of this was a planned collaboration with Robert Flaherty (another filmmaker who, after the success of *Nanook*, had become increasingly unhappy with the insistence of Hollywood studios that he make his films more "commercial") on a film to be set in the South Seas and ultimately financed to a considerable extent by Murnau himself. It is now generally agreed that the central concept and realization of the film that resulted from this, *Tabu*, should be attributed primarily to Murnau and that Flaherty's role in the production became a relatively minor one.[40]

Tabu transforms the familiar city-country contrast into a conflict between the unspoiled natural surroundings and behavior of the Polynesian

The autocratic father (David Torrence) in *City Girl* expresses his disapproval of his son's bride (Mary Duncan), but the film ends with a somewhat unconvincing reconciliation all round.

....

islanders and the exploitation and corruption brought into this setting by white civilization. On the personal level, however, the dramatic conflict brought about by the separation of the young lovers is caused by a custom within Polynesian society: the choice of the girl Reri as the tribe's sacrificial virgin. The structure of the film thus parallels *City Girl* quite closely in that—in contrast to Murnau's earlier films—it does not simply present the love theme as part of the overall clash between a "good" and a "bad" way of life and the choice that has to be made between them. In other respects, however, the film most closely resembles *Die Finanzen des Grossherzogs* in its presentation of an idyllic island setting threatened by unscrupulous exploiters and in its rapturous celebration of the senses and the beauty of the human body. Murnau seems to have reveled in the freedom from conventional sensual (and sexual) restraints that the South Seas environment offered: the camera sculpts the bodies of the men and the young boys with the kind of delighted ardor that in Hollywood had been reserved for the female figure, and though the film—out of commercial necessity—follows the fortunes of a heterosexual love affair, it is able to set this in a context that permits Murnau's own homosexual sensibility far greater rein than usual.

Though it was shot well into the full sound era, *Tabu* was designed deliberately as a silent film with a musical sound track—though Hugo Riesenfeld's atrocious score, full of "Mickey Mouse" effects, Hawaiian restaurant–style melodies, and hoots-and-hollers in the dances that are more suited to a campfire hoedown in a Western, is blatantly inauthentic and a major affront to the ear throughout. The opening sequences in particular, showing the islanders bathing, fishing, quarreling, relaxing, courting, and collecting food from the palm trees, present the rhythm of their life in images that are exquisitely composed and lit and sparkle with sensual beauty. As the canoes move out to welcome a boat that has arrived in the bay, the camera goes with them in a complex montage sequence that shifts the viewpoint from one canoe to another and constantly alters the angle of vision in a celebration of the flow and freedom of movement. The same sense of spontaneity and lack of inhibitions continues as the islanders scramble on to the boat and perch contentedly in the rigging.

As the plot gets under way, however, it becomes clear once again that Murnau's interest in narrative is perfunctory and conventional and that his main talent is for the *visual* dramatization of conflict and relationship. As in other films, he works partly through contrast: the debased Western dancing of the island to which Reri and Matahi flee, set against the graceful movements of the traditional dances of their home; Matahi forced to dive for

*P*ristine innocence and beauty, on both the human and natural level, in *Tabu*.

pearls in order to take Reri to a more secure refuge, in contrast to the care-free diving and swimming of the opening sequences. Images reflect or convey states of mind: the canoes bound joyously out to greet the arriving ship in a series of shots that recall the townspeople of Odessa bringing provisions to the *Potemkin*, while the boat carrying the avenging priest to the lover's refuge glides ominously to the pier from the left of the frame, in a setting of skeletal black trees, like the death-ship arriving in *Nosferatu*. Matahi's vision of escaping his servitude takes place "inside his head" in a manner similar to the doorman's muddled imaginings in *The Last Laugh:* on a close-up of the youth's face Murnau superimposes a shot of the shopkeeper displaying the bills for the provisions Matahi has bought from him; this gives way to a wish-fulfillment dream in which Matahi defies the local tabu and

finds an immense pearl that the shopkeeper accepts as cancellation of his debt, with the sequence ending on a return to the young man's face.

The major difference from the immediately preceding films, of course, is that, in an independent production, Murnau was able to follow the logic of his fictional situation through to an unhappy ending: the priest carries off Reri as Matahi vainly pursues them along the seashore, then plunges into the water to swim after their boat; he catches up with them, but the priest cuts the rope by means of which Matahi is trying to scramble on board and the youth is left further and further behind until he is finally overwhelmed by the waves.

Murnau's death a week before the New York premiere of *Tabu*, which had been acquired for distribution by Paramount, leaves unanswered the question whether he could ever have found a place in the American film industry without compromising, perhaps fatally, his own artistic integrity. On the evidence, this seems unlikely: the historical and economic situation of Hollywood in the early 1930s was rarely favorable to directorial independence and though Paramount (which, according to Eisner, was prepared to offer Murnau a ten-year contract on the strength of *Tabu*) allowed Lubitsch considerable freedom during this period and even tolerated Von Sternberg's excesses for several years, both men usually performed satisfactorily at the box office—and when Von Sternberg ceased to do so, he found himself edged rapidly out of the studio's graces. Murnau had never, at any stage, been "box office"; his reputation was based on the artistry and innovative quality of his films and though critics and reviewers continued to find these virtues in his American work, the mass public, bored and baffled by films that were too "artistic," sought easier sources of satisfaction.

The pattern of classical Hollywood narrative cinema, with its emphasis on action, movement, clearly defined psychology and motivation and the protagonist's successful achievement of his or her goal, together with its subordination of pictorial values to visual pragmatism, was not one with which Murnau could ever have felt much at home. Though Lubitsch's American films were often accused of being too subtle and esoteric for the mass audience, they at least told a story that the average spectator could follow and presented characters and situations that the audience could easily recognize. Murnau's conservative ideology[41] and his concentration on "personal" themes (especially the romantic theme of the young couple separated and then reunited) were perfectly in accord with the mainstream of audience expectations at the time and would not, on their own, have caused him any major difficulties. In this respect, in fact, he was probably closer to

American popular taste than Lubitsch, with his ambiguities and knowing "European" ironies. With *Sunrise,* Murnau even made an attempt to accommodate himself to the standard narrative codes of intermingling comedy with drama and moving with increasing obviousness toward a happy ending once the crisis of the narrative is over. He did not, then, deal with particularly unfamiliar or disconcerting subject matter, and he was not overly intransigent or unwilling to attempt to accommodate himself to the wishes of either studio or audience. Yet he and his films were steadily marginalized by the end of the decade, while Lubitsch flourished.

The problem for Murnau lay neither in subject matter nor in outlook, but in the overall tendency of his film style, with its emphasis on lighting and composition at the expense of narrative drive, and its concern to represent psychological crises visually and allusively rather than through physical action. In these respects he had remained true to the German tradition in which his earlier films had been made—but this was not a tradition with which American audiences, or, in the long run, critics, were comfortable. Janet Bergstrom has remarked, with respect to *Sunrise,* that

> The "problem" [of the film] in the United States lay in the
> fact that the American public was presented with a film made
> according to the conventions of another cinema that were signifi-
> cantly different from its own. The success of Murnau's reworking
> of conventions—overlaying narrative and stylistic conventions
> from the Weimar cinema with pictorial conventions from another
> tradition—was dependent on an audience willing to look at a film
> with the pace and attention required in looking at paintings. This
> meant, for the Weimar cinema, an audience that recognized and
> valued art and was also accustomed to cinematic conventions of
> abstraction and ambiguity. The American audience, on the other
> hand, was in the midst of a cinema that was perfecting conven-
> tions of narrative and visual action and economy of detail.[42]

Murnau himself was fully aware that his kind of cinema demanded a specialized audience if it was to be fully appreciated, hence his suggestion, quoted earlier, that there should be different kinds of film theaters, geared to the needs and tastes of different audiences. A chain of art cinemas of this kind could well have been his salvation (assuming he had lived) and would have allowed him to capitalize on his high critical reputation without having to cater constantly to an undiscriminating mass audience. But that was not, in the 1920s and 1930s at least, the American way.

Victor Sjöström

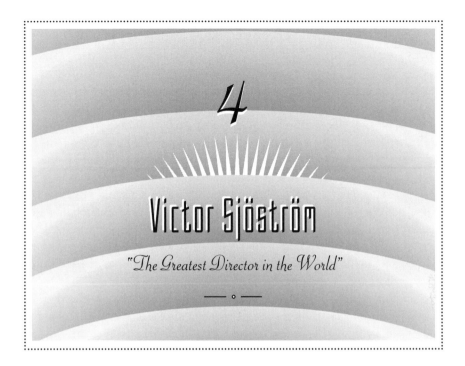

4

Victor Sjöström

"The Greatest Director in the World"

— ○ —

hen he arrived in New York in January 1923 on the invitation of the Goldwyn Company, Sjöström was much less well known to the American film-going public than Lubitsch or even Murnau; he did, however, possess one major advantage over both of them that made it easier for him to settle down and adjust to a new way of life, and that was his command of the English language. Though he was born in Sweden, he had spent virtually all of his life up to the age of thirteen in the United States and had maintained contact with his relatives there, even paying them a visit in the summer of 1905. That he had not lost his mastery of the language was noted immediately by an early interviewer, who commented that "his English, though perfectly fluent, has at times a noticeably American accent, and an occasional American phrase."[1]

Cautious and reserved by nature, Sjöström hesitated for considerable time before accepting the Goldwyn offer and, with the encouragement of his Swedish production company, Svensk Filmindustri, seems to have convinced himself initially that he was going more with the intention of studying American production methods than with the hope of establishing a career for himself there.[2] Svensk Filmindustri also planned to use Sjöström's presence in America as a means for securing the distribution rights to Goldwyn films in Sweden, though this too did not work out quite as was originally intended. American attention had been drawn to Sjöström mainly through *Körkarlen (The Phantom Chariot)*[3] which had its New York

premiere on 4 June 1922. Far from being even a relative commercial suc-
cess like *Passion, Deception,* or *The Last Laugh,* the film nevertheless
attracted a good deal of attention for its artistic qualities, and June Mathis, a
scriptwriter and editor for the Goldwyn Company, who had also admired
Sjöström's more recent *Vem Dömer* (*Love's Crucible,* also known as *Mortal
Clay,* 1921) proposed that the director himself should be invited to work in
America instead of the company taking further risks on distributing Swedish
films that she considered unlikely to have much popular appeal. After
weeks of vacillation, Sjöström cabled acceptance on 4 December 1922 and
set sail on 10 January 1923 to find himself, to his utter amazement, welcomed as a celebrity on his arrival in New York thanks to an astute public-
ity campaign by his new employers.

    Bengt Forslund suggests that Sjöström felt that his career in
Sweden had reached an impasse at this stage and that he was discouraged
and uncertain about his future. There certainly is evidence to confirm that
he felt this way on a purely personal level; it would be a mistake, however,
to assume, as earlier Swedish critics in particular have done, that he had
also reached a stage of artistic exhaustion and that after 1921 he never
"made any original motion pictures any more."[4] An overview of Sjöström's
career is bedeviled, even more than Murnau's or Lubitsch's, by the sheer
quantity of material that has been lost: only a dozen of the several dozen
films he made in Sweden between 1913 and 1922, and only four of his nine
American films, one of them *Name the Man* in an incomplete version, still
survive.[5] Retrospectives of his work at the National Film Theatre in London
and the Museum of Modern Art in New York, among others (usually in the
context of Swedish silent cinema as a whole), have drawn attention to the
quality of the films that still exist, and *The Wind* and *The Scarlet Letter* are
slowly building a long-overdue reputation as two of the finest American
films of the 1920s, yet most standard English-language film histories still
devote little more than a few paragraphs either to Swedish silent films or to
Sjöström's career as a whole.

    Swedish critics have often, with justifiable indignation, drawn
attention to the combined arrogance and condescension with which one of
the most powerful and original stages of early film history has too often been
treated by English-language film critics. One of the most striking characteristics of Swedish silent films, their spectacular use of outdoor settings, has
been variously attributed to the influence of Griffith or to imitation of
American Westerns.[6] Though Sjöström in particular certainly knew
Griffith's work, this central tendency in Swedish films had been established

even before he began to work for the Svenska Biografheatern in 1912; Charles Magnusson, who became production manager in 1909 and was responsible, along with Julius Jaenzon (cameraman and occasional director, who photographed most of Sjöström's Swedish films) for an emphasis on artistic quality in the films he made, operated according to criteria that can be summarized as follows: "The Swedish public should have good films, and these good films should, as far as possible, be Swedish and express the national characteristics." Films, wherever possible, should be made out-doors and in natural surroundings, with an emphasis on "real" people. Artificial, studio scenery should be avoided, for the background played a leading part. "Thus Charles Magnusson, prompted by his own good taste and experience, came to lay the foundations of a style in which nature and reality were an essential part of the performance—and the actors as natural as nature itself." This style "was to be the hallmark of Swedish films and leave a deep impression on the development of the film in other countries."[7]

Sjöström's earliest first major success, *Ingeborg Holm* (*Give Us This Day*, 1913),[8] follows these precepts quite closely, even though it has an urban rather than a "natural" setting. The film was not only his first interna-tional success; with a running time of ninety minutes it was unusually long for the period, and it demonstrates at a relatively early stage in film history many of the qualities conventionally associated with film realism in subject matter, setting, and emotional power. Though it was based on a stage play and contains several melodramatic elements, the play itself had been writ-ten by a public official involved firsthand in poor-relief and was based on an actual case; as Bengt Idestam-Almquist puts it: "The play attacked the seri-ous abuses which still existed in Swedish poor-relief and which, among other things, permitted the sale by auction of the children of the poor and destitute to speculators in free labour."[9]

The film follows the central character through the tribulations that she suffers after her husband, who has borrowed money to open his own gro-cery store, suddenly dies and she is left to deal with his creditors. Despite her hard work she is unable to keep up with their demands and is forced into bankruptcy, poverty, and finally the workhouse; though the film's primary focus is on social abuses, an effective comment on personal indifference to her plight is provided by the detail of her shop assistant yawning in boredom in the background of the scene as she is faced with the final demand to pay up. Her children are taken away from her and she is given the job of clean-ing the workhouse; hearing that one of her children is seriously ill, she pleads with the officials for a chance to visit her, but is refused. She escapes from the workhouse and after eluding the pursuing officials reaches the foster home only to find that the child has died. Back in the workhouse she is insulted by the officials and stands rigid and unresisting before them. Later, after she discovers that her youngest child no longer recognizes her, she goes mad and is confined to an asylum. Some slight mitigation of her sufferings is provided in an epilogue set some fifteen years later when her eldest son returns from sea to visit her. Though she is still insane, nursing a piece of wood to replace her lost child, she is finally brought to recognize her own photograph, and then her son himself.

The film was a great popular success at home and, though it made no impact in America, it gained Sjöström considerable recognition in Britain and Europe. Critics at the time praised in particular the realistic treatment, the restraint of the acting, and the imaginative lighting and photography. Idestam-Almquist summarizes its effect as follows: "In the exteriors—as with all the films Magnusson produced—the picture is animated and dynamic and contains beautiful natural scenery. The settings throughout were realistically convincing. But above all, the film was impressive for the acting of Hilda Borgström which, even today, is deeply moving. Her acting was free from melodramatic tricks."[10] Sjöström made over twenty films, all but one of them now lost, between *Ingeborg Holm* and *Terje Vigen* (*A Man There Was*, 1916), based on a narrative poem by Henrik Ibsen set in the Napoleonic Wars. By 1916 Svenska Bio had sharply reduced its rate of production from around twenty-five films a year to four features for 1917 and three for 1918,[11] as part of a policy of emphasizing quality above quantity. Sjöström himself seems to have been going through both a personal and an artistic crisis at this period and he initially rejected Magnusson's suggestion that he should film Ibsen's poem. Instead he made a journey to the area in which he had spent his adolescence after his family's return from the United States, discovering on the way some hitherto unknown facts about the hardships suffered by his mother during his infancy, when she had to provide for the family on her own while waiting to join her husband in America. He then traveled to Grimstad in Norway, where Ibsen had lived at the time when he heard the story on which *Terje Vigen* was based. The firsthand encounter with the actual environment in which the poem was set provided a catalyst for Sjöström, and he informed Magnusson that he was ready to make the film.[12]

The story is revealing in its confirmation of the centrality of landscape to Sjöström's artistic personality, and *A Man There Was*, which was the biggest Swedish success to date on the foreign market and was eventually (in 1920) shown in America, is considered the harbinger of the great period

*T*he social realism of Sjöström's first surviving film, *Ingeborg Holm*, is central to his work.

of the country's cinema in which the visual qualities of the films, and especially the use of landscape, were to attract widespread attention.

A Man There Was is divided into two contrasting yet parallel sections. In the first, related partly in flashback, Terje attempts to evade the blockade of the Norwegian coast by the British navy, in order to obtain food for his family. He is detected, pursued, and arrested and, despite his pleas, the British captain has his boat and the supplies it contains sunk. Terje is sent to prison and discovers on his release that his family has meanwhile died of starvation. The second half shows him leading a bitter, solitary existence until one day he goes out to help a ship in danger during a storm; its captain is the same officer who was responsible for his misfortunes, and Terje at first plans to kill him and his own family in revenge. He is softened, however, by the sight of the captain's young daughter and saves their lives

*O*ne of the most
striking features
of Sjöström's Swedish
films is the use of
natural locations to
intensify and reflect
the emotions of his
characters: *Terje
Vigen (A Man There
Was)* and *The Outlaw
and His Wife.*

instead; the film ends with Terje reconciled to society once more and taking an amicable farewell of his former enemy.

Most of the film takes place out of doors, with spectacular scenes of human beings set against the elemental forces of nature; in some of these, as in the storm at the end, Sjöström puts his camera not only on board the threatened ship but into Terje's small rowing boat as it sets off to the rescue. The film is also full of beautifully composed shots that reinforce the contrasting themes of community and isolation around which the film is constructed: the villagers gather on the shore as a British soldier reads the proclamation imposing a naval blockade of the coastline; later Terje is seen setting off in his boat as his wife waves goodbye (a shot that is balanced at the end by Terje waving goodbye to the British family whose lives he has spared). The second half of the film concentrates on Terje wandering alone among the rocks and along the coastline or silhouetted in the graveyard against a background of crosses and a gaunt tree as he contemplates the loss of his wife and child.

Berg-Ejvind och hans Hustru (The Outlaw and His Wife, 1917), which is based on an Icelandic play, also falls into two parts, divided by an interval of several years, and once again Sjöström shows his characters integrated into and inseparable from their natural environment. The film offers a curious mixture of some obviously staged and artificial winter scenes and location shots of mountains, streams, lakes, forests, and waterfalls that powerfully emphasize both the splendor and the hardship of the characters' struggle to survive in the wilderness. Though Berg-Ejvind and his wife are forced to leave the farming community and establish a miniature community of their own, consisting of themselves, their child, and the opportunistic and unreliable Ames, the dramatic conflict centers around parallel scenes of sexual jealousy and rivalry as much as it deals with themes of social justice. The brutal sheep farmer at the beginning who wants to marry Halla tries first to discredit then to imprison the intruder, Berg-Ejvind, thus forcing the couple to flee into the mountains; when they are joined by Ames (whose dishonesty has earlier been established by a scene of him stealing wool) their harmonious existence is threatened by his (unreciprocated) attentions to Halla and the opportunities offered by their precarious situation to rid himself of her husband.

The characterizations in themselves are not particularly subtle, and Berg-Ejvind (played by Sjöström himself) is an outlaw in the romantic tradition: he stole a sheep to feed some starving peasants after the local priest had refused to give them any help. Halla remains loyal and trustworthy throughout, sharing the hardships of his life without complaint (except for some mutual recriminations near the end) and, in the final scenes, killing their child rather than allow her to be captured with them, and sharing her husband's fate to the very end as they freeze to death together in the snow. The villainous farmer displays no redeeming qualities, though Arnes is rather more equivocal: tempted to cut the rope by which he is hauling Berg-Ejvind to safety after a fall, he finally resists; yet he continues his advances to Halla until forced to leave and then, seeing the approaching search party, returns to warn the couple.

In contrast to Murnau's highly stylized presentation of rural life, Sjöström attempts authenticity in clothes, faces, acting style, and settings throughout, usually with remarkable success. The opening scenes of tension and conflict take place in a harsh, mountainous landscape, as does the flash-back showing Berg-Ejvind's solitary life as an outlaw. The later scenes integrate the figures into the landscape rather than setting them in opposition to it: though the mountains and waterfalls remain majestic and overpowering, the characters are photographed so that they blend into the landscape instead of being dwarfed by it, or they are seen drawing sustenance from it, bathing, fishing, or cooking. Though the stage-like sets and unconvincing snow of the ending detract somewhat from this impression, they do not destroy it entirely, and the dominant images of the film remain those showing the couple living in harmony with each other and with the world around them.

The remainder of Sjöström's Swedish films fall basically into two categories: those based on the novels of Selma Lagerlöf (who offered exclusive rights to her work to Charles Magnusson and Svenska Bio in 1917), and those scripted by Hjalmar Bergman, usually based on his own novels. Though Lagerlöf enjoyed a considerable international reputation at the time, her work is much less well known in the English-speaking world today, and it might be helpful to quote Hans Pensel's summary of its main features:

> Lagerlöf's work has certain characteristics which have been associated with silent Swedish films. She writes in a simple, narrative way; and, like the Swedish films, her books could be described as folk tales. Her style is very visual, almost like a series of cartoons in a comic strip. At the same time she manages to present a penetrating psychological observation of the human mind that can be represented on the screen only by the most subtle and realistic acting.
>
> Lagerlöf often lets physical action reveal the thinking of her characters. She pays a lot of attention to nature—a common trait in Swedish art and literature. Nature becomes an active part in the

life of her characters: sunshine, snow, wind, rain, dusk, dawn, and night are described more like characters in a fairy tale than mere physical phenomena. Lagerlöf often uses her home province, Värmland, as a setting for her stories. Born in Värmland, Sjöström was also very familiar with this province and its people.[13]

Tösen Från Stormyrtorpet (*The Girl From the Marshcroft,* also known as *The Girl From Stormycroft,* 1917) demonstrates many of these qualities and also, in its handling of themes of sexual conflict and jealousy, renunciation and self-denial, and social prejudice and intolerance, helps to explain, not only why Sjöström should later have been attracted to a work like *The Scarlet Letter,* but why he filmed it in the way he did. A peaceful rural community is scandalized when a young woman from a poor family has an illegitimate child. The father, a married neighbor, refuses to help her, and when she tries to name him in court in front of a hostile and contemptuous audience, he denies responsibility. The community treats her as an outcast, and when the son of a wealthy landowner tries to help her by finding work for her in his parents' home, he and his fiancée also become the topics of village gossip and scandalmongering. Hildur, the fiancée, insists on having Helga sent away and his mother reluctantly complies. At a stag party before his wedding, Gudmund becomes involved in a drunken brawl with some local farmworkers, as a result of which one of the workers is killed. Gudmund wrongly blames himself for the death and confesses to Hildur on the day before their wedding. Instead of sympathizing or helping, she abruptly rejects him and calls off the wedding; he turns to Helga for consolation, but she self-sacrificingly attempts to reconcile him with Hildur and provides proof that he was not responsible for the death. She manages to convince Hildur, too, who belatedly apologizes, but Gudmund chooses to marry the loyal Helga instead.

The landscape of the film is peaceful and pastoral in contrast to the elemental and awe-inspiring settings of the two previous films; perhaps because life is simpler and the struggle for existence less harsh, the villagers have more leisure for the social arts of petty slander and small-minded intolerance. Nature remains important, but it is less of an animating and controlling force than before; instead Sjöström draws from his performers (who include two of the most important Swedish actors of the period, Lars Hanson and Karin Molander) a series of psychologically convincing relationships that are portrayed with a restraint and subtlety considerably in advance of most other contemporary directors—and certainly superior to most of the acting in the films that Murnau and Lubitsch were making around this time. The sequences in which Gudmund comes to think that he is a murderer, confesses to Hildur, and is rejected by her, show Sjöström employing silent-film techniques in a refined and sophisticated way to convey states of mind. Gudmund emerges from the fight at the inn disheveled, injured, dazed, and too drunk to know clearly what had happened; the next morning he reads a newspaper report of the worker's death, drops his coffee cup in agitation, and gropes guiltily in his pocket for his knife. The blade is broken and he assumes that this results from his stabbing the worker; in a panic he throws the knife into the pond and hides the clothes that he fears might incriminate him. His father finds the knife, but does not understand its significance and the wedding preparations continue. Against a background of festivity and merrymaking, with boats garlanded with flowers sailing across the lake, Gudmind unburdens himself to Hildur; not only does she refuse to help him, she cannot bring herself to touch him or be touched by him any longer. Later Helga clears up the mystery by revealing that she broke the knife while using it to cut wood.

Ingmarssönerna (*The Sons of Ingmar,* 1918–1919) was originally filmed in two parts and was based on Lagerlöf's novel *Jerusalem,* from which three other films were also made—Sjöström's *Karin, Daughter of Ingmar,* and two directed by Gustaf Molander. Prints of the film shown today condense the original two parts into one film of normal feature length. The central themes are again those of sexual tension and misunderstanding, public intolerance of sexual lapses by unmarried women, and female self-sacrifice and renunciation. Brita has been imprisoned for killing the child born out of wedlock to Ingmar after their marriage had been postponed; the repentant Ingmar had acknowledged his responsibility at the trial and wishes to marry her on her release. Brita is conscious of the fact that the townspeople still consider her guilty and feels that she will be a disgrace and a liability to Ingmar; she tries to leave town without his knowing, but her plan is thwarted and they finally marry.

As with *A Man There Was* and *The Outlaw and His Wife,* much of the first part of the story is told in flashback, this time in a fantasy sequence in which Ingmar climbs by ladder to heaven and asks advice from his ancestors as to how to handle his problems. The climb to heaven shows Sjöström working for the first time (in the extant films at least) with sophisticated special effects and trick photography on a large scale; as Idestam-Almquist demonstrates, the scene is built up "by a skilful montage of a real ladder in a field, ordinary scenery shots, a map, and trick shots of a miniature landscape and a ladder."[14] Heaven itself is presented in a tongue-in-cheek manner as a replica of Swedish peasant life on earth, complete with grazing cows, a farm, and a log cabin in which Ingmar's ancestors are seated all round the walls waiting for him.

Nature is again subordinated to personal relationships, with the main outdoors scene the one in which the pregnant Brita runs away from Ingmar, tries to throw herself off a cliff but is prevented by an old woman, and Ingmar searches for her by a lakeside in whose waters he imagines seeing her reflection. As in *The Outlaw and His Wife* and *A Man There Was* too, events in the flashback are paralleled by incidents in the remainder of the film: when Ingmar escorts Brita to his home after her release, he opens the gate for her in a manner that recalls an earlier scene, and her previous flight and his search for her are reflected at the end of the film when the townspeople search for the missing couple to announce that they will accept their marriage after all. Brita's mental conflict as she tries to decide whether to accept Ingmar's offer of marriage or not is portrayed visually and effectively as she begins to write a letter saying she is leaving the country, hesitates, remembers her trial and her own face during it, and as a sunbeam slides down the wall and on to the paper, lowers her head again and writes.

The sequel to this film, *Karin Ingmarsdotter* (*Karin, Daughter of Ingmar*, 1920), is often considered the most conventionally moralistic of Sjöström's Swedish films, and its relentless harping on the evils of alcohol, and its rather mechanical application of rewards and punishments according to a system of poetic justice, certainly make parts of it appear rather strained today. Karin mistakenly believes her fiancé Halvor to be a drunkard and rejects him, marrying instead the hypocritical Eljas, who soon begins to mistreat both her and her younger brother, Ingmar (named after her father, who dies in the course of this film). The patient Halvor befriends the young boy and even tries to look after Eljas when he injures himself in a fit of bad temper. Eljas, however, dies after rejecting medical advice to avoid alcohol; Halvor is wrongly blamed for his death by the local community and gossip about his relationship with Karin threatens to separate them until her father's spirit appears to her in a vision and advises her to obey her conscience. She publicly acknowledges her feelings for Halvor and the couple receive the blessing of the community, whose puritanical standards are treated rather more forgivingly than in earlier films.

The style of the film displays most of the elements that were by now characteristic of Sjöström's work: gravity and seriousness of tone, methodical pacing, linkage between landscape and human relationships and moral values (as in the opening shots of the farmers resting from their work in the fields and bowing their heads in prayer), and careful attention to lighting and composition (the film makes striking use of deep-focus shots through door-ways to the interior of rooms). It is a style that is basically realistic in setting, subject matter, psychological motivation, and the handling of space and time, though there is also what is usually referred to as the sense of a "mystical" bond between nature and human beings, and occasionally dreams and super-natural visions are used to further the plot development or denouement.

Körkarlen (*The Phantom Chariot*, 1920), the last of Sjöström's Swedish-made adaptations of Lagerlöf's work,[15] combines this kind of real-ism with a fantastic premise and a far more complex use of flashbacks and special effects than Sjöström had ever attempted before. The film moves freely back and forth between several different time levels and includes scenes that are straight memory, scenes that are pure fantasy, and scenes that indicate potentiality rather than actual events; the overall structure is dreamlike and revealed as possibly being a dream at the end, yet the bor-derlines between dream and reality are teasingly difficult to identify. Sjöström and his cameraman, Julius Jaenzon, indicate some of the transi-tions by means of visual clues: dissolves to signal the beginning and end of flashbacks; multiple superimpositions and an ethereal photographic quality for the more fantastic scenes, with a starker, more strongly contrasted visual image to indicate "reality"; and, in the restored and tinted print that I saw at the Swedish Film Institute, an additional coding by means of color—a warm red tinting for the scenes of happy family life, a dull yellow for the lapse into poverty and misery, and so on. Nevertheless, it is hardly surprising that con-temporary audiences found it hard to follow: in America, where it was released as *The Stroke of Midnight*, it was extensively re-edited to give the flashbacks a coherent and sequential chronological pattern, with a short and clearly defined "dream sequence" at the end.[16]

The film goes one stage further than *Intolerance*, which had already intercut freely between four different centers of interest, widely separated in space and time; *The Phantom Chariot* moves back and forth between five separate narrative threads, three of them in the present and two in the past, as well as including a purely imagined sequence in which David Holm (played by Sjöström himself) recounts the legend of the phantom chariot that collects the souls of the dead and whose driver can be relieved of his task only by someone who dies at the stroke of midnight on New Year's Eve. The opening of the film brings the three present-time narratives together before splitting them up and following each of them as they move in "real" time through what is virtually a simultaneous pattern of events. Sister Edit, a Salvation Army officer, lies on her deathbed on New Year's Eve, and wishes to see David Holm before she dies. David, a wastrel and an alcoholic, is sought for at his home and in the tavern, but cannot be found. Meanwhile his haggard, despairing wife comes to Edit's bedside to comfort her. All this time David has been drinking with friends in the churchyard; he talks of a dead friend of his, a poverty-stricken intellectual, and then tells them about the phantom chariot which, in an elaborate fantasy sequence built up from double, triple, and even quadruple exposures, is seen collecting souls from various locations, including the bottom of the sea. The Salvation Army officer who is looking for David finds him and urges him to see Sister Edit, but he refuses to move. His friends try to persuade him, both verbally and then by force, to go; in the struggle which follows he is struck by a bottle and his panic-stricken friends flee, leaving him for dead. Midnight sounds and the phantom chariot, driven by David's dead friend, appears.

On one level, time now stands still for the remainder of the film: David's spirit rises from his body and he is told that, as punishment for his evil life, he will now have to drive the coach. He pleads for a reprieve and is shown his life in flashback and reminded of the harm and suffering his behavior has caused to others. The flashbacks both take place "outside time" and cover, in chronological fashion, the main events of David's life after his marriage; they are also themselves divided into two main centers of interest, one dealing with David's family and one dealing with his meetings with Sister Edit. At frequent intervals the flashbacks are interrupted, not only by returns to the churchyard, but by reminders of the present-time action that, paradoxically enough, continues: Sister Edit dies and David's wife returns home, where she prepares to poison herself and her children. In an added level of complexity, David's spirit is allowed to visit both Edit's deathbed and his own home, where he is forced to confront the *present* consequences of his actions as well and is tormented by his inability to intervene and prevent them. These scenes are distinguished from present-time reality by means of superimpositions that make David's body less solid and substantial than his surroundings. There are thus really three interacting time levels in the film: David's past; his "ghostly" present; and the real present—the last two of which occasionally overlap.

The total effect is remarkable and, in its own way, unmatched in world cinema before the 1960s. Sjöström goes far beyond what was to become the typical flashback structure for the next forty years (most clearly incarnated in Hollywood films of the 1940s and 1950s), in which we begin in the present, move to a chronological and generally uninterrupted presentation of the past, and then return to a denouement in the present where the problems revealed in the flashback are given a tidy solution or explanation. Sjöström's method is much closer to a film like Alain Resnais's *Je t'aime, je t'aime* (1968), in which the time pattern created by the editing forces the main character into constant confrontation with and reassessment of his past actions. Sjöström, of course, has no equivalent of Resnais's obsession with the arbitrary and fallible nature of memory, and the flashbacks in *The Phantom Chariot* are assumed to be accurate representations of past events; likewise he does not venture into blurring the borderlines between past and present, dream and reality, the actual and the imagined or anticipated, in the manner of films like *Last Year in Marienbad, Persona,* or *8½.* Yet the ending of the film reveals something of the incompatibility between mutually contradictory explanations of the film's events that is characteristic of much modern cinema. David "dies" near the beginning of the film, but his spirit is given a moment of suspended time in which to explore the actions of his past life; simultaneously with this exploration, however, two important actions take place, both of which David witnesses, but neither of which he is able to prevent: Sister Edit dies and David's wife prepares to take poison. Yet Sister Edit is aware of his spiritual presence and dies comforted by it. The ghostly coach driver (who has been revealed as initially responsible for David's descent into alcoholism) takes pity on him and agrees to reprieve him, both from the task of replacing him and (presumably) from death itself. David wakens in the churchyard (from death? from a dream?) and hurries home in time to save his wife from carrying out her intention. Sister Edit's death, on the other hand, appears to be irrevocable. The genuine modernity of the film lies in its unwillingness to settle for one "logical" explanation for the action, as much as from the complexity of its structure and time-scheme.[17]

Alcoholism is as central to the moral theme of the film as it was with *Karin, Daughter of Ingmar,* yet the treatment is much less strident than in the earlier film. Though the moral seriousness remains, the emphasis is much less that of a tract against alcoholism than on the concept of moral responsibility. The coach driver acknowledges his own responsibility for David's downfall by continuing to drive the coach for another year, until a more suitable victim can be found; and the evocations of David's past force him to recognize the harm he has done to others, most of it irrevocable. After an idyllic introduction to the contentment of his early married life, which is shared by his brother, we discover the brother in prison for killing a man in a drunken brawl as a result of David's pernicious influence on him. His wife leaves him after failing to persuade him to mend his ways and he responds by drinking even more than before. The family strand of the flashbacks then begins to interweave with that involving Sister Edit; David wanders into her Salvation Army hostel and allows her to try to help him by mending his jacket. The jacket, however, is tainted with germs of the disease from which Edit will later die. On leaving the hostel David contemptuously rips up the jacket again and sneers at Edit and her associates.

It is at this point in the present action that David is told by the coach driver that he must visit Edit's deathbed so that he can be directly confronted with the actual consequences of his deeds. He tries to resist and to return to his "dead" body, but is overpowered by the driver; when they arrive in her room Edit is aware of the driver's presence and, thinking that he is Death, pleads for a delay so that she can still be reconciled with David. The film returns again to the past, with David in a tavern mocking Edit's attempts to reason with him. The wife of one of his friends arrives and tries to make her husband return home; David tells him to stay, but the contest of wills is won by Edit, who not only persuades the young man to leave but gets him to sign a temperance pledge at the next Salvation Army meeting. David turns up at the meeting to jeer at his friend's weakness and fails even to recognize his own wife, who is in the audience too.

Edit now tries to bring David and his wife together again and David undergoes a brief period of repentance. He quickly slips back into his old ways, however, and resorts to violence when he comes home drunk one day, and his wife locks him up in the kitchen while she prepares for herself and their children to leave him for good. David starts to break his way out with an ax, and his wife collapses under the stress and terror that he has caused her. He restores her to consciousness before resuming his verbal abuse and storming out of the house. We return to Edit's room in the present as she again says that she must see David to make amends for her previous mistakes and try once more to reconcile him with his wife. In the churchyard David's spirit feels true remorse for the first time and breaks free from the coach driver's restraints to return to Edit's bedside. Though nothing can be done to avert her death, she is aware of his presence and his repentance and dies content. The coach driver then takes him to his home, where David sees his wife living in misery and poverty and preparing poison for herself and her children. He wants to intervene, but is told that he cannot turn aside the course of fate and must return to the churchyard; by this time, however, his repentance is complete and genuine. A fade returns him to the churchyard, where he wakes up restored to life in his physical body. He rushes home in time to save his wife and is reconciled with her; they pray together that this time his reformation is complete.

The intricate structure of the film thus forces David literally to relive his past actions and become aware of their consequences—both those that cannot be changed and those that there is still time to modify or reverse. His reformation as a result is much more clearly motivated and much more convincing than the arbitrary poetic justice meted out in *Karin, Daughter of Ingmar:* it is seen as a process, at first partial and unconvincing; then more seriously, even desperately intended but coming too late to avoid the inevitable consequences of his earlier actions; finally, through force of will, it is strong enough to effect what should be a genuine change. In this respect, as well as in the visual qualities of those parts of the film that deal with David's relationships with his family and with Sister Edit, the film successfully works within the realistic framework established by Sjöström in *Ingeborg Holm* (whose leading actress, Hilda Borgström, played the role of the wife in *The Phantom Chariot*). Sjöström, who gives one of his own best acting performances before his final appearance in Ingmar Bergman's *Wild Strawberries,* used no makeup, thus accentuating the "natural" quality of his appearance in contrast to the prevailing codes of the period, where film stock and lighting generally required even men to be heavily made-up; clothes and appearance are convincingly scruffy and unkempt; and the scenes at the Salvation Army in particular, with their harsh visual contrasts, their starkness and bleakness, are powerfully reminiscent of nineteenth-century photographs of doss-houses and slums with their destitute, despairing inhabitants. Though it was the more obviously photogenic elements of superimposition and trick photography that aroused most widespread comment and admiration at the time, it may be those other aspects that prove most striking to an audience today.

Most commentators on Sjöström find his films between *The Phantom Chariot* and his departure for America in January of 1923 very disappointing and attribute this either to the belief that he was less at home with the work of Hjalmar Bergman, who wrote the scripts for most of them, than he was with the themes and atmosphere of Lagerlöf, or to the deliberate policy of Svensk Filmindustri (which succeeded Svenska Bio in 1919) of capitalizing on the international success of Sjöström's and Stiller's work by making films with a presumed "international" appeal and so neglecting the specifically national characteristics that had brought Swedish film acclaim in the first place.[18]

His first collaboration with Hjalmar Bergman had been in 1919, in between two of the Lagerlöf adaptations, *The Sons of Ingmar* and *Karin, Daughter of Ingmar,* and had been, uncharacteristically for Sjöström, a comedy. *Hans Nåds Testamente (His Lordship's Last Will)* has the visual elegance

and lightness of touch found in Stiller's comedies at the time and is in striking contrast to the sobriety and seriousness of the overall tone of Sjöström's
work in general. The action takes place on the count's birthday, as the iras-
cible and rather self-important old man decides which of the competing
claimants among his relatives is to be favored in his will. The humour is primarily visual, conveyed through background details (a little girl desperate
to go to the toilet but restrained from leaving until the count has finished a
long speech to the crowd that has assembled to greet him); facial expressions; and clearly defined character types, with his madcap young niece, for
example, contrasted with his prissy, extremely conventional butler. The
opening beautifully establishes the tone of the film, with the camera showing us a tramp sleeping at the castle gate, then some pigs, also asleep, the
sleeping cook indoors and the slumbering servants, and then the count himself dozing in bed—while outside the young lovers who will eventually be
rewarded in his will romp happily together.

Mästerman (*A Lover in Pawn*, 1920), from an original script by
Bergman rather than an adaptation of one of his novels, was shot after *The
Phantom Chariot* but released some months before it. The film is a rather
curious mixture of "sordid" realism (in the setting of the shop belonging to
Mästerman, the miserly pawnbroker, and his own clothing and appearance—the role is played by Sjöström himself); psychological realism (in the
development of the relationship between the pawnbroker and the young
heroine); and boisterous physical comedy (in the practical jokes played on
the pawnbroker by the heroine's sailor fiancé). The somewhat grotesque plot
has the heroine agreeing to put herself in pawn to the old man until she has
worked off money borrowed from him to pay her fiancé's gambling debts.
The pawnbroker begins to fall in love with her and misinterprets her instinc-
tive kindness as a sign of reciprocal affection; when her fiancé returns from
a voyage they play cards for the possession of the young woman and the
pawnbroker wins. At the last moment, however, he relents and yields her up
to her lover. While he is clearly "wrong" for Tora as a lover himself, a certain degree of ambiguity surrounds his renunciation and he appears, in
some respects, morally superior to her brash and insensitive fiancé.

The film's exterior scenes are shot with the crystal-sharp clarity
typical of Sjöström's work, while the interior of the pawnshop is a bizarre
clutter of largely useless objects, including a stuffed crocodile and a caged
bird that functions both as a symbol of Tora's entrapment and a sign of the
pawnbroker's potential for affection. (Tora soon empties the shop of most of
its contents, giving them away to customers who she feels needs them more

than Mästerman does.) Sjöström himself creates a convincing portrait of someone hardened to public indifference and even dislike (as when the young men of the town publicly ridicule the pawnbroker as he is on his way to give Tora her wedding gift) and who is willing to lie to Tora about Knut's feelings for her in an attempt to alienate her from him. Yet his final change of heart is convincing and handled without undue sentimentality: his habitual gruffness persists almost to the very end and is softened only by a closing smile as he looks back at the lovers standing at the church door.

Vem Dömer (*Love's Crucible*, 1921) is a costume drama set in Renaissance Florence, some of whose images of a burning at the stake inevitably recall (or anticipate) Dreyer's *The Passion of Joan of Arc* and Bergman's *The Seventh Seal*. The film is generally seen as marking an attempt to cash in on the success of such films elsewhere, especially those of Lubitsch in Germany, and as being pictorially magnificent but cold and empty. Its visual beauty is undeniable, not only in the sumptuous costumes and elaborate sets and in the fine handling of the crowd scenes, but in the texture of light and shadow throughout, and especially in the final scenes, with the townspeople silhouetted on the skyline as they gather fuel for the pyre and the heroine herself outlined against a background of swirling smoke and leaping flames. The formality of the composition is matched by what, for Sjöström, is unusually stylized acting, with emphatic gestures and carefully designed poses, and by an almost excessive pattern of crucifixion imagery: the deceived husband, learning of his wife's treachery, strikes a crucifixion pose against a doorway before collapsing; the heroine is suspected of murdering her husband when a crucifix starts to bleed; and the final scenes are crowded with crucifixes, some actual, some imagined by the heroine, and some suggested by the shape of the swords and halberds carried by the soldiers.

While the films that first brought Sjöström fame established the link between human beings and an awe-inspiring natural environment that came to be seen as representative of Swedish cinema, his later Swedish films focused more strongly on moral and psychological themes, often in an urban setting. Guilt, repentance, confession, self-sacrifice, punishment, atonement, and redemption occur again and again, usually within a context that establishes the social pressures and expectations that condition, for good or evil, the characters' conduct. Looked at in this light, *Love's Crucible* is less atypical of his work than it first appears. Though Ursula is not technically guilty of murdering her husband, who dies of a heart attack after learning that she had planned to poison him, she comes to accept moral responsibility, both for her sexual infidelity and for the intention of murder.

Sjöström's prestige production, *Vem Dömer* (*Love's Crucible*), clearly influenced Ingmar Bergman's *The Seventh Seal* three decades later.

She thus agrees to submit to an ordeal by fire and rejects her lover's offer to take her place; the final images suggest physical death but spiritual redemption as she visualizes her husband on the cross and he descends to lead her by the hand through the flames to kneel in prayer at the foot of a crucifix beside her lover.

Eld Ombord (*Fire on Board*, 1922) is generally treated by critics with even more disdain than *Love's Crucible*, yet, without being a neglected masterpiece, the film has some interesting aspects to it. The climax recalls *A Man There Was*, with the hero Dick about to take vengeance on the cruel Captain Steen by tying him to the mast and leaving him to be blown up with his ship, but changing his mind on seeing a doll belonging to the captain's little daughter lying on the deck. After a spectacular explosion that sinks the abandoned ship,[19] a somewhat unconvincing reconciliation takes place on shore between the two men. The lighting and composition of the film are often impressive, both in the scenes on board ship and in the smoke-filled tavern on shore; and the sexual rivalry (Dick, a mate on the ship, having previously been a suitor to the captain's wife) is handled with genuine intensity at times. A major difference from *A Man There Was* however, comes in the role of nature, which is here largely a backdrop to the action rather than a participant, in accordance with the overall tendency of Sjöström's films at this period.

The VIP treatment accorded Sjöström on his arrival in New York[20] bore very little correlation to firsthand knowledge of his work by the American film-going public and even by his new employers. *The Phantom Chariot*, under the title of *The Stroke of Midnight*, had received favorable reviews, but had been shown in America in a re-edited form that successfully destroyed all the film's true originality and left it to be admired primarily for its visual qualities and the special effects, though the *New York Times* (5 June 1922) also drew attention to the realism of the scenes in the Salvation Army hall and in David's home. *Love's Crucible*, which, like most of Sjöström's major Swedish films, had enjoyed considerable success in Europe, was noticed favorably from London by *Variety* on 30 June 1922, and prominent figures in the film industry like June Mathis of the Goldwyn Company saw and admired it. Like most Swedish films, however, it seems not to have been seen very much more widely than in private screenings to critics and others professionally involved in film. Frances Taylor Patterson, writing about "the Swedish photoplay" in *Exceptional Photoplays* (December 1922, 3–4), complained vigorously about this limitation. Of four films highly praised in the article (Sjöström's *Love's Crucible*, *The Phantom Chariot*, and *Secret of the Monastery*, and Stiller's *Sir Arne's Treasure*) only *The Phantom Chariot* had been publicly screened at that date, and in, as Patterson pointed out, a mutilated version. *Pictures and Picturegoer* (September 1920, 46) claimed that *Love's Crucible* (under its American title, *Mortal Clay*) had also "suffered complete metamorphosis" in the United States, and that, instead of being a murderess, the heroine became "an innocent young thing wrongfully accused," while the film was also given a happy ending. Sjöström himself quickly discovered that the Goldwyn Company was much more interested in having a Swedish director on American soil than in buying Swedish films for distribution. Offers of more of his own and Stiller's work were firmly rejected and he was told that only substantial re-editing could make them suitable for American taste.[21]

Like Lubitsch (whom Sjöström met shortly after his arrival in Hollywood in March 1923) and Murnau, Sjöström was given unusually favorable terms in his first contract. This was to involve him in making three films in his first year and gave him script approval, initial choice of cast, selection of cameraman and assistant director, and the right to supervise the editing.[22] Whereas Murnau, however, had brought his own production team with him and Lubitsch was able to use Hans Kraly as his scriptwriter for much of his early Hollywood career, Sjöström had to work without familiar faces around him. Talk of bringing over Julius Jaenzon came to nothing and, though Hjalmar Bergman joined him for a few months at the beginning of 1924, he found it impossible to settle and the experience was not a happy one. Later on, of course, Sjöström was to work with two prominent Swedish actors who had come to Hollywood, Greta Garbo and Lars Hanson; but he had never worked with Garbo in Sweden and Hanson had appeared in only one of his major films there.

Sjöström spent some time studying, and rejecting, proposed script material before deciding on a novel called *The Master of Man* by the prolific and popular writer Hall Caine, who was taken much more seriously by critics in the 1920s than he is today, as his work is virtually forgotten. Melodramatic as the material is, it was a shrewd choice in that its themes of sexual betrayal, guilt, suffering, confession and atonement, and the emphasis on public opinion and its condemnation of moral lapses, tie it in firmly with the Lagerlöf adaptations and *Love's Crucible*.[23] Sjöström was largely responsible for the script himself, altering certain elements under pressure of censorship fears by the studio, and was rather indignant that his script assistant Paul Bern was given the major credit for it.

The extant prints of *Name the Man* (1924), as the film was retitled, are all incomplete, lacking the final scenes; but even so it is clear that the immense acclaim that the film received on its initial release was far from unmerited. Like Murnau and Lubitsch, Sjöström wisely steered clear of tackling an American setting and subject in his first Hollywood work: the film is supposed to take place in the Isle of Man, which is sufficiently exotic for American audiences to accept both the peculiar criminal code that forms the crux of the plot and the vaguely "old-world" costumes and sets that represent "peasant life" in the film. *Name the Man* is in fact remarkably close to Murnau's *Phantom* and *Sunrise* in juxtaposing a sophisticated modern urban setting, complete with "flappers," against a supposedly timeless rural society with its own, very different, customs and moral standards. Like Murnau, Sjöström brings the two sets of value into conflict and directs our sympathies—with reservations—toward the more traditional of them.

The plot, a watered-down version of Tolstoy's *Resurrection*, that also bears striking similarities to Carl-Theodor Dreyer's first film, *Praesidenten*

*S*jöström's first American film, *Name the Man*, deals with his perennial themes of sexual betrayal, guilt, remorse, confession, and atonement.

....

(1918), concerns Victor, the son of a judge who is a pillar of the community, who quarrels with his girlfriend Fennella and has a brief affair with Bessie, a young girl from the countryside. Bessie becomes pregnant, does not tell Victor (who has meanwhile been reconciled with Fennella) and kills the baby. Victor replaces his father as a judge and his first case is to try Bessie for child murder. She refuses to name Victor as the father, but Fennella and Victor's best friend (who is acting as Bessie's lawyer), guess the truth and are horrified when Victor is too cowardly to admit his guilt and condemns Bessie to death. Extant prints of the film end at this point; originally it went on to show Victor helping Bessie to escape from prison (accompanied by his friend, who has fallen in love with her), then confronting an enraged mob in the town square to confess both his part in the escape and his original responsibility for Bessie's plight. He is thrown into prison, but his action regains him Fennella's respect and love. (In Dreyer's film the woman accused of child murder is the illegitimate daughter of a judge who refuses to try the case himself. She is condemned to death by an unsympathetic colleague, but the judge helps her to escape and then resigns from his own position.)

Studio shooting did not allow Sjöström much opportunity to display the Swedish touch with landscape, and the supposedly rural setting of Bessie's home, with its blatantly picturesque mill wheel, is very unconvincing. The only scene to capture something of the natural grandeur of his earlier work is a flashback during the trial that sets Bessie's killing of her child in a bleak tableau of rocks, cliffs, and sea. Interestingly enough, this scene, related by an eyewitness to the crime, is presented in an ambiguous enough way to leave doubts in the minds of both the audience to the film and the audience in the court as to the witness's reliability.

Victor's inner conflicts and torments, on the other hand, are effectively and powerfully handled and, as with David in *The Phantom Chariot*, Sjöström takes the character through several stages of partial repentance before allowing him final absolution. Contrasts between town and country, rich and poor, privileged and deprived, are made through extensive cross-cutting, some of it quite effective. Most of Bessie's tribulations are associated with rain: she is maliciously locked out by her father when she is a few moments late coming home; Victor finds her homeless in the street during a rainstorm and takes her to his house for shelter. Later she is out in the pouring rain in search of a lost lamb; shots of her cradling the animal on her lap are intercut with shots of Fennella seated comfortably at home caressing a lapdog. When Bessie returns home she is attacked by her brutal father, who tries to drive her out into the rain again; in a scene that is more effectively handled than it can possibly sound in description, the girl's fragile mother rises to her defense and throws the father out of doors instead. When Bessie is arrested for the murder of her child and taken off in a police carriage, the scene is intercut with shots of Victor and Fennella setting off for a drive in a car together. Bessie's mother clings to the back of the carriage and is dragged some distance behind it before finally losing her hold and, in a scene reminiscent of the ending of Chaplin's recently released *A Woman of Paris*,[24] car and carriage pass each other on a country road, neither set of occupants aware of the other, before Victor comes across the mother and stops to help her.

The seduction scene is also imaginatively filmed, with Bessie changing out of her wet clothes behind a screen and her body visible in shadow behind it; the resulting action is hinted at by an exchange of glances between herself and Victor. And contemporary reviews agreed that the now missing ending was powerfully and skillfully directed. Overall the film received considerable approval from the critics, though the *New York Times*

(4 February 1924), while agreeing that several scenes were "portrayed with telling emphasis," had considerable reservations about the film as a whole. *Moving Picture World* (15 December 1923) anticipated the film's opening with photographs of Hall Caine and Sjöström on its front page and nominated both for its "Hall of Fame": Caine "because his latest and most popular novel, 'The Master of Man,' has been made into the most thrilling motion picture of many years," and Sjöström "because this great Scandinavian director is the supreme master of human sympathy in the motion picture drama. Because he has just produced "Name the Man!" a picture that the years will not forget."

The magazine's own review (12 January 1924, 136) was equally laudatory, praising story, acting, photography, sets and the "intense suspense of the picture." A month later (16 February 1924, 550) it reported that the film was a huge commercial hit: "there is no doubt that it is going to achieve one of the biggest successes of the year." The article went on to quote admiring comments from the major New York papers and a week later (24 February) the magazine reaffirmed that the film was doing "tremendous business" in New York. *Variety* agreed that the film was "among the screen achievements of the period," "a gripping story handled flawlessly," and "sure fire to the box office." It added that the film gave "another proof that the foreign directors when given American casts and American cooperation in production can come pretty near topping all of the regular run of American directors with the exception of a few in the matter of detail."[25]

An article by Jim Tully in *Motion Picture Classic* headlined "The Greatest Director in the World" announced that Chaplin, Lubitsch, and Tourneur all granted this status to Sjöström.[26] The article gave a sympathetic portrait of Sjöström both as an artist and as a person: "There is that something about him—a subdued majesty—that commands mingled awe and respect. An oak in a forest of pines, he is one of the very few big men that the cinema world has produced." "In painstaking application, in mental capacity, in magnificent background, in a thoro and relentless drilling in the fundamentals of his art, Seastrom leads that brilliant array of foreigners who are the chief glory of the American screen." Tully compared him favorably with Griffith, praising the intelligence, emotional power, simplicity, truthfulness, and lack of sentimentality of his work, and called him "the most self-effacing and modest individual in pictures today." A brief interview at the end of the article, though it elicited little of significance about the director's ideas on his art, confirmed this impression of reticence, even shyness, and stressed Sjöström's simple tastes and love of his family in contrast to the glitter and extravagance of the normal Hollywood style of living. Tully's final comment on the obvious pleasure that Sjöström took in the actual filming of a picture is echoed in Bengt Forslund's emphasis on his personal contentment at this period of his career, and the admiration and love with which he was regarded by those who worked with him. Each, however, chooses different, even contradictory, examples to illustrate this: Tully speaks of Sjöström's "loud laughter" while directing a humorous scene, while Forslund quotes Conrad Nagel (the leading actor of *Name the Man*) on his own sense of shame when someone broke the mood established by "this taciturn, strange, lonely individual" by making an inappropriate joke just when shooting was about to begin.[27]

Successful as *Name the Man* had been, there was a longer delay before Sjöström's next film appeared than had been anticipated in his contract primarily because of the upheavals within the Goldwyn Company attendant on the financial problems caused by von Stroheim's *Greed* and the merger with Metro and Mayer to form MGM in April 1924. He worked on a script with Hjalmar Bergman (before the latter gave up and returned to Sweden) which came to nothing and then was offered the play *He Who Gets Slapped* by another popular literary figure of the period, Leonid Andreyev. Forslund quotes from an interview for a Swedish newspaper at the time that shows Sjöström both aware of, and apparently reconciled to, the fact that he would have to work in America in a very different way than he had been accustomed to in Sweden:

> One thing I've learnt to acknowledge out here, and that is that it's absolutely meaningless to try to make Swedish films for America. It's an utter waste of energy. One realizes that, when one stays in America and the American film world and sees how vastly separated their ideas are from ours. They don't recognize themselves in the foreign milieu, they are totally ignorant of it, uninterested, yawn, and talk about something else.[28]

His comments here seem to place him somewhere in between Murnau and Lubitsch: like Murnau, with his desire for a chain of "art" cinemas, he seems aware that the American mass audience had little interest in adjusting to ways of thinking and behaving that differed significantly from those presented by their own cinema; yet, as his subsequent career proved, he was temperamentally unable to accept the kind of adjustment and compromise that allowed Lubitsch to appeal to an American audience and yet retain a "European" touch.

Despite his forebodings, however, Sjöström made few concessions to popular taste in *He Who Gets Slapped,* which illustrates even more clearly than *Name the Man* that his American films were not the unmitigated disasters that (with the conventional exceptions of *The Wind* and *The Scarlet Letter*) they are commonly presented as. Once again there is the distancing effect of a foreign setting (in this case, France), and the fact that the action takes place almost entirely indoors perhaps accounts for the film's neglect at the hands of critics who associate Sjöström exclusively with themes of Man and Nature. Its analysis of a profoundly masochistic personality takes it considerably beyond *The Phantom Chariot* in its psychological insight and, though it lacks the structural intricacy of that film, it operates through a complex pattern of repetition and variation of images, motifs, gestures, actions, and character relationships that goes far beyond the intermittent use of these devices in the Swedish films.

The film is built around two parallel and interlocking sets of action and character relationships. Paul Beaumont (brilliantly played by Lon Chaney) is a shy and passive person whose wife Marie first of all cuckolds him with Baron Regnard, then helps the latter to steal the documents relating to Paul's scientific research. In a deliberately nightmarish and grotesque sequence, the Baron presents Paul's work as his own to an audience of admiring scientists and, when Paul attempts to intervene and protest, the Baron publicly ridicules and humiliates him, slapping him on the face to the applause and laughter of the onlookers. When the bewildered Paul returns home and appeals to Marie for consolation, she too mocks and insults him, calling him a "fool" and a "clown." Instead of protesting or fighting back, Paul accepts this designation and becomes a circus clown whose act consists of an elaborate and endless series of ritual humiliations: he enters on stilts and is knocked off them by the other clowns; he then tries to offer the audience a series of what he calls "scientific" propositions, but is interrupted and silenced by a barrage of slaps from his fellow performers. When things have reached the point that he cannot even open his mouth without being greeted by a rapid series of blows, he is made to remain immobile while a line of clowns, ending with a small boy, file past and slap him. The next part of the act begins with Paul (who by now is known and advertised only as "HE WHO GETS SLAPPED") being thrown back into the circus ring bound and gagged; the other clowns gather round and one of them rips off a cloth heart sewn on to Paul's costume, squeezes it, and buries it in the sand of the ring. They then conduct a mock funeral for him and carry him off on a stretcher, but even this cannot be performed with dignity, for the canvas on

*P*aul (Lon Chaney), the scientist-turned-clown of *He Who Gets Slapped*, seems deliberately to court humiliation at the hands of Consuelo (Norma Shearer), by inviting her to slap him.

the stretcher must break and send him sprawling to the ground while the others march off triumphantly with the empty framework.

It is possible to see at least some of this as a social comment on the ineffectiveness of the intellectual in the face of public ignorance, disdain, and even hatred, or as an acknowledgment that sadism and cruelty often lie at the wellsprings of comedy; yet the mechanical intensity with which Paul persists in acting out in detail both his personal and his professional degradation points to an astonishing degree of masochism and self-pity. The heart motif refers back both to his betrayal by Marie and to the pattern that dominates the second half of the film: the heart is sewn on to his costume before each performance by Consuelo, the beautiful bareback rider (played by Norma Shearer), with whom he is secretly and hopelessly in love, knowing that she prefers her partner Bezano (played by John Gilbert).[29] As a symbol of his despairing love, he keeps a smaller "heart" hidden in his pocket. The Baron meanwhile reappears, having grown tired of Marie; he witnesses a circus performance, without recognizing Paul, and is attracted to Consuelo, whom he negotiates to "buy" from her degenerate father, the impoverished Count Mancini.

Once again Paul invites rejection and humiliation by confessing his love to Consuelo as she sews his cloth heart on one day. She responds with astonishment and amusement, refusing to take him seriously, and slaps him playfully on the face; after a moment's hesitation, placing his hand on his cheek, Paul laughs too and invites her to slap him again. They are interrupted by Mancini and the Baron, who tell Consuelo to prepare for her marriage immediately after she has completed her performance. Paul then loses all sense of self-preservation and deliberately antagonizes the two men; consequently the Baron finally recognizes him and a scuffle takes place in which Mancini stabs Paul with his swordstick. As he collapses, he pulls the miniature heart from his pocket and tries to staunch the flow of blood with it. He has already prepared his revenge, however, though it is a typically indirect and passive one: as the men leave they are confronted and killed by a circus lion that Paul has released from its cage.

Paul begs the lion to give him "the last slap" but the animal is driven back into its cage by its trainer. The other clowns dance into the ring for Paul's performance and he staggers in to join them; when he starts to talk about his love for Consuelo they think he is merely changing his act a little and begin the routine of slapping. It is only after he has been knocked down several times that they realize the true situation and he is allowed to die in Consuelo's arms, with a close-up revealing his outstretched hand clutching the bloodstained heart. Nevertheless the show continues, with the oblivious audience applauding Consuelo and Bezano as they ride on horseback together.

The overall structural pattern of the film presents a relentless series of symbolic and actual humiliations, on both the public and the private level, performed on a character who makes no real attempt to resist them and seems in fact to invite even more persecution as the action proceeds. In the first half of the film, he is betrayed by his wife and thwarted in his professional life by his wife's seducer; in the second half he is rejected by the woman he loves, who seems at one point destined to belong to his previous tormentor. His attempt to avert this leads to a second failure, parallel to the earlier lecture hall scene, where once again he struggles to communicate his ideas to an audience and is greeted with laughter; and this failure is followed by death.

The larger parallels are linked together by an intricate series of motifs such as the various forms of slapping already mentioned, or the hearts. Audiences and applause punctuate the film at regular intervals and

𝒫aul can win Consuelo's affection and concern only in death. John Gilbert
plays Consuelo's lover, Bezano.

in many ingenious ways: in the lecture hall the Baron's speech is applauded
by an audience seated in steep tiers of seats who are shown mainly in close-
ups of grotesque, toothless, wrinkled faces; after Paul has intervened and
the Baron has slapped him, close-ups of his bewildered face are intercut
with shots of the mocking audience. When Paul is giving his circus performance, Sjöström cuts repeatedly to a particularly fat member of the audience (accompanied by his equally overweight family) who goes into convul-
sions of mirth at each successive humiliation and ends by almost choking on
an apple that he is eating. At one point the faces of Paul's fellow clowns as
they mock him dissolve into the faces of the audience in the lecture hall.
When the Baron and Mancini are being attacked by the lion, their shouts for
help are drowned out by the applause of the audience for Bezano and
Consuelo; and in the final scenes the audience unthinkingly applauds as the
dying Paul tries to express his thoughts on what a title calls "Hate, Life,
Love," and is repeatedly knocked down by the other clowns.

As in *Name the Man*, Sjöström also uses crosscutting for ironic or dramatic effect, particularly when a love scene in a forest glade between Consuelo and Bezano is intercut with the negotiations between Mancini and the Baron as to how much the Baron is prepared to pay for Consuelo. Consuelo is coy and flirtatious, making Bezano pursue her; Mancini suggests that the Baron should marry his daughter; an iris shot closes in on the Baron fingering a string of pearls and this dissolves to an iris opening out on Bezano making a daisy chain; the lovers are observed by a woodcutter who plays a joke on them; the Baron says he will marry Consuelo; Bezano proposes and Consuelo says she must have her father's consent; Mancini asks his prospective son-in-law for a "loan." Though there are conventional elements in the scene, especially in Consuelo's maidenly reluctance to be won too easily, it is well handled overall; the woodcutter, however, introduces a jarring note of broad comedy that had already occurred rather inappropriately in the trial scene of *Name the Man* and was to mar certain scenes of both *The Scarlet Letter* and *The Wind*. As Sjöström had rarely included comic interludes of this kind in his Swedish films, it seems likely that they were a deliberate concession to the presumed taste of an American audience and its unwillingness to sit through ninety minutes of unrelieved seriousness.

The film begins with a shot of a clown spinning a huge globe; this dissolves into a shot of Paul in his study with a smaller globe on his desk.[30] At crucial points in the story, the clown and globe reappear: after Paul is spurned by Marie, we see the clown and the globe, then a host of clowns superimposed on the rim of a spinning globe, and then this dissolves to a shot of the circus ring. After Mancini and the Baron have concluded their bargain over Consuelo, there is a shot of the clown vigorously spinning the globe; the Baron then takes his leave of Marie, and as she looks at the check he has given her for her services, the clown is seen thumbing his nose at the globe. The last shot of the film is of the globe, with a group of clowns tossing Paul's body off into the void—a startlingly bleak ending for a Hollywood film of this period.

He Who Gets Slapped was made on a relatively low budget and seems to have been written, shot, and released as Sjöström intended it to be and without studio interference. Stylistically it has much in common with his Swedish films, particularly in the cutting and the lighting; he is reported to have insisted on atmospheric lighting rather than the purely naturalistic style that he had used in *Name the Man*, and this helped greatly to create the sense of loneliness, despair, and isolation around the main character. One of the most striking shots of this kind shows Paul alone in the ring after a performance; he listlessly digs the cloth heart out of the sand with his toe and puts it in his pocket. The spotlights go out, leaving him in darkness, with only the white clown make-up of his face visible.

Once again the critical response was overwhelmingly favorable. *Moving Picture World* (15 November 1924, 267) called it "one of the most human, gripping and at the same time artistic motion pictures that it has been the pleasure of the writer to witness this year." The reviewer also thought it "real box office stuff." He praised the script and the acting, but concluded with the main reason for the film's success: "Victor Seastrom's direction is of finest craftsmanship. His staging of each scene is well night *[sic]* perfect and the backgrounds are marvels of beauty and artistry." *Motion Picture Classic* (January 1925, 50) agreed that "the Scandinavian director has not missed a single trick in establishing the deep well of pathos which governs the life of the clown—superbly played by Lon Chaney." While acknowledging that the picture was "off the beaten path," it felt that it was "certain to be appreciated by all thinking people." And the *New York Times* (10 November 1924) fully atoned for its lukewarm response to *Name the Man:*

> At the Capitol this week there is a picture which defies one to write about it without indulging in superlatives. It is a shadow drama so beautifully told, so flawlessly directed that we imagine that it will be held up as a model by all producers. Throughout its length there is not an instant of ennui, not a second one wants to lose; it held the spectators spellbound yesterday afternoon, the last fade-out being the signal for a hearty round of applause. This celluloid masterpiece is Victor Seastrom's picturization of Leonid Andreyev's play "He Who Gets Slapped."

After describing the plot, the reviewer (Mordaunt Hall) concluded:

> Mr. Seastrom has directed this dramatic story with all the genius of a Chaplin or a Lubitsch, and he has accomplished more than they have in their respective works, "A Woman of Paris" and "The Marriage Circle," as he had, what they did not have, a stirring, dramatic story to put into pictures.[31]

Neither of Sjöström's next two pictures, both made for MGM, is known to exist at present. *Confessions of a Queen* (1925), which was based on a novel by Alphonse Daudet, appears to have him working in territory more usually occupied by Lubitsch. The *New York Times* (25 March 1925) called it "another mythical kingdom story, which is by no means as strong as some of the similar vehicles" and suggested that it might have been improved with Adolphe Menjou in the cast. It also remarked that "comedy is an unknown quantity" for Sjöström and described what might have been a strikingly erotic scene in which the king brands a young woman (at her request) on her leg with the royal coat of arms inscribed on his cigarette case. Though the *Times*'s low opinion of the film may have been merited, it might be unwise to accept it without question, knowing that Sjöström had indeed made a perfectly respectable comedy already in *His Lordship's Last Will*.

The *Tower of Lies* (1925) was based on *The Emperor of Portugalia* by Lagerlöf and contained the familiar ingredients of sexual guilt, public pressure, and persecution, shame, repentance, and reconciliation. It starred Chaney and Norma Shearer and dealt primarily with the relationship between a father and daughter; the father adores and idealizes the young woman and goes mad when she leaves to work in the city in order to pay the rent on their farm and is not heard from for several years. When she does return, there are rumors that she has lived as a prostitute in the city and the indignant country people unite to drive her away again. Her father pursues her, but is accidentally drowned, as is their landlord, who had been responsible for corrupting her in the city. The girl returns to the farm and marries her childhood sweetheart.

Critical response was mixed, but on the whole favorable. *Moving Picture World* (10 October 1925, 498), called Sjöström "one of our best directors," and praised the acting, direction and photography. While acknowledging that the first half moved very slowly, it found that the film ended "in a whirlwind of effectiveness" and that it was "tremendous drama" overall. It did, however, call it "a high-class production" about which "the so-called intelligentsia" might be more enthusiastic than "the average audience"—though "young and old, shop girl and sophisticate" should be won over to it by the end. *Variety* (30 September 1925, 42) was less enthusiastic. It found the acting and direction satisfactory enough, but, notwithstanding the film's excellence from "the artistic and literary viewpoints, it is too heavy for the picture audiences." The theme was "ponderous," the plot "silly" and "illogical," the setting unconvincing, and the picture as a whole "soggy." This particular review seems to reflect the growing separation between "popular" (i.e., American) films and "artistic" (i.e., ponderous, gloomy, and foreign) ones that has already been noted in chapter 1. It also appears to confirm Sjöström's foreboding that "it's absolutely meaningless to try to make Swedish films for America" in the reviewer's offhand comment that "the locale is apparently some Scandinavian country" and his adamant refusal to make any allowance for different patterns of moral and social behavior when contemptuously dismissing the "silly" plot.

Sjöström's next film, made at the beginning of a new contract for MGM, was his first attempt at tackling a purely American subject and setting, though once again it was shrewdly chosen in that it allowed him to work with thematic material that related very closely to his Swedish films. Critical commentary on *The Scarlet Letter* (1926) has tended to concentrate on its faithfulness or otherwise to either the spirit or the details of Nathaniel Hawthorne's novel; I will be less concerned with that here than in trying to see the film in the overall context of Sjöström's career and as a work that retains the best qualities of his Swedish films while applying them to a specifically American context. The film reunited him with Hanson, who had been working in America for some years, and of course starred Lillian Gish, then at the height of her career, as Hester Prynne. It was photographed by Hendrick Sartov, who had been closely associated with Griffith's recent work and had been responsible for some of the finest images of Gish in *Broken Blossoms* and *Orphans of the Storm*.[32]

The film has the Lagerlöf elements of adultery, illegitimacy, the pressures of an intolerant public opinion, guilt, punishment, atonement, and repentance—though Sjöström remains faithful to the spirit of the book by making the adulterous pair suffer the full consequences of their actions with no suggestion that the threads of a normal life can be picked up again once the crisis is over. There is even a literal "name the man" situation, as Dimmesdale, unable to admit his guilt publicly, tries to persuade Hester to name him as the father of their child, which she refuses to do. All this, however, takes place in Puritan New England, presented with a brilliant sense of time and place, even if some of the details are symbolic or deliberately comic rather than historically accurate. Church groups alarmed that the film might be either an attack on "religion" or an apology for "immorality" were appeased by MGM before production began and without involving any major alteration to Sjöström's own concept of the film. It is the comic elements, in fact, that provide almost the only blemishes, especially in the tedious subplot involving Giles and his fiancée.

Besides its "Swedish" themes, the film allows for more interplay between human beings and their natural environment, again along the lines of the Lagerlöf adaptations, than had been the case in Sjöström's American work so far (even if the limitations of what was largely studio shooting prevented the sense of scope and natural grandeur of *A Man There Was* or *The Outlaw and His Wife*). The film opens with a succinct series of images that summarize the main elements that will be in contention throughout the story: flowers, church bells, the pillory. The camera tracks with the towns-people (there is much more extensive and elaborate camera movement throughout this film than had been usual for Sjöström) as they gather for church, and the community's penalties of ostracism and public shaming are indicated when we are shown one of its victims. Hester meanwhile (who dresses throughout in a lighter shade of clothing than the others) is more concerned with her appearance and is seen admiring herself in a mirror only imperfectly covered with a motto warning against vanity. The fact that her pet canary is singing on the Lord's day scandalizes a passerby, and when the bird escapes from its cage, Hester chooses to pursue it rather than make her way to church. She follows it into a forest glade with a stream and a waterfall that clearly represents her true environment; she fails to capture it, arrives late for church, and receives a public rebuke from Dimmesdale, the minis-ter, and then is placed in the stocks for running on a Sunday. In the mean-time, in a foreshadowing of her own later acceptance of her fate, the bird has returned voluntarily to its cage.

Dimmesdale's involvement with Hester begins when he comes across her while she is busy washing her underwear in the stream. Her attempt to conceal a garment attracts his attention and he forces her to reveal what she is hiding, to the embarrassment of both of them. Sjöström makes the latent sexuality (which would have been blatant with von Stroheim) perfectly evident, but does so with both delicacy and humor. Dimmesdale says he wishes to discuss her errant behavior with her and they set off to walk together, Hester first trying to throw the offending item of underwear out of sight. Their mutual embarrassment and uneasiness, together with the growing sexual attraction that neither feels free to acknowledge, is suggested by a series of fast tracking-shots as they pace back and forth over the same stretch of ground, the camera first following behind them, then retreating as they turn, then following again. Finally they yield and touch each other, holding hands, the camera panning sardonically to the undergarment, which has caught on a branch rather than falling out of sight; then they embrace, half concealed from view by a bush. The natural-ness of this scene, which of course takes place out of doors, is immediately given a grotesque contrast in the courtship rituals officially approved by Puritan society, with Giles and his fiancée allowed to communicate only by means of long speaking tubes, and the young woman so horrified by his unbridled lust that she rushes to her parents for protection when he attempts to embrace her on taking leave at the doorway of her house. Unfortunately

Sjöström, perhaps still uncertain as to just what level of sophistication to aim at in his audience, overplays the comedy of the scene, with Giles being smothered in a fall of snow from the roof as he leaves.

Hester and Dimmesdale meet again, this time in her house, and she admits that she is already married. He leaves in anger, and she runs vainly after him in the snow, then returns home. In one of the most strikingly beautiful and powerful shots in all of Sjöström's work—and indeed in the whole of silent cinema—the shadow of her spinning wheel is cast web-like on her dress, centering exactly on her womb, in a brilliant and multifaceted summation of her relationship with Dimmesdale and its eventual consequences. The imagery of entrapment is picked up immediately in the following scene as the camera tilts down and tracks toward a barred window, through which we see a crowd assembling in a courtyard. Hester has borne her child and is in prison awaiting punishment, and on the day that this is to take place, Dimmesdale returns home after a long absence. He offers to confess but (like Bessie in *Name the Man*) she prefers to suffer alone rather than destroy his public reputation; she walks with dignity to the scaffold, carrying her baby, to submit to public reproach and to receiving the letter "A" that she will have to wear as a permanent badge of shame. Not content with this, some of the townswomen try to take her child away from her so that she cannot contaminate it with her influence, but she resists so fiercely that they retreat and Dimmesdale is able to intervene and baptize the child, stipulating that she should keep it.

The child, Pearl, is seen growing up, innocently curious about the "A" that her mother wears and shunned by the local children, who throw mud at both her and Hester. In another strikingly lit and composed shot, Dimmesdale punishes himself for his cowardice and his guilt by branding an "A" into his flesh with a poker. A shot of the house in which Hester now lives, framed to show a gallows on the hill behind it, is followed by the return of her husband, Roger. He helps to cure Pearl, who has fallen ill, but learns of Hester's relationship with Dimmesdale and threatens vengeance. Contrasting images of repression and freedom accumulate as Hester and Dimmesdale decide to flee and begin a new life somewhere else. Hester removes the "A" from her dress, throws it away, and releases her hair from its normal confined state; but Pearl finds the discarded letter and pins it back on her mother's dress. After another unnecessarily comic interlude involving Giles (in which he tricks the church elders into ducking one of the most vicious of the local gossips in the town pond), Dimmesdale preaches a sermon on tolerance to the assembled community. Roger reappears and says

*T*hree faces of Lillian Gish from *The Scarlet Letter:* the innocent maiden, the victim (note the web-like shadow of the spinning wheel centered on her womb), and the devoted and outcast mother.

he intends to take Hester and Pearl away with him, and the tormented Dimmesdale (in a scene presumably similar to the lost ending of *Name the Man*) ascends the scaffold to confess his guilt publicly, standing with arms outstretched. Hester attempts once again to protect him and denies that he is telling the truth, but he tears open his shirt to reveal the "A" branded on his chest. He rips the "A" from her dress and as he collapses, it falls to rest on top of the letter burned over his own heart. As he dies in Hester's arms, the men of the town remove their hats in what is presumably intended as a gesture of respect and thus a rather overoptimistic suggestion that they will have more tolerance for such sinners in future. On the personal level, however, the film offers a less easy consolation, with a close-up of Hester's face as she stands beside her lover's body on the scaffold followed by a long-shot of her, the scaffold, and the subdued, motionless crowd.

Whether or not the film adequately conveys the ambiguities and peculiar tensions of Hawthorne's novel, it certainly assimilates the subject matter into a form that Sjöström had made very much his own and presents it through images of unforgettable power and beauty. Comparisons with the Lagerlöf adaptations come most obviously to mind, but there are also evident similarities to *Name the Man, He Who Gets Slapped* (Paul dying in Consuelo's arms clutching his "heart" and Dimmesdale dying in Hester's arms with the two brands of shame and guilt united), and even *Love's Crucible* (in the acceptance of public penance at the end). Even the suggestion at the end that the townspeople have been sufficiently moved by the sight before them to set aside (for a moment at least) their habitual prejudice and intolerance is at least consistent with the world of Lagerlöf's novels, even it is not easily reconciled with Hawthorne. *The Sons of Ingmar* and *Karin, Daughter of Ingmar* both end with the members of the community accepting a character or a relationship that they had previously condemned; in *The Scarlet Letter,* however, Sjöström denies the surviving character any hint of consolation in the prospect of personal happiness.

If there are any signs of commercial compromise in the film, they are to be found in the comic interludes, and even these are not totally gratuitous in themselves, in that they are intended to illustrate an extreme aspect of the sexual repression that condemns and destroys Hester and Dimmesdale. It can certainly be argued that they are damaging to the overall mood of the film and yet Sjöström, like Murnau, was probably correct in suspecting that American audiences and reviewers would be only too quick to condemn any film that was too unrelentingly "heavy," "ponderous," or "gloomy."

The result, in any case, seemed to satisfy most of the critics at the time, and the film received the kind of praise that had greeted Sjöström's first two American productions.[33] *Moving Picture World* (21 August 1926, 484) thought it "destined to be one of the outstanding pictures of the season" and praised the scene in which Hester resists the women trying to take her child from her as "the finest thing [Gish] has done." "She has more securely placed herself in the ranks of the leading American players in this picture than in any previous endeavor, for she avoids here to a very large degree the tricks of personality which have at times marred the fineness of her earlier work." Sjöström's direction was "admirable" and the film itself was "a milestone in the development of the picture; a thing to endure."

Variety (11 August 1926, 11, 14) doubted the film's box-office strength after what it predicted would be a successful opening engagement, but agreed that "the direction of Victor Seastrom is pretty near perfect and the composition in some of the scenes bespeaks the highest art in picture photography." The rather pedestrian review in the *New York Times* (10 August 1926) approved of almost everything in the film, including the comic elements, to which, in fact, almost half the review was devoted. Sjöström ("an earnest Swedish director") was credited with "some cleverly pictured scenes in the church" and "imaginative direction, both in the handling of the players and in their arrangement according to the shades of their costumes."

After a brief visit to Sweden with his family, in the course of which he sorted out some visa problems that the American Immigration Service had raised about his status in the country, Sjöström returned to make *The Divine Woman*, starring Garbo and Hanson. Garbo was already an important figure in Hollywood and reportedly asked for Sjöström as director and Hanson as co-star.[34] The script was loosely based on an episode in the life of Sarah Bernhardt and was written by Sjöström in collaboration with Frances Marion, who had also worked on *The Scarlet Letter*. Once again accurate assessment of the film's worth is impossible, for no prints survive and contemporary reviews offer contradictory judgments of it.[35] *Variety* (18 January 1928, 16) concentrated on Garbo's performance, which it found satisfactory on the whole, and offered some vague comments on "considerable comedy," "hefty emotionalism," "perfect" photography, and "scenic ambitions" directed at "realism rather than magnificence." The *New York Times* (17 January 1928), however, found "an absence of spontaneity" and "a tendency toward hysteria in the more emotional sequences." It also condemned the "lethargy" of the production, its "artificial situations," and the occasional "overacting" of both Garbo and Hanson. The few comments on the direction suggest that Sjöström made a good deal of use of editing for ironic contrast, along the lines of *Name the Man* and *He Who Gets Slapped:* "You see Marianne, who has won wealth and fame on the stage, wearing a sparkling bracelet and this ornament fades out into a glimpse of the handcuffed wrist of Lucien, the hero. Mr. Seastrom does a similar thing again when he takes the spectator from a stage banked with flowers to the shafts of light in Lucien's cell."

In much the same way as Garbo had selected Sjöström as director for *The Divine Woman*, it was Gish who secured for him the job of directing *The Wind*, preferring him to the studio's original choice, Clarence Brown.[36] Sjöström insisted on filming the exteriors on location in the Mohave Desert, and—rather surprisingly for a company many of whose executives had suffered through the filming of *Greed*—he was allowed to do so. Conditions of shooting were often almost intolerable, with temperatures of up to 120 degrees and a battery of wind machines whipping up the sand that became the dominant physical presence of the film; Gish later described it as "one of my worst experiences in film making" and comparable to the torments of the ice floes in Griffith's *Way Down East*.[37] Yet Sjöström emerged from it with the film that he wanted and still retained the affection and respect of his coworkers: he felt he had made his best American film and the one that had ended up closest to his original conception of it. Though he was once again awarded double the normal bonus by a satisfied studio, problems soon arose over the original ending (which had left the heroine insane after the wind had relentlessly exposed the body of the man she had killed in self-defense) and over the release of a film that had been shot as a silent at a time when a sound track of some kind was rapidly becoming obligatory. As a result, although the film had been completed in 1927, it was not released until November 1928, with a happy ending providing a reconciliation between Letty and her husband, and some added sound effects. Sjöström had to accept both the delay and the alterations, but the experience offered the first major disillusionment of his Hollywood career and contributed substantially to his decision to leave the country two years later.

Nevertheless, *The Wind* is almost certainly Sjöström's best American film and perhaps his finest film overall; it is also one of the masterpieces of American silent cinema. Critics who see the Man against Nature theme as central to Sjöström's work have called it the closest in spirit to his Swedish films; it would perhaps be truer to say that it picks up one facet only of his Swedish work, with *The Scarlet Letter* exploring in an American context the equally important themes of the Lagerlöf adaptations. Moreover, there are some major differences between the role played by nature in films like *A Man There Was* and *The Outlaw and His Wife* and its function in *The Wind*. In the Swedish films nature dwarfs and overwhelms human beings, reducing them to insignificance; yet there are occasions in which they can either live in harmony with nature or rise to meet the challenge that nature offers them. In *The Wind*, on the other hand, there is little grandeur in the natural environment; rather it is a relentless, omnipresent force that steadily saps the willpower and the energy of the central character and demonstrates in its unpredictable eruptions into violence that human attempts to resist it are puny and ephemeral. Nature here is neither an awe-inspiring, almost mystical force as in the Swedish films, nor a challenge to be overcome through human courage and endurance as in an American Western; and the happy ending, which attempts to give it the latter connotation, with Letty standing firmly in the doorway of her home, braving the full force of the wind and proclaiming that she is "not afraid," runs totally contrary to the sombre implications of the film as a whole.

The film opens with a title referring to man's "conquest" of nature, a statement that would normally be taken at face value in an American movie but which is here quickly shown to be a premature and overconfident assumption. One of Sjöström's most striking achievements is his ability to keep the wind as an all-pervasive, inescapable presence throughout the film, without resorting to crudely repetitive devices to remind us of this. Wind and sand blow through the open window of the train in which Letty is travelling to meet her cousin; at one and the same time a basic motif of the film is established and an impetus is given to the plot as the city slicker Wirt Roddy takes advantage of the opportunity to do her a favor by closing the window and then strikes up a conversation with her. As they talk, Sjöström cuts insistently to shots of sand gusting against the windowpanes and then to long-shots of the train itself, almost lost in the immensity of the desert, with only the lighted patches of its windows to distinguish it from the obscurity around it. The visual motif of the loss of spatial distinctions, with sky and sand merging into one continuous blur, becomes central to the film, mirroring (and even helping to cause) the confusion and disorientation that Letty experiences in her new environment, where the assumptions and behavior patterns of her Eastern world no longer seem to apply. She is met at the station by neighbors of her cousin, in a whirl of wind, sand, and darkness, utterly bewildered and almost ready to yield to the temptation offered by Wirt to retreat to the comparative security of the train. Another thematic pattern of repeated motifs is inaugurated as Sourdough and his companion quarrel about who is to sit beside her; the argument is decided by a shooting contest as the men vie to extinguish a nearby lantern and the triumphant Sourdough takes his place by her side. As they drive, he tells her of the legend of the "ghost horse" that rides the wind, and a superimposition shows the gigantic white animal whose image will recur at a crucial moment later in the film.

As in *He Who Gets Slapped* and *The Scarlet Letter*, Sjöström builds the remainder of the film around thematic variations of these initial motifs: Letty's inability to cope with the harsh realities of her new natural environment and her corresponding disorientation in a world lacking the social graces and polite conventions of the civilized East. Cora, her cousin's wife, treats her as an unwelcome intruder from the start; the physical contrast between the two women—tight-faced, unsmiling Cora, old before her time, with dark hair drawn severely back and tied into place, and shy, youthful, vulnerable Letty, with fair hair framing her face in an ethereal halo—establishes their sexual rivalry in a manner reminiscent of Murnau's contrast between the Wife and the Woman from the City in *Sunrise*. Sjöström, however, allows us to sympathize with both women and to understand Cora's resentment that the years of drudgery as housewife and mother that have aged her and brought about the loss of her good looks should not only be taken for granted but even count against her as the men, her husband included, flock around the newcomer and compete in offering her the gastronomical delicacies of sow belly and intestines. Letty, far from gloating over their attentions as the jealous Cora assumes, is embarrassed by them, but is unable to find a polite way of rejecting them; once again her sense of disorientation is compounded by the intrusion of the alien natural world around her, as sand seeps in through the windows and on to the bread that she eats, the wind gusts against the glass, and twigs and broken branches scurry past outside.

Cora's unspoken hatred of Letty intensifies as the young woman innocently starts to supplant her in those aspects of her role that involve giving and receiving affection, leaving to her the thankless, and unthanked, mechanical tasks that keep the household going. In one of the scenes that, in its resolute deglamorization and close attention to physical detail, establishes *The Wind* as a valid precursor of neorealism, Cora is shown cleaning out a pig carcass (sleeves rolled up, her arm plunged up to the elbow in the animal's body) while Letty fastidiously irons some clothes, the camera singling out her delicate hands in close-up. Cora's children arrive home and immediately rush to greet Letty, ignoring their mother; when her husband enters, Cora makes a point of embracing him possessively and kissing him with unaccustomed warmth; he quickly disengages himself, however, and goes over to speak to Letty. Cora, watching them balefully, slowly wipes the blood-stained butcher's knife clean on her apron.

At a community dance Letty once again becomes the innocent focus of sexual competition, this time between Sourdough (a figure played entirely for comedy in the manner of Giles in *The Scarlet Letter*), and Lige, a local farmer (played by Lars Hanson). In a variation of the scene at the station, they try to decide by means of a shooting contest which of them will propose to her and, when this ends in deadlock, they toss a coin—methods which, understandably enough, Letty regards as a joke, rather than taking them with the seriousness that the men do. Meanwhile Wirt Roddy has reappeared bringing a welcome (from Letty's point of view) touch of urban sophistication into a situation that is becoming increasingly bizarre. Both

The Wind picks up the social realism of Sjöström's Swedish films, as Letty (Lillian Gish) is made aware of the hostility Cora, her cousin's wife (Dorothy Cummings), feels toward her.

Sourdough and Lige make fun of him, mocking his fastidious gesture of brushing dust from his sleeve, while Sourdough carefully spits tobacco juice on to his highly polished shoes. These maneuvers, and the dance itself, are interrupted by a cyclone that does a certain amount of damage to the dance hall; the local inhabitants accept it philosophically, filing down to the safety of the cellar while a few of the men barricade the doors and windows.

When Cora learns that Letty is refusing to take Lige's proposal seriously, she loses control, attacks her, and tells her to leave. Confused and frightened, Letty seeks out Wirt in town and asks him to take her away. He is only too delighted to accept, but warns her that he is already married—a minor consideration in his own eyes, but enough to send Letty back to her cousin's. Cora comes to collect her in a scene that maintains the unobtrusive

presence of the wind as a factor in almost every shot of the film, with the women's clothes fluttering and rustling round them with each step that they take. Far from mellowing, Cora is even firmer now: there is no place for Letty in her household and she will have to marry Lige. The sequence of the marriage and the wedding night is one of the most brilliant in the whole film, merging perfectly the two major visual and thematic motifs that emphasize Letty's continuing alienation from both her natural and her social setting. A close-up of the wedding ring being placed on her finger dissolves into a shot of her new home, Lige's cabin, disordered and untidy, with piles of unwashed dishes waiting to be cleaned: the road that will lead her to being a second Cora is clearly visible before her. Lige boisterously slings her wedding hat on to a coat hook and Letty nervously begins to prepare for bed. She lets down her hair and tries to wash, but the basin is full of sand that has to be cleared out first; sand has also infiltrated the marriage bed, foreboding the disasters that are to follow.

As in *The Scarlet Letter*, Sjöström crates a sense of sexual tension and embarrassment through purely visual means. The couple hardly even know each other yet; Letty instinctively shrinks from physical contact with this man who is virtually a total stranger to her, and Lige clumsily attempts to calm and reassure her, offering her coffee which she finds undrinkable and secretly pours into a basin (where Lige finds it and realizes the total extent to which he has been rejected). Letty tries desperately to evade the sexual contact that she knows is imminent, seizing on every opportunity to distract Lige and avoid his touch: when he attempts to embrace her, she snatches up a comb and busies herself with her hair. Angry and frustrated, he leaves the room, and Sjöström alternates shots of each of them pacing uneasily back and forth, physically separated and yet, as close-ups of their feet moving in the same direction across the screen suggest, emotionally linked despite their overt antagonism. Shots of the wind swirling outside the cabin emphasize that Letty is struggling against a whole way of life and not just an individual; they might also suggest her growing lack of self-control. Lige finally loses patience, kicking aside the discarded coffee cup and rushing into her room; he tries to kiss her and she responds as if to a rape, resisting and breaking away from him; wiping her mouth, her face contorted into a grimace of physical disgust, she reproaches him for having "made me hate you; I didn't want to hate you." Defeated, Lige agrees to leave her alone and says he will let her go back East as soon as possible. Though Letty's reaction may seem excessive to a modern audience (or even to contemporary spectators of Lubitsch's *The Marriage Circle* or *So this is Paris*), the sequence still carries considerable power. The intensity of Gish's performance combines with Sjöström's directorial skill to create a complex pattern of repulsion and attraction, conciliation and antagonism, evasion and misunderstanding, through gesture, movement, facial expression, camera angle, and the bare, uncluttered setting that both allows the emotions to evolve without visual distraction and serves as a reminder of the bleak future awaiting Letty in her married life. Neither character really wishes to hurt or offend the other, yet each does so almost irrevocably; partly through a mis-guided defense of his or her "rights" (as a virgin, as a husband), partly through circumstances that have forced them into marriage without truly knowing each other, and partly through sending out ambiguous signals that are easily, or willfully, misinterpreted.

After an exterior sequence that serves mainly to emphasize the vast-ness and barrenness of the hostile desert that surrounds them, Letty comes into contact with Wirt again, when he is brought to their cabin after being injured in an accident. He immediately starts to flirt with her, offering a con-spiratorial smile as he is brought in and later drawing attention to the meager-ness of her possessions and her lack of basic comforts as she wears an old, stained dress while scouring the dishes with sand to clean them. His advances are interrupted by Lige, who makes him join with the other cattlemen in rounding up the cattle and some wild horses before a threatened storm strikes; Wirt pretends to cooperate but leaves the group at the earliest opportunity.

As the storm gathers force Letty is left alone in a cabin buffeted by the wind, as inescapable indoors as it is outside. She becomes increasingly frantic as crockery and even shelves sway around her; a window breaks and she stuffs a cloth into the gap, but the wind finds another entrance and blows over a lamp, setting fire to the tablecloth. She manages to put out the fire, but by now she has almost completely lost control; holding her hands over her ears to block out the insistent howling, she sees (in a series of sub-jective shots reminiscent of parts of *The Last Laugh*) the whole room roll and tilt around her. Wirt arrives and as she opens the door for him, she is knocked over by the force of the wind. When he tries to embrace her, she rushes outside and, hurled this way and that by the power of the wind, she sees the ghost horse of the legend striding across the sky. The wind knocks her back through the doorway and Wirt picks her up and places her on the bed. A necessary (for the period) ellipsis covers the ensuing rape, but it has been clearly enough signaled through the physical violence of the wind itself and the traditional sexual symbolism of the stallion. Apart from its intrinsic power, the sequence demonstrates the symmetrical, balanced structure that characterizes much of Sjöström's best work, bringing together

the three elements introduced in the opening sequence of Letty's arrival: the destructive power of the wind, on both a physical and psychological level; the constant sexual advances offered to a largely uncomprehending heroine; and the association of the wind with sexuality through the mediating figure of the white horse.

With the storm over, Letty is seen sitting on a chair, her back to the camera, which tracks in toward her from a high angle, then pans to show a gun on a nearby table. Wirt offers to take her East with him, and when she makes no response he hits her. Letty seizes the gun and threatens him with it. He responds with contemptuous amusement and comes closer to her, daring her to shoot, and, to his amazement, she pulls the trigger. A series of close-ups on their faces follows: Wirt, still uncomprehending, barely registering what has happened to him; Letty, wild-eyed and disheveled, showing fear and astonishment, then a childlike vulnerability, and then panic as Wirt slumps to the floor, dead. Sand blowing in through the open doorway suggests a means of disposing of the body; she frantically digs a grave outside then retreats to the cabin, peering through the window, one hand resting on the pane and a close-up revealing only her eyes and forehead, the rest of her face blocked out by the cloth covering the broken glass. Shots from her point of view show the wind gradually stripping away the sand concealing Wirt's body, uncovering clothing, a hand, his face. It must have been at around this point that the film originally ended, but the tense atmosphere is held for a few moments longer as we see a hand clutching the half-open door and an unseen body outside trying to force it open. Terrified, Letty refuses even to look, struggling to free herself as a man grabs hold of her; the tension then dissipates entirely as she realizes that it is Lige. She tells him what she has done, but the sand has re-covered the body and there is nothing to be seen; reconciliation follows and an embrace ends the film in the obligatory Hollywood manner.

The commercial failure of the film and its subsequent neglect by critics until very recently[38] can be attributed partly to the delay in releasing it, with the result that it was generally overlooked on its appearance at the end of 1928[39] when critics and audiences were already looking on a nontalking film as obsolete and unworthy of serious attention. The reviews of the time, however, suggest that another important reason was that it was perceived as being too "foreign" in its style and subject matter and that the happy ending and the elements of comic relief did little to shield it from the stigma of not being "entertaining." Welford Beaton, in the *Film Spectator,* was one of the few to welcome the nonformulaic elements of the film, calling

𝒩 ature, at the end of the film, thwarts human effort as Letty struggles to bury Wirt's body.

....

it "one of the most powerful pictures that Hollywood has ever turned out." He found the comic relief irrelevant and hoped that it might have been inserted against Sjöström's wishes, and remarked: "Seastrom's entire treatment of the story suggests the foreign school, tempered, as much as the story would allow, to the tastes of the American public."[40]

Most other reviewers, however, did not have to dig very deeply into their bag of clichés to come up with an appropriate response. For *Variety* the film was "lifeless and unentertaining," and "the story is too morbid, the background too dreary in picture form for popular appeal." The brief review in *Motion Picture Classic* (which had hailed Sjöström as "the greatest director in the world" a few years earlier) employed the same vocabulary: the story is "morbid," "cannot be called very entertaining," "tells nothing but a sordid story of domestic conflict without revealing very much of spiritual value." In case its readers have missed the point, the review (which ironically enough accuses Sjöström of being heavy-handed) repeats all this in the last of its four paragraphs: "It's too morbid to attract any untoward interest from fans desirous of being entertained . . . the story is driven home with heavy blows—there being insufficient shading to vary the drab monotony of the plot." A scathing and flippant review in the *New York Times* made similar charges of overemphasis, monotony, artificiality, tedium, and drabness. It also suggested that the sound effects added by the studio did little to enhance the film's commercial appeal:

> The sound effects with this production are not calculated to increase the demand for such ideas. There are a couple of songs which come forth as if they were being sung by somebody behind the screen, and then there is an Airedale which emits a few barks and a howl, and a train conductor who quite nervously ejaculates, "Board!"[41]

Though few reviewers explicitly drew attention to it, one reason for the hostility to the film may well have been its "non-American" attitude to nature. Sjöström's presentation of the landscape, as has been pointed out, differed significantly from that in his Swedish work, but it remained an outsider's perspective (and valuable for that very reason) rather than reflecting the traditional American optimism that sees man "mastering" or "conquering" nature or, at the very least, living in creative harmony with the grandeur and magnificence of his surroundings, Whatever the reasons, however, the whole experience must have been profoundly disillusioning to Sjöström: first to succeed in making a film that fully satisfied his original intentions; then to have its potential impact seriously diluted in pursuit of commercial appeal; and finally to see the film in its altered state flop because it still wasn't sufficiently "entertaining." He may well have begun to suspect that "it's absolutely meaningless to try to make Swedish films for America," not just in the sense of making films with a Swedish setting, but in trying, in the context of the late 1920s, to make any film at all that went against the grain of popular American culture.

The one major exception to the generally negative response to *The Wind* came in a remarkable article for one of the few specialist film magazines of the period, *Close-Up*, an English publication that provides one of the finest contemporary assessments of Sjöström's work. "Film Imagery: Seastrom" by Robert Herring demonstrates familiarity not only with Sjöström's Swedish films (seen in England and France) but with the tradition of Scandinavian cinema as a whole.[42] The complete article is reproduced in Appendix B, but some of Herring's perceptive comments on *The Wind* are worth isolating here. He notes that in Sjöström's films "people are against the

community in which they live, solely because of their finding themselves in it. His people are trying to stand up against the storm, and the film resolves itself into whether, in face of the storm, they will bend or break, oak or willow" (17). Applying this to *The Wind*, he finds that Gish is struggling

> against a destructive force. Against the type of life it produced, the type of men the life produced, and the woman she would be if she stayed, married to one of the men. The storm in her mind is produced by the storm of the wind. Inner and outer conflict, the outer in this case serving to throw up the inner. Like a chord or a subsidiary colour, an image. The wind is an image, the fields of snow are images, the roads and woods of *The Scarlet Letter* are images. Landscape is image in Seastrom. . . .
>
> The landscape is not only a mauve to throw up a blue. It is a darker blue itself. It is of the same colour, it is the same mood, as that colour or mood it brings into prominence. What I said of *The Wind* shows this. Wind causes the psychological stress, but that stress is in terms of wind . . . Seastrom's landscapes are used psychologically, but they connect logically. They could never be mistaken for "visual subtitles" as the spring shots in *Mother* have been. He achieves this by a very subtle adjustment between conception and execution. In the first place, he sees the wind, or some other element or surrounding, as responsible for the states of mind of his characters. BUT, the characters having been treated as influenced by these, these things in their turn have to be treated to relate to the people's minds, in order to bring it all out. In order to express what they are, Seastrom makes them be something else. But they have to be themselves, too. And because of this, because they are fact it is not always seen that they are image too. They have to partake of something of what they have caused for us to see that the results visible in the people were latent in them. In fact, "there is a blending of the two sets of images, the apparent and the real." (9–20)

This is followed by analyses of three major sequences: the wedding night, the scene where Cora is butchering the carcass and Letty is ironing ("watch the way Gish draws her skirts as she passes the carcass to fetch an iron . . . you have a state of mind pure before you"), and Letty alone in the cabin struggling against the intrusion of the wind, all of which subtly demonstrate Sjöström's use of objects and settings to convey states of mind.

A sympathetic response of this kind, whether or not Sjöström would have been aware of it, was nevertheless of little practical value at a time when commercial considerations and the reactions of a mass audience were the primary factors in determining the course of his career. His next film, *Masks of the Devil*, starring John Gilbert, appeared almost simultaneously with *The Wind*, at the end of November 1928. Once again this is a "lost" film and contemporary judgments of it provide contradictory assessments of its quality. Reviewers compared it variously to Oscar Wilde's *The Picture of Dorian Gray* and to Eugene O'Neill's *Strange Interlude* and *The Great God Brown* in its attempts, by means of mirror shots and double exposures, to suggest the dual personality of the main character and the disparity between his true thoughts and true self and his facade. The film was released with a synchronized music score (on discs that broke down during the screening viewed by the *New York Times* critic) and intermittent and apparently unconvincing sound effects. *Motion Picture Classic* found it "worth seeing," though "a trifle sombre, after the fashion of all of Seastrom's pictures." The *New York Times* thought it "quite a good entertainment, but it has its short-comings—quite a number, in fact." Its comments on the handling of land-scape suggest that this was done in a much more conventional manner than was usual with Sjöström: "Blossoms and the sunshine invariably accompany a love-lorn scene in motion pictures, and so they are not neglected here." *Variety*, while deriding it as "composed of pseudometaphysics, deep-breathing passion and a lot of everyday nonsense," nevertheless found much to praise in it and felt it had "high promise as a silent box office fea-ture" (though audiences were already being "educated to the real thing in sound and dialog pictures"). For *Photoplay* it was "a creditable effort to delve into the minds of a group of strange, Continental characters," and the English periodical *Film Weekly* remarked that "This superficially rather ordinary story is rendered psychologically interesting and 'worth-while' by the expressionist treatment it receives from its director Victor Seastrom."[43]

A Lady to Love (1930) was Sjöström's only full-scale American talkie, and also the last film he made in the United States. Although no prints of the film survive, it seems legitimate to assume that he had no strong commitment to this particular production. He was clearly disillu-sioned with Hollywood by this stage and, as with *Masks of the Devil*, he was not closely involved with writing the script, as he had been on all the previ-ous films, whether credited for this or not. The film, which starred Vilma Banky and Edward G. Robinson, created little interest, with the *New York Times*, for instance (1 March 1930), reserving its positive comments almost entirely for the acting, "arising out of the mist of only fair direction." The film seems to have been limited by the cumbersome technology of early sound cinema and lacked "a pictorial mobility." Sjöström left America on 24 April 1930, a few weeks after its premiere, and never returned.[44]

The reasons he himself gave for leaving were both personal and professional. He was by now over fifty and wanted "to give himself time to be a human being";[45] moreover the "Swedish circle" with which he had been associated in Hollywood had begun to break up as Hanson, Sven Gade and others made the decision to return home. He was also unhappy with some of the consequences of the introduction of sound and the increasing restrictions on the creative freedom of the director that were being imposed by the studios as a result of this.

Sjöström's career in Hollywood has often been seen as emblematic of the problems faced by a filmmaker struggling to maintain his personal and creative integrity in the face of a system either indifferent or actively hostile to his endeavors. His talent is said to have been "nearly ruined" or "destroyed" by the studios, his abilities "wasted" or "squandered" on unsuitable projects. One of the strongest statements of this viewpoint can be found in an article by the Marxist critic Seymour Stern in *Experimental Cinema,* where Sjöström's fate is used to bolster a fierce attack on the defects of Hollywood cinema as a whole. The sections referring to Sjöström are as follows:

> the wearisome, unequal struggle of such men as F. W. Murnau, Robert Flaherty and Von Stroheim, against the stupidity, tyranny, ignorance and rattlesnake politics which characterize the Hollywood racket, definitely checked whatever constructive influence might have been forthcoming from the best of the intellectuals. In my opinion the defeat of the Swedish director, Victor Seastrom, was the most significant setback in this connection, unless we include the recent rejection of Eisenstein. . . . But the crushing of first-rate men like Flaherty and Seastrom, who fought the barbarians in a fight lost from the start, was not in itself a basic cause. It was merely a dialectically inevitable result of an entire process of corruption and decay. The "fruits" of this process are manifest in the present wholesale disintegration. . . . The whole mountain of celluloidal rubbish heaped up under the electric sign of "HOLLYWOOD" is a dialectical product, a crazy but inevitable monument, of the decayed culture of the American bourgeois class.

After contrasting the "condition of artistic conquest" of the contemporary Soviet cinema with the "decadent *avant-garde* cinema of France," Stern returns to his attack on "the 'film' developed by Hollywood":

> Degenerative impulses from the beginning; misunder-
> standing of the basic principles of film-form; relentless abuse
> and persecution of the small minority of useful and creative men
> involved (Seastrom, Flaherty, Stroheim, Dupont, Murnau); exten-
> sion of false technique; growth and deliberate encouragement of
> technical creative methods (cutting, photography, direction and
> scenario writing) that are essentially non-filmic and that have
> been obviously inspired by purely commercial exigencies during
> the industry's periodic panics.[46]

From this purist Marxist viewpoint, which argues that the very nature of Hollywood as an "industry" renders it inherently inimical to genuine creativity and originality, there is clearly little more to be said, and there is obviously a good deal of uncomfortable truth in Stern's charges. Though he acknowledges *The Wind* (along with *Greed* and *Moana*) as one of "the high marks of attainment on this side of the Atlantic," he sees it as an exception, one of "certain isolated achievements after Griffith," and presumably would see Sjöström's other Hollywood work as flawed by the necessity for commercial compromise.

It is interesting that Stern associates Sjöström with Murnau as one of the "first-rate men" defeated by Hollywood and nowhere mentions Lubitsch in his article; for another way of looking at the situation is to see that, in the eyes of the reviewers who both shaped and reflected popular tastes and prejudices, both Sjöström and Murnau remained irredeemably "foreign," while Lubitsch was seen as giving "a Continental flavor" to films that in all important respects responded to the tastes of the American public and met the essential requirement of "entertainment." *Photoplay's* contemptuous dismissal of *Sunrise*, for example, reinforces the point made in the first chapter of this book: that by 1927 (and, in many cases, earlier) foreign directors were expected to conform fully to "the American psychology of entertainment" and forget all the "fancy," "artistic," "morbid," "gloomy," "depressing" stylistic and thematic concerns that had given them their original prestige and distinguished them so sharply from the run-of-the-mill domestic product. According to *Photoplay, Sunrise* was:

> The sort of picture that fools high-brows into hollering "Art!" Swell trick photography and fancy effects, but, boiled down, no story interest and only stilted mannered acting.
>
> F. W. Murnau can show Hollywood camera effects, but he could learn a lot about story-telling from local talent. The only American touch is a fine comedy sequence in a barber shop.[47]

The complacent assumption here that "local talent" is best and that the film should stand or fall on its ability to produce the "American touch" (the scene cited is, though amusing enough, probably the least subtle in the whole film) suggests that, rather than accusing Sjöström and Murnau of "failing to adapt" to American taste, it would be more accurate to chide American critics, audiences, and studios for failing to accept—or even attempting to understand—the challenge that their films posed to stereotyped acceptance of the superiority of "the American way."

Though Sjöström ultimately gave up the struggle to work in Hollywood in his own way and on his own terms, his American career—or at least what survives of it—contains as much success as failure. His personal life appears to have been happy and contented throughout, as the comments by Gish and others quoted by Pensel indicate.[48] The quality of his best American work—*The Wind, The Scarlet Letter, He Who Gets Slapped*—is very high and would place him firmly among the major directors of the silent period, even if his Swedish films were not taken into consideration. *Name the Man* is far from a failure, and some of the "lost" films, especially *The Tower of Lies* and *Masks of the Devil*, might well provoke further favorable reassessment if they were ever to be rediscovered. Moreover, as with Murnau and Lubitsch, he was able to carry over into his American films many of the best and most characteristic elements of his Swedish work, in theme, visual style, and narrative techniques. Like Murnau, he attempted to remain true to the sources of his own creative inspiration while making a realistic accommodation to what he perceived as the legitimate requirements of a new country and a new audience and, perhaps even more than Murnau, he succeeded in doing this with dignity and integrity. If he was ultimately "defeated," the defeat was an honorable one and the result of circumstances beyond his, or any individual's, control.

Mauritz Stiller

5

Mauritz Stiller and Others

"They Are a Sad-Looking People, These Swedes"

— ○ —

The careers of Murnau, Lubitsch, and Sjöström in Hollywood neatly encapsulate the three major fates suffered by almost all the European directors lured to America in the 1920s: by the beginning of the next decade Murnau was dead; Sjöström had returned to Sweden and would direct a mere handful of films during the remainder of his life; and only Lubitsch was to forge for himself a successful and long-lasting Hollywood career. The overall casualty rate is in fact even greater when more of the major figures from Scandinavia, Germany, France, and Hungary (the major sources of foreign talent during this decade) are taken into account. Mauritz Stiller, who died in 1928 after a particularly frustrating time in Hollywood, is the saddest and most striking example; but Leni too was dead by 1929, while Christensen, Fejös, Alexander Korda, and Jacques Feyder all left Hollywood after working there for less than six years in each case, with some of them, like Christensen, showing little further taste for filmmaking after their return home. Only Michael Curtiz,[1] who arrived at the very end of the decade, enjoyed a Hollywood success comparable—in commercial terms at least—to that of Lubitsch.

The natural assumption—and the one made by most film historians—is that these blighted careers provide an object lesson in a basic incompatibility in sensibility, technique and intentions where European and American filmmaking are concerned. The Europeans on the whole, it is argued, failed to understand or adjust to the essentially commercial nature

— ○ —

of the American film industry, and fell by the wayside as a result. Though there is a considerable amount of truth in this viewpoint, it is much too easy to assume, as most film historians have done by virtually ignoring or summarily dismissing the work the Europeans produced, that they contributed little of lasting interest to the American cinema of the period. Once again, any overall judgement is limited by the fact that, as with Murnau and Sjöström, several potentially important films—such as Fejös's *The Last Moment*, which appears, by all accounts, to have been a remarkably advanced work for its time—have been lost; nevertheless many of those that do survive deserve serious and sympathetic attention.

The pattern with most of these directors was similar to that experienced by Murnau and Sjöström on their arrival in the United States. They were given a warm initial reception by both studios and press, with the latter expressing genuine interest in the "foreign" quality of their work and speculating how this could provide a welcome stimulus and challenge to the standard Hollywood product. In most cases they were allowed a considerable degree of freedom on their first films, which were generally praised by the critics but often enjoyed only a mediocre commercial success. As a result, studio pressures on them increased and, if they refused to mend their ways, they found their films altered and tampered with and their initially privileged status removed so that they were soon assigned projects like ordinary mortals instead of being allowed to initiate them themselves. Meanwhile the once sympathetic critics were complaining that their films were too "foreign," too "arty," too "depressing," to fit the mold of American popular entertainment. The most usual consequence was a break with the studio, either to work—with little greater success—somewhere else, or to return to Europe. Christensen's career fits this pattern almost perfectly, though its essence can be found in the experience of most of the other directors under consideration.

This apparent failure, however, should not blind us to the often quite considerable merits of those films that were made with a certain degree of creative autonomy, or to the significant contribution made by the European directors in developing—and sometimes even inaugurating—some of the most popular film genres of the period, in particular the sexual comedy, the comedy-mystery, the circus film, and the historical romance. The work of Christensen, Leni, Fejös and Stiller is of considerable interest in this respect though some of the films discussed in previous chapters, such as *He Who Gets Slapped* and most of Lubitsch's American films, would obviously fall into some of these categories too. An approach by genre at this

Benjamin Christensen

point should help to clarify some of the ways in which the foreign directors could, or could not, adjust to "the American psychology of entertainment," and is probably the most useful way of examining the contributions made to Hollywood cinema of the period by men who, on the whole, suffered even more frustrations and restrictions that did Lubitsch, Murnau, and Sjöström. As they were all, however, gifted filmmakers, it is only fair to offer a summary of their careers as a whole, before examining their attempts to cope with the Hollywood system.

Until relatively recently, Christensen was known to film historians only for *Heksen* (1921), shown to English-speaking audiences in a heavily mutilated version entitled *Witchcraft through the Ages* and regarded as something of a curiosity rather than an important film in its own right. In the mid-1960s the rediscovery of his first and second films, *Det Hemmelighedsfulde X (The Mysterious X,* 1913) and *Haevnens Nat (Night of Revenge,* 1915), prompted renewed interest in him as a significant film stylist whose work was remarkably advanced for its time. Even in 1966, however, John Gillett, writing about these films in *Sight and Sound,*[2] suggested that all Christensen's American films were lost, and a flurry of correspondence in subsequent issues of the magazine, though it clarified the situation somewhat, left many questions unanswered. In fact at least three of the American films survive, *The Devil's Circus* (1927), *Mockery* (1927), and *Seven Footprints to Satan* (1929), and together with the three Danish and Swedish productions mentioned and the German-made *Seine Frau, die Unbekannte* (1923), these provide a reasonable basis on which to survey his career as a whole.

Christensen was born in Viborg in 1879[3] and, after a brief period of studying medicine, trained as an opera singer at the Royal Theatre. A mysterious illness that affected his vocal chords, however, thwarted both this career and an attempt to act on the stage, and he finally entered the film industry in 1912 after a few years as a wholesale dealer in champagne. He worked as an actor on at least two films before writing, directing, and acting in *The Mysterious X* in 1913.

This film's complex and melodramatic plot, which deals with a virtuous naval lieutenant who is unjustly accused of spying, and saved from a firing squad at the last moment when his young son provides evidence of his innocence, is efficiently enough handled; but Christensen's major innovations come in the area of lighting, camerawork, and editing. The most striking sequence is probably that in which the son sneaks into the prison to visit his father in his cell, with strong contrasts of light and shade throughout and the camera invariably placed in the most effective position to provide the maximum dramatic impact: in one shot the boy is shown climbing the prison wall on the left-hand side of the screen while the oblivious guards are seen on the right. Many scenes are shot either through windows or doorways, looking to a scene outdoors; or with these providing the only source of illumination for an interior, in a manner rarely seen at this period. Camera movements are well-motivated and used to reinforce the action, and the editing moves the story forward unobtrusively and efficiently. Close-ups are used to isolate objects or details of significance to the plot, and objects themselves are sometimes given a metaphoric rather than simply a functional significance: the spy is twice seen talking to the lieutenant's wife with a serenely classical statue of a young woman visible on the mantelpiece behind and between them. The statue's presence creates an unsettling effect in the context of the spy's attempts to manipulate the wife into carrying out his intentions against her husband's interests, and anticipates the much better-known example of this device in the conversation between the Marquis and Geneviève in Renoir's *La Règle du Jeu*.

The Mysterious X enjoyed considerable international success, in both Europe and the United States, as did Christensen's next film, *Night of Revenge* (titled *Blind Justice* for its U.S. release)[4] whose plot develops the themes of mistaken identity, deception, false accusation, revenge, and mystery which were already evident in the earlier film and were to remain central to Christensen's work for almost the next twenty years. The story takes place over a period of fourteen years and deals with a man falsely accused of, and imprisoned for, murder who, on his release, vows revenge on the couple who were responsible for his arrest. The couple, in the meantime, in a belated attempt to made amends, have adopted his young son. Flashbacks are used at strategic moments to clarify the complex plot, and lighting, camerawork, and editing all display the sophistication of the earlier film. An interest in the bizarre and the macabre—already evident in *The Mysterious X* in scenes in which the half-dead spy, trapped for several days in a cellar, is shown with rats swarming all over his body—is also seen here. The convict and his associates break in to the couple's house and indulge in a strange orgy of childlike foolery that involves, among other things, dressing a monkey in baby's clothing and placing it in a crib. A last-minute change of heart on the convict's part brings about reconciliation and mutual forgiveness just before he dies.

The film's success brought Christensen an invitation to the United States and the offer of a job with the Vitagraph Company. Though he actually visited New York and received several other offers of employment while

$\mathcal{T}$he melodramatic poses and glances in *The Mysterious X* are remarkably restrained for this early date (1913), and Christensen uses the bust on the mantelpiece to introduce a subtle sense of dramatic and visual tension into the scene.

....

he was there, he chose to return to Denmark. His next film, *Heksen,* which was the result of extensive research into the subject of witchcraft, was made for Charles Magnusson's Svensk Filmindustri, for which Sjöström and Stiller worked. The film combines documentary and fictional techniques, uses both professional and amateur actors, and attempts to treat the subject from virtually every possible viewpoint: religious, historical, legal, sociological, and psychological, probing into both the facts and the folklore of the subject, and surveying it from a modern perspective that interprets it as the result of hysteria and neuroses yet also makes use of historical documents to validate the information provided.

The beautifully restored and tinted print of the film held by the Royal Danish Film Museum makes it possible to correct some of the wide-spread assumptions about its incoherence and its apparently naive and random mixture of documentary and fictional techniques, largely based on the heavily cut versions that circulated in a scandalized Europe and America after its release.[5] It begins with a sequence that uses medieval texts and woodcuts to introduce the beliefs about witchcraft held in the Middle Ages, then moves to illustrating these concepts in fictional form by showing a "typical" witch and her clients and activities, especially the preparation of love potions. A visually complex sequence presents popular superstitions about the Devil through such devices as superimpositions, reverse motion and stop motion. The film then moves from the general to the particular as it follows the arrest and trial of one old woman, on the instigation of jealous neighbors and a group of monks.

The scenes of her interrogation and trial are among the most power-ful in the film and may well have had a strong influence on Carl-Theodor Dreyer (who saw and admired this film) when he made *The Passion of Joan of Arc* a few years later. Close-ups of the old woman's wizened and wrinkled face alternate with shots of the judges, who are often grotesque and characterized by physical peculiarities of features and hair style. Scenes of torture are implied rather than shown directly and her confession of participating in a witches' Sabbath is vividly visualized in some of the scenes that caused most controversy at the time, especially one in which young women are seen embracing demons and then filing past the Devil and kissing him on the arse.

Another pattern of denunciation and trial is followed in the arrest of a woman for the supposed murder of her husband by witchcraft. In scenes that once again anticipate Dreyer's film, the woman is tricked into confess-ing and sentenced to be burned at the stake. After a brief return to a semi-documentary display of torture instruments and a demonstration of their use, the film ends with scenes of sexual hysteria, mass possession, self-mortification, and the defiling of sacred objects by nuns. These are then "explained" in the light of modern medical and psychological theory, and episodes from the film are repeated, then reenacted in a modern setting so that they can be properly accounted for. Even so, the film admits that super-stitions linger on and concludes with examples of these, rather than with the enlightened rationalizations just offered.

Christensen apparently refused an offer from Charles Magnusson to continue working for him on a long-term basis, and his next film, *Seine Frau, die Unbekannte* (1923), was made for UFA in Germany. The film once

*C*hristensen's *Heksen (Witchcraft through the Ages)* caused a scandal at the time, for reasons that are obvious enough from this still. *Variety* pronounced it "absolutely unfit for public exhibition."

again centers around a case of mistaken identity, but it is taken to more elaborate lengths than in earlier films. A young painter blinded during the war marries a nurse in the mistaken belief that she is another woman, of much less reputable character, whom he has briefly met. When he recovers his sight, some years after his marriage, he is made to undergo a lengthy period of testing by his wife (who has meanwhile learned about the misunderstanding) before he is allowed to take up his life with her once more. She pretends to be his child's nanny and teasingly punishes him for his flirtatious attentions to her and to one of his models before revealing her true identity and permitting him to "marry" her once more, this time understanding fully what he is doing. The tone of the film is very uncertain, pre-

°

senting potentially painful and emotionally disturbing scenes in terms of rather heavy-handed comedy, and the chance to explore the inherent masochism of the wife's behavior is passed over in favor of some superficial role and game playing.

Christensen seems then to have worked on another film at UFA, a British production called *The Woman Who Did,* which was never completed, as well as playing the leading role in Dreyer's German-made *Michael* in 1924. Meanwhile MGM had offered him a Hollywood contract on the basis of private screenings of *Heksen,* and he arrived in America in February 1925. His first film for MGM, *The Devil's Circus,* starred Norma Shearer and was based on an original story by Christensen, though, in standard Hollywood fashion, it went through several rewritings at the hands of "about twenty American scriptwriters" before being filmed.[6] Although John Ernst, in his booklet on Christensen, calls the film a "resounding flop," it was in fact very well received by many of the major reviewers. *Moving Picture World* was particularly enthusiastic, calling it "an unusually powerful and intense drama that will appeal especially to the highest class of theatregoers" and praising Christensen for having "handled this rather grim story superbly." The review ended by emphasizing "the strong human note, the deep pathos, the beautiful romance, the excellent direction and splendid acting" as major factors in creating "excellent and absorbing entertainment." *Variety* was less impressed by the acting and felt that "it could have been a better film than it is," but nevertheless "it's foreign and it's different." It felt that "Christianson" (as his name was now metamorphosed for American audiences) had made a good enough start: "It won't do [him] any harm, for they'll make allowances for his initial effort and this work should establish the fact that he knows what he's doing." The *New York Times,* noting, like *Variety,* that it was the director's first American film, found it "a somewhat ponderous but nevertheless absorbing story of circus life" and thought that the "dismal happenings" were effectively handled throughout.[7]

His next film, *Mockery* (1927), starred Lon Chaney, a fact which may have given rise to the widespread and erroneous belief that it is a horror film. It is in fact set during the Russian Revolution and presents Chaney as a slow-witted peasant who is mistreated by the Reds when he tries to help a White countess and then becomes involved in the events of the revolution when he feels that she has not kept her promise to reward him. This time the reviews were almost uniformly hostile, with critics drawing sarcastic parallels between the "lumbering, dull-witted and, on the whole, unconvincing" character and the story itself and its treatment.[8] *Variety* was scathingly contemptuous of every aspect of the film—"The theme is dull, trite and uninspiring on account of the limitations in handling"—and *Moving Picture World* agreed that Chaney's performance was "hopelessly encumbered by the amateurishness of the plot development and handling." Almost the only dissenting voice was that of *Picture Play*, which found it "one of the best pictures of the new season" and praised the "thoughtful direction," the "honesty of treatment," the lack of "hokum," and the authentic Russian atmosphere.[9]

Nevertheless, Christensen was assigned by MGM to direct Jules Verne's *The Mysterious Island*, an elaborate and expensive production to be shot on location in the West Indies. Disaster struck, however, as *Motion Picture Classic* reported in "Movies You Will Never See" in November 1927:

> Huge sets were built, costly arrangements for taking undersea shots were devised, and half the picture had been made when a hurricane destroyed two hundred thousand dollars worth of equipment in five minutes. The financial loss was too great to risk repeating in such a temperamental climate. Now half of a remarkable and imaginative photoplay is stored in the Metro-Goldwyn vaults awaiting the decision to finish the film. If it is ever done, the West Indies will be built on the Culver City lot.[10]

After being shelved for two years, the film was in fact completed in 1929, but with a different cast and under the direction of Maurice Tourneur and Lucien Hubbard. It is impossible to know if any of Christensen's footage survived into the final version, though some of the events near the beginning of the film, dealing with an attempted uprising by characters dressed in cossack costumes, bear a strong similarity to parts of *Mockery*.[11]

By the time that *The Mysterious Island* was released, Christensen had moved on to First National, where he made four films, one in the newly popular gangster genre, and three capitalizing on the vogue for the comedy-mystery inaugurated by the success of Leni's *The Cat and the Canary* (1927). Only the last of these films, *Seven Footprints to Satan*, appears to survive today.

The Hawk's Nest (1928), according to the somewhat flippant review it received from *Variety*, dealt with underworld rivalries in New York's Chinatown and centered around the murder of one of two competing nightclub owners. The gang boss, the "Hawk," saves one of his henchmen from being wrongly executed for the crime by tracking down the real killer.[12] *The Haunted House* (1928) starred the comedian Chester Conklin and was explicitly compared to *The Cat and the Canary* by the *New York Times* reviewer, though he found it considerably less successful than Leni's film. The *Film Spectator*, however, thought it "a clever picture" and praised the camerawork and the intelligent treatment of the story.[13] Chester Conklin also starred in *House of Horror* (1929), which boasted a few moments of dialogue in the opening scene. The film was damned by *Variety* as "one of the weakest and most boring afterbirths of pseudo mystery-comedy grinds out of Hollywood."[14] With none of these films available for viewing today, it is difficult to tell how justified these largely contemptuous assessments were; certainly, however, *Mockery* is considerably more interesting than most contemporary reviews would indicate, and *Seven Footprints to Satan*, Christensen's last comedy-mystery and his final Hollywood film, has many attractive features. Like its three predecessors, it was written by Christensen himself and photographed by Sol Polito, and, like *The Haunted House* and *House of Horrors,* it starred Thelma Todd. It was released in both silent and sound versions, and John Ernst credits Christensen with being one of the first to experiment with a mobile microphone by attaching it to the end of a bamboo pole.[15]

The more detailed treatment later on will offer an opportunity to examine the quality and significance of Christensen's American work. It seems clear, however, that, either in serious or comic vein, he maintained the interest in mystery, superstition, crime, mistaken identity, disguise, and revenge evident in his European-made films, and that the fact that he acted as his own scriptwriter enabled him to pursue these interests consciously and deliberately. Like Sjöström, when he returned to Denmark in 1929, it was for business reasons (to clear up problems over his part-ownership of a film theater) and, unlike Sjöström, he returned to America a year later, intending to continue with his career there. This time, however, he wanted to go into independent production with a Danish partner rather than remain under contract to a major studio. Plans were well advanced for making his first film under these conditions when the National Industrial Recovery Act introduced by the newly elected Roosevelt government in 1933, which favored established companies against independent producers and exhibitors, thwarted their project. Disappointed, Christensen returned to Denmark for good in 1934.

He made no more films until 1939, when he began to work for the Nordisk Company. Between then and 1942 he shot four films, three of them with largely sociological themes, dealing with problems in middle-class family settings, and a spy thriller. The last of these (the thriller) was apparently

Paul Fejös

very badly received in Denmark on its release, and Christensen retired from filmmaking for good, spending the last fifteen years of his life as the manager of a movie house.

Of the directors studied in this book, Fejös is the only one with whom it is impossible to adopt a before-and-after approach when dealing with his American films for the simple reason that none of the films that he made before arriving in the United States still exist. His American work, nevertheless, is of sufficient importance to merit his inclusion, though, like so many other Europeans, he finally abandoned the struggle to make films in Hollywood on anything like his own terms, and—again like Christensen and Sjöström—continued to direct films for barely another decade before retiring to spend the remaining twenty-odd years of his life in other pursuits.

Unlike the German and Scandinavian directors, and unlike his compatriots Korda and Curtiz, who had worked in Germany before reaching the United States, Fejös had no advance reputation as a filmmaker and in fact came to America on his own initiative and with no specific intention of working in films. Born in Budapest in 1897, he attended medical school, obtained his degree, and fought in both the cavalry and the air force in the First World War.[16] After the war he worked in the theater and then directed some half-dozen feature films between 1920 and 1923, none of which survive today. Curtiz and Korda had already left Hungary in 1919, and Fejös followed them into exile in 1923, inspired, among other reasons, by a distaste for the reactionary government that had come to power after the collapse of the brief Communist-led insurrection in 1919.

America had fascinated him since his childhood and it was thus natural for him to choose to try his fortune there; his first few months, however, were spent in acute poverty, as he had no friends or connections and was unable to find work of any kind. Finally he obtained a job as a laboratory assistant at the Rockefeller Institute and then became involved with some theater groups in New York. He became obsessed, however, with the idea of working in Hollywood and set off for California in 1926; once again poverty and some medical work in Los Angeles hospitals followed, though he apparently also wrote some scripts for Hollywood westerns. By his own account, his break into film directing occurred in almost fairy-tale fashion when he met up with a young man called Edward M. Spitz who had five-thousand dollars that he wished to invest in a film and was looking for a director and script. Fejös, who was a man of considerable personal charm, instantly offered to oblige and managed to persuade Georgia Hale (of Chaplin's *The Gold Rush*) to work for him for nothing, but only on days when she had no other commitments. He then rented studio space on an hourly rather than a daily basis, undertaking to make use of whatever sets, which were being used as backgrounds for other films, happened to be on stage at the time. He obtained raw film stock on credit, and also a camera—as well as a cameraman, Leon Shamroy,[17] who was looking for a break on a feature-length film. He then wrote a script that allowed him to juggle the various resources available, with a double standing in for Hale for anything other than full-face shots, and still obtain a coherent story. Within three months *The Last Moment* was completed.

The next problem was distribution. Fejös invited Welford Beaton, the influential editor of *Film Spectator*, and Tamar Lane of *Film Mercury*, to attend a private preview, and both immediately went out and wrote glowing reviews of the film. Beaton's article in *Film Spectator* for 26 November 1927 (11–12) was headed "Introducing to You Mr. Paul Fejos, Genius" and called *The Last Moment* "one of the most outstanding works of cinematic art that ever was brought to the screen." Fejös's "extraordinary ability as a director" was acclaimed, as was Shamroy's camerawork and the film's production values, despite its tiny budget. Fejös, Beaton concluded, "had won his right to immortality even if he never makes another picture." Distribution was arranged, according to Fejös, by Beaton's persuading Chaplin to view the film at his own house; Chaplin was impressed and arranged for United Artists to release the film. It opened in New York in March 1928 to considerable critical acclaim, and Fejös found himself a celebrity. The film later turned up on several "ten-best" lists for that year.

Unfortunately, *The Last Moment* is another "lost" film at present, and the originality of style and structure that so intrigued contemporary critics can be judged only by the accounts of the film given in reviews at the time.[18] The *National Board of Review Magazine* for February 1928 gives a detailed summary of its most important aspects that suggests that Fejös was using almost subliminal flashbacks to convey the apparently chaotic processes of memory in a way that seems to anticipate by almost forty years the techniques of Alain Resnais:

> The film is, briefly the history of events in a person's life at the moment of that person's death. It has thus a psychological import, although we have scant evidence at best of what a man can think about while he dies. But the theory is familiar to everyone, and it is an interesting theory which in this case has been used in a way to provoke the imagination and in a medium pecu-

liarly suited to its artistic expression. In any event, the only subtitle in the film is the one at the beginning that sets forth this psychological assumption, and it is the only one that is necessary.
The first scene shows bubbles rising from the pond as a man's
head vanishes beneath the water. Then follow, with lightning-like
rapidity, flashes—faces, objects, snatches of scenes—an apparently disconnected phantasmagoria of life. These slow down to
connected rhythmic sequences of action which compose the
experienced incidents and situations out of which arose these
mind images of the drowning man. These again, at the end of the
picture, speed back in the lightning flashes of the brain. Thus at
the beginning and ending, the mechanism of the mind is plausibly and vividly exposed, the effect being that of peering into the
secrets of cerebral action, while throughout the intervening
stretches of the film the sense is preserved of a dream interlude,
not quite real, but real enough, like reflections in a dark strange
mirror before which a human life passes at its illuminating and
crucial moments. Nothing quite like this film has been done
before. The significance lies in the fact that its method is the
chiefly interesting and compelling thing about it. The story it
tells is hazy, sketchy, nothing in itself extraordinary. But the
method allows the medium to hold sway in a technical virtuosity.
This manipulation of pattern and image, light and shadow, in a
constant shifting and convolution, is of itself enough to cast a
thralling spell. The pictures alone count—or rather the moving
pictures. In short, it is cinema on its own, distinct, like painting,
poetry, music. The medium is permitted to achieve its own
results. Here we see a motion picture cut free of its established
mould and striving for a purer form. We see that the acting,
which, even interpreted as stylization, could for the most part be
improved, is not after all of prime importance, the idea being, not
to represent characters, but to present them as part of the mood,
movement and intention of the film. They are but images used
like objects to hold the sequences together. Perhaps they may be
likened to pervading notes in a harmony, something that threads
the production like a theme. Again the relationship of music and
cinema is suggested, not as mediums that go hand in hand, as
supplements or complements, but as distinct, independent ways
of awakening emotions and evoking imagination. So too with the

story. It is simply an outline that gives the pictures cohesiveness. One technical feature is extraordinary. The film may be said to have been cut in the camera box. There is little splicing together of scenes. Continuity is photographed not assembled, separate shots dissolve one into the other. This gives an unusual flow to the composition. One can only assume that a very perfect continuity was worked out and closely followed by director and cameraman. *The Last Moment* is another milestone at which our hopes for the motion picture can be replenished and our enthusiasm renewed.[19]

Variety agreed that

> The film does introduce a novel technique. Instead of following the screen formula of dramatizing a theme in orderly sequences, leading up to a climax and concentrating dramatic action upon one personal or story element, it goes on the basis that a human life—any human life—has a large content of drama. That being the case, a brief prolog crystallizes a whole lifetime by the device of picturing the operation of a man's mind as he is drowning.

Though he found this aspect of the film intriguing and thought the production values remarkable for a film made on such a low budget, the reviewer was skeptical of the commercial possibilities for "an interesting, freaky and slightly morbid arty picture" of this kind, and felt it was strictly something for "the Greenwich Village faddists to chew over."[20]

Such non–Greenwich Village faddists as the heads of almost all the major Hollywood studios were so impressed with the film, nevertheless, that Fejös found himself inundated with offers to work for them. His insistence on retaining control of script, casting, and editing of any future project proved a deterrent, however, and only Carl Laemmle, Jr. of Universal was willing to accept him on these terms. Fejös politely declined Laemmle's suggestion that he begin with a "clean sexy" picture and spent some time instead wading through the scripts on hand at the studio, finding all of them totally uninteresting. At last he came across a three-page outline of a story that appealed to him, chose for his leads an unknown actress called Barbara Kent and the currently popular Glenn Tryon, and made *Lonesome*.

This film too was a huge critical success and firmly established Fejös's reputation as one of the top directors of the day (interestingly enough, a new critical magazine called *Close-Up* proudly advertised its intellectual respectability at the end of 1928 by announcing that it was read by Lubitsch, Murnau, Leni, Henry King, and Fejös). Like so many films of this period of transition to sound, it was released in both silent and part-talkie versions; some of the fairground scenes also made use of hand tinting of selected details within the image—in a relatively rare use of this device by this time. Though the sound effects and the music enhance the effect of the film considerably (in much the same way as the simple yet evocative music score does for *Sunrise*), the brief dialogue scenes are weakly written and poorly delivered, and the static camera setups that they necessitate contrast harshly and unfavorably with the fluid visual style of the remainder of the film.[21]

The *New York Times* (2 October 1928) offered one of the few sour notes on *Lonesome* by complaining that Fejös had "paid more attention to his interesting dissolves and double exposures than . . . to the characterization of his story," and a similar objection was raised by *Photoplay* to his next film, *The Last Performance* (sometimes shown under the title of *Erik the Great*). "Paul Fejos had the time of his life figuring out weird camera angles in this film," it observed, adding that "everybody overacts and a striking plot has been wasted to make a director's holiday."[22] Fejös himself claimed later that he had little interest in making the film beyond the opportunity it gave him to work with Conrad Veidt, and it is certainly a fairer observation on this film than it was with *Lonesome* that he shows himself more interested in elaborate visual effects (many of them very striking) than in the highly melodramatic plot.

By the time that he came to make *Broadway* (based on a successful stage musical) in 1929, Fejös had moved, within two years, from the five-thousand dollar budget of *The Last Moment* to the million or more dollars spent on making the later film.[23] Like many other directors, he found that the degree of creative freedom permitted him shrank in almost exactly inverse proportion to the costs involved, and he spent a good deal of his time simply trying to spend the huge budget that had been assigned to the film. A considerable amount of this went toward the construction of an elaborate nightclub set that, as Fejös ruefully admitted, made nonsense of the basic premise of the film: "In this horrible abortion, this dreadful big nightclub, the Paradise Club, Glenn Tryon, who played a small hoofer, was constantly dreaming about 'big time.' He was in a nightclub which was bigger than anything that was ever built, and he was there dreaming of the big time."[24] Nevertheless, he managed to make spectacularly successful use of this set

*T*he elaborate nightclub set for Fejös's *Broadway* and the specially built crane.

and the film (released in both sound and silent versions and with a last reel in the early Technicolor process) displayed an astonishing degree of camera mobility at a time when most other directors might as well have had their cameras bolted to the floor. In particular, Fejös, in collaboration with his cameraman Hal Mohr, had a self-propelled crane with a fifty-foot arm designed to his own specifications, and the nightclub scenes are generally introduced with overhead shots displaying the whole vast set, with the camera then moving into and around it to follow details of the action.

Although Fejös was still highly regarded by Universal and was encouraged by Laemmle to continue with his experiments with camera and lighting effects, he was beginning to fret under the restrictions imposed on him in his choice of subject matter. He accepted another assignment, *The Captain of the Guard*,[25] but suffered a thirty-foot fall from a platform during shooting and the film was completed by John Stuart Robertson. He had great hopes of being given *All Quiet on the Western Front* to direct, but this went to Lewis Milestone instead and Fejös was asked to make *King of Jazz*, a tribute to the musician Paul Whiteman. That film is now credited to John Murray Anderson, though Fejös talked extensively about working on it in the interviews he gave to Dodds.

Fejös was now thoroughly dissatisfied with Universal and decided to break his contract with them, suffering some months of blacklisting as a result. He then signed with MGM, but here he was given even less freedom than with Universal, and his only work for the company was the direction of the German- and French-language versions of the prison film *The Big House*, whose English version was made by George Hill. Effective as Fejös's contributions are, they can hardly have involved very much more than putting the German and French casts through the actions and setups already laid out by Hill for the primary shooting.

By 1931 Fejös had abandoned any hope of being able to work in Hollywood with any genuine degree of creative freedom, and he returned abruptly to Europe. As he told Dodds:

> I simply didn't fit into the Hollywood picture. I found Hollywood phony, not just the people but the city itself. I found everything artificial, I found the people impossible; I mean, for example, the people in the story departments; writers, so-called writers, utterly unintelligent, utterly uneducated, stupid hacks who sat down in afternoons in an office for story conferences and tried to build a drama.[26]

He went first to France, where he filmed a version of *Fantomas*, then back to Hungary, where he made the beautiful and moving *Spring Shower* (also known as *Marie*) and the recently rediscovered *Itel a Balaton*;[27] but his uncomplimentary picture of the Hungarian bourgeoisie in the former film aroused considerable hostility and he moved on to Austria. Here again he made two films, one at least of which, *Sonnenstrahl* (*A Ray of Sunshine*, 1933) ranks among his best work. His career as a maker of feature-length fiction films ended in Denmark, where he made three films. In 1935 he persuaded a Danish film company and Svensk Filmindustri to allow him to set off for Madagascar to shoot, at his own discretion, material for a series of ethnographic films. For the next six years he worked in the Far East and

Paul Leni

South America on projects of this kind, some of which, like *A Handful of Rice* and *The Yagua*, present an essentially anthropological subject in fictional form. In 1941 he retired from filmmaking altogether to become head of the newly established Wenner-Gren Foundation for Anthropological Research, where he spent the years until his death in 1963 in mainly academic activities.

When Paul Leni died of blood poisoning in September 1929 at the age of forty-four, his film career in Hollywood was not in the stage of crisis, or even despair, that had afflicted both Murnau and Stiller at the time of their own early deaths. He had made four successful films and seemed to have adapted well to the commercial requirements of Hollywood while pursuing his own interests in the fantastic and bizarre (in both subject matter and visual treatment) that had originally brought him to the attention of Laemmle and Universal.

With the exception of *Das Wachsfigurenkabinett* (*Waxworks*, 1924), the film that brought Leni international success, the films that he directed in Germany have all vanished. He worked extensively, however, as set designer and scriptwriter on films directed by Dupont, Joe May, and others (including two of Curtiz's Austrian films), and some of these still survive. Born in Stuttgart in 1895, his original interests were in stage design, and he worked with Max Reinhardt for some time before moving into film in 1914. He directed six, now lost, films between 1916 and 1921, and can be credited as "co-creator" of *Hintertreppe* (*Backstairs*, 1921), directed by Leopold Jessner, but with Leni contributing the "visual conception" that remains the most striking feature of the film.[28]

Acclaimed in its time as the first film to deal with the lives of ordinary people in a straightforward and uncondescending manner, *Backstairs* is irretrievably flawed today by its grotesquely overemphatic acting and the ridiculously contrived poses struck by the characters at moments of high emotion (a far cry from the relative naturalism that Lubitsch and Murnau were beginning to attain at the same period). Its story of a love-struck postman who tries to destroy the romance between the woman he silently adores and her lover is handled in a way that reduces the "humble emotions" of the characters to an almost childlike level, and it is only Leni's sets that make the film watchable today. The careful contrast between the stark, bare surroundings of the lower-class characters and the lush rooms inhabited by the rich, and especially the scenes in the courtyard with their barren angularity and meticulous lighting effects, still give the film considerable visual impact.

Another film on which Leni worked, *Der Weisse Pfau* (*The White Peacock,* 1920), directed by Dupont, has a conventional enough story, but again offers considerable visual distinction. Built around a contrast between luxury and squalor, it follows the career of a young gypsy girl who becomes a nightclub dancer and attracts the attention of an English nobleman (who rejoices in the unlikely name of Lord Cros in Field).[29] He becomes her protector and later marries her, though both are anxious to conceal the truth about her past. She is recognized by a former acquaintance, however, and leaves her husband in order to spare him disgrace. The story is set within a flashback structure that begins and ends with the dancer trying to escape from both aspects of her past and earn a living on her own, but once more she is recognized, and the film ends with her shooting her would-be blackmailer and then dying. The low-life scenes of the gypsy encampment and the sordid nightclub in which she is performing when the nobleman discovers her are particularly well created; in the latter setting the aristocrats arrive for a night's slumming and are greeted with a mixture of amazement, ridicule, and mockery by an audience of authentic ruffians who are watching the wrestling match that precedes the heroine's performance.

Backstairs was not shown in America till 1926, five years after it had been released in Germany, and by that time the American audience was not disposed to welcome with much favor a film that *Variety* dismissed as "a drab affair" and "not for American consumption." The review began with the now-fatal linking of European films with depressing atmosphere and subject matter: "Imbued with the Continental touch of stark tragedy, this picture grinds out its story and lets it go at that, disregarding any attempt at a happy ending."[30] *Waxworks*, however, released in the same year, was able to exploit the earlier success of such films as *The Cabinet of Dr. Caligari* and Fritz Lang's *Der Müde Tod* (*Destiny*, 1921), the latter of which shared a similar multipart structure.[31] The comic treatment of the story of the caliph Haroun al Raschid (shown first in the original German version, but last in the American print reviewed by the *New York Times*)[32] also helped to heighten the commercial appeal for the American public.

The Arabian section of the film makes no more attempt than do Lubitsch's Oriental films to create any kind of realistic setting or atmosphere. The world presented is that popularly associated with *The Arabian Nights,* but Leni pushes his visual stylization to extremes that go far beyond the conventionally "exotic" decor of Lubitsch's and similar films and are clearly intended to recall the expressionistic devices of *Caligari.* Circular shapes abound, in the houses of the poor and the domes and cupolas that dominate the city, while the houses and streets take on a twisted, demented, writhing life of their own. Windows and doors mirror the shapes of the bodies and even the turbans of the people outlined against them, and the characters make their way through tunnels that curve like waves, rising and falling. The interior of the caliph's palace, as Freddy Buache points out, resembles the anatomy of the human body, with its corridors and stairs and tunnels playing the role of veins and arteries. Extravagant lighting effects and strange angles abound: the Caliph is seen fully lit as he flirts with the baker's wife, while she stands in the foreground blacked out completely except for her eyes. And, in a device which was to become a favorite of Leni in such later films as *The Last Warning*, the characters split and fragment into multiple images of themselves, as when the caliph's reflection is refracted in the facets of the ring he wears.

The second story, concerning Ivan the Terrible, is brooding and intense in tone, and both its mood and its visual style clearly influenced Eisenstein's treatment of the subject some twenty years later. Conrad Veidt's Ivan, lean and angular, with pointed beard and wild staring eyes, anticipates Nikolai Cherkassov's performance; and Leni, like Eisenstein, exploits the low-ceilinged architecture of the czar's palace and the vaulted chambers that force him to stoop as he enters them, to reflect the character's inner torment in the physical poses that he is forced to strike. The climactic banquet scene in which Ivan changes clothes with a rival and avoids assassination as a result also anticipates Eisenstein (though the circumstances are slightly different in each case), and while there is no equivalent in Eisenstein's *Ivan* films of the scenes of the czar's madness (endlessly reversing an hourglass in the belief that when the sand finally trickles from one half to the other he is doomed to die), a remarkably similar portrait of a brooding, solitary, anguished personality emerges from both films.

The third and shortest segment, a treatment of the Jack the Ripper story, has a deliberately nightmarish quality, and is in fact revealed to be a dream at the end. Multiple superimpositions against a variety of oddly distorted sets give the characters an almost hallucinatory transparency, and the villain appears in a series of multiplied images of himself that give him an omnipresent and inescapable quality.

After completing *Waxworks* Leni continued to work as set designer on a variety of films in Germany and Austria, until the success of *Waxworks* on its American release brought him an invitation from Laemmle to join Universal. Wisely, Laemmle allowed Leni to work on a thoroughly congenial subject for his first American film, and *The Cat and the Canary* (1927) was a smash hit with both critics and audiences. Most critics agreed that the film was even better than the successful stage play from which it was adapted,

and Leni was variously praised for his handling of actors, his camerawork, his creation of mood and atmosphere, his lighting, and his ability to keep the audience guessing and produce a genuine surprise with the dénouement. *Moving Picture World*, crediting "the superb direction of Paul Leni, a noted European director," felt that he had successfully combined the "Continental touch" of "weird lighting and unusual camera angles" with "the straight dramatic bits and the comedy" that characterized "the American technique of picture production."[33] The emphasis in this review and others on "the fine comedy relief" recalls the almost exclusive attention paid by the *New York Times* review of *Waxworks* to the comedy of the Arabian section and serves as a reminder that by 1927 Continental directors were expected to adjust to American expectations and subordinate their artistic "touches" to the requirements of a good, entertaining story.

The Chinese Parrot (1927), Leni's next film for Universal, is now lost, but the *New York Times*, praising its "eerie atmosphere and forceful camera effects," found it "a worthy successor" to *The Cat and the Canary*. Leni was "a master of camera technique" and had created "the eerie atmosphere necessary" through "an ingenious use of shadows, lights and photographic angles."[34] *The Man Who Laughs* (1928), however, moves away from comedy-mystery to costume film in its adaptation of Victor Hugo's story of a man whose mouth is deliberately mutilated in childhood to form a perpetual grin so that he can be exhibited as a carnival freak. The critics were more divided on this than on Leni's earlier films, ranging from the enthusiasm of *Picture Play* for its "atmosphere of evil beauty" to the unmitigated distaste of the *Film Spectator:* "It is a sombre tale to begin with, and it is treated in a sombre manner—dull, heavy, Germanic. Its tempo is funereal. . . . It merely is the kind of foreign picture that American audiences have refused to accept. The fact that it was not made in Europe does not in itself make it any more interesting."[35]

Variety, while somewhat ambivalent about the film itself ("will appeal to the Lon Chaney mob and to those who like quasi-morbid plot themes. To others it will seem fairly interesting, a trifle unpleasant and intermittently tedious") and warning that it might suffer from a reaction against a recent surplus of costume pictures, nevertheless found that "production, direction and photography are excellent." The *New York Times* thought it "a gruesome tale in which the horror is possibly moderated but none the less disturbing." It too, however, praised Leni's "quite expert" direction.[36]

The Last Warning (1929), a mystery rather than a comedy-mystery, met with a less favorable reception than Leni's first two American films, though part of the reviewers' discontent sprang from the inadequacies of the sound system in the version that was released as a part-talkie. *Variety* complained that the sound recording was scratchy and "painfully distinct" and that "Leni should learn that dialog must have pace." The *New York Times* praised "some finely directed passages," but found the story as a whole uninteresting and unconvincing, with "too many outbursts of shrieking."[37] Despite this rather cool reception, however, there seems to be no evidence that either Leni or Universal was in any way regretting their association, and Mohr, his cameraman on *The Last Warning*, remembered him at this period of his life as "a charmer; he was a wonderful little old guy and a lot of fun. He had a grand sense of humour and we had a very close relationship during the making of the picture."[38] If he had lived, then, it is entirely possible that, like Lubitsch, Leni would have settled down to a balance of "European" and "American" qualities that would have continued to bring his films favorable attention and allowed him to pursue a successful career in his new environment.

While Sjöström, Murnau, and all the other directors discussed so far made a confident start to their American careers with a critical and often popular success, Stiller's association with Hollywood was dogged by misfortune virtually from the moment of his arrival. Though he signed his contract with MGM on 9 July 1925 with the stipulation that he was to start work for the company in September of that year, he never completed a film for MGM and it was over a year later, in September 1926, that he finished work on his first American film, *Hotel Imperial,* which he made while on loan to Paramount. MGM then released him from his contract and he continued to work for Paramount, but the critical and commercial success of *Hotel Imperial* was not repeated and Stiller, whose health had been poor all through his stay in America, returned to Sweden at the end of 1927 and died there almost exactly a year later.[39]

Stiller had been hired by Charles Magnusson to work for Svenska Biograf early in 1912, shortly before Sjöström joined the company. He was not in fact Swedish, either by birth or nationality, and it was not until 1921 that he became a Swedish citizen. He was born in Helsinki on 17 July 1883 of Russian-Jewish parents, and his original Christian name is variously given as Mowscha or Mosche. Both his parents died when he was very young (his mother committed suicide upon learning that her husband was fatally ill), and he was brought up by a Jewish family called Katzmann who ran a small business making caps and bonnets. After eight years of schooling he began working in the family shop, but he had already developed an interest in the theater and started to play bit parts in a Swedish-speaking theater in Helsinki in 1899 at the age of sixteen. He later moved to a similar theater in Turku until 1903 and was then, as a Russian citizen, called up for military service in 1904 during the Russo-Japanese War. To avoid being sent to the front line, he fled to Sweden under a false name and with a false passport, and resumed his theatrical work there till 1907, when he returned to Helsinki.[40]

In 1910 (according to Pensel; 1911 according to Werner) he became artistic manager of the avant-garde Little Theater in Stockholm; he was then contacted by Charles Magnusson and joined the Svenska Biograf film company in 1912. In his first year with the company, "he wrote at least six scripts, which were filmed either by himself or others, played in at least four pictures, three of which he directed himself, and during the summer directed six films."[41] By the beginning of 1917 he had made thirty-three films, only one of which survives in a complete form, though fragments and stills from others do exist.[42] His early films appear to have been mainly thrillers, melodramas, and comedies, and Gösta Werner, in his examination made on the basis of surviving evidence of what these lost films must have been like, suggests that his first attempts at comedy were "coarsely humorous" and "slightly grotesque," showing little sign of the subtlety and elegance that were to mark Stiller's mature work.[43]

The earliest of Stiller's films to survive, *Kälek och journalistik* (*Love and Journalism*, 1916), demonstrates the "quieter and more subtle means of expression" that Werner sees developing in Stiller's work of 1915–16,[44] and the film remains fresh and enjoyable today, partly at least as the result of the fine acting of Karin Molander, who had appeared in previous Stiller films and was to continue a fruitful association with him over the next few years. She plays a young journalist determined to produce a story about an extremely uncooperative explorer, who refuses to grant interviews and whose privacy is guarded by a fiercely protective housekeeper. The young woman dresses in her fifteen-year-old sister's clothes and obtains a job as assistant to his housekeeper, prying into his papers whenever she has the opportunity. Discovered by the housekeeper while doing this, she is dismissed, but the explorer, who has become attracted to her, tries to hunt her down—without success, as she has given a false address. Finally he comes across her, as herself, in a fashionable restaurant and she explains that she regrets her deception and intends to return the material she had appropriated and tear

up the story she had written. He forgives her and both acknowledge their love for each other.

After some rather grotesque physical comedy in the opening scenes, the film settles down to the style of sexual sparring and visual implication that Stiller was to make firmly his own, and which is considerably more sophisticated than the more exuberant type of comedy that Lubitsch was producing in Germany at this period. The explorer's interest in his housemaid is signaled by sly glances at her legs and by some open flirtation as she goes about her business in his house; their growing but unacknowledged attraction to each other is delicately and subtly handled, yet it cannot be admitted until each has either made some kind of concession to the other's needs or confessed to carrying out a deception or pretence—a pattern that Lubitsch's German comedies were also to develop as his style gained more assurance.

The two paired films, *Thomas Graals bästa film* (*Thomas Graal's Best Film*, 1917) and *Thomas Graals bästa barn* (*Thomas Graal's Best Child*, 1918), extended Stiller's comedy range and methods even further. Both starred Karin Molander once again, with Sjöström as the hero, and were written by Stiller in collaboration with Gustaf Molander. In the first film Graal is a film scriptwriter who meets up with a young girl who has run away from home, and he starts to write a story about her that freely embellishes her own account of her domestic situation. The film employs a structure that mingles actual incidents, flashbacks, and scenes imagined by Graal for his film in a manner that often deliberately tricks the viewer into accepting as reality something that is later revealed to be imagined. The acting by both principals is restrained and naturalistic, and there is some good-natured satire on the exaggeration and heavily melodramatic situations of the films that Graal is making that implicitly contrasts with the film which Stiller much more elegantly constructs around him.

Thomas Graal's Best Child is more clearly a social satire, beginning with the chaotic preparations for his wedding in the course of which Graal ends up wearing two pairs of trousers, with the wedding ring firmly in the pocket of the pair underneath; he manages, however, to turn the attention of the guests elsewhere for long enough that he can whip down the outer pair and retrieve the ring in time for the ceremony to take place. The newly married couple promptly quarrel over the bride's insistence that their first child is to be a girl called Lilian, and on their arrival home they take up residence in separate rooms and communicate by means of notes. A few days later Graal comes to his wife's defense when a drunk propositions her as she is

*S*tiller's early comedies combine an elegance and sophistication remarkable
for their period with touches of the grotesque behavior and appearance more
commonly associated with the development of silent comedy. Karin Molander as
the aspiring journalist in *Love and Journalism* and with Victor Sjöström in *Thomas
Graal's Best Film*.

taking air on her balcony. In the ensuing scuffle Graal is arrested and is only released when Bessie, after denying that she has ever seen him before, agrees to acknowledge him. The scene, which ends in mutual recognition that they have been behaving foolishly, is a forerunner, not only of much of Lubitsch, but of a whole series of 1930s American films in which a couple who understand each other perfectly at heart, nevertheless delight in embarrassing each other and deflating pompous or inconsiderate behavior.[45] There is also a good deal of Lubitsch-like byplay concerning doors and the ambiguities created by the separate bedchambers, as when Bessie's mother, summoned by the valet to try to reconcile the couple, discovers to her surprise that she has been forestalled and meets Graal emerging from his wife's room while she is vainly trying to find him in his own.

The second half of the film, dealing with the early upbringing of what turns out after all to be a son, pokes fun at "modern" educational theories and the concept of the "modern woman." Bessie scolds her husband for trying to kiss the baby (an unhygienic practice) and later for playing with him instead of trying to develop the baby's mind. Unfortunately, her attempts to introduce the boy to Beethoven's music reduce him to tears and only a romp with his father will console him. Bessie continues, nevertheless, to read books on child care and to dress in a dowdy, "unfeminine" manner that upsets her husband. In an attempt to restore her to her "real" self, he tricks her into believing that he is contemplating an affair with someone who will play a more conventional female role, and Bessie has to revert to dressing and behaving like the woman she once was in order, as she believes, to recapture his affections. As usual, however, Stiller attempts to maintain a balance between the couple and to avoid the suggestion that one wins out over the other; and the final scene is preceded by one that deflates Graal's pretensions as a hunter and provider when he is forced to buy in a shop the game that he failed to shoot when he was out on a hunting expedition.

In between the two Graal films, Stiller made another comedy, *Alexander den store* (*Alexander the Great*, 1917), which I have not seen, but which was described in the program notes for the showing at the Museum of Modern Art in February 1977 as "a subtle comedy of manners, morals and aspiration," in which "the characterization has grotesque affinities" and "Stiller's talent for elegance could not be used." The film appears to have been the victim of censorship, unlike *Erotikon* (1920), where Stiller's talent for erotic comedy reaches its peak. (*Erotikon* will be discussed more fully later in this chapter.)

As well as comedies, Stiller turned his attention at this period to literary adaptations, including three films based on books by Selma Lagerlöf which, unlike Sjöström's treatment of her work, were disliked by the author for the liberties that the director took with the material. *Sangen om den eldröda blomman* (*Song of the Scarlet Flower,* also known as *Across the Rapids,* 1918) brought Stiller his first international success.[46] The film makes striking use of natural locations and has a famous set piece depicting the hero's dangerous journey downriver balancing on a log, which stretches action that would in reality have taken only a couple of minutes into a sequence four or five times that long by means of skillful crosscutting that anticipates Eisenstein's methods in the Odessa Steps sequence of *Potemkin.* Shots of three parallel lines of action—the hero, seen in longshot from the bank, making his way through the rapids; spectators watching from a bridge; and another group of spectators trying to keep pace with him as they run along the shore—are cut together in a way that corresponds to the psychological time experienced by the characters rather than clock time.

The story itself is, however, less adventurous: forbidden to marry his family's serving girl Ellie, Olaf (played by Lars Hanson) becomes a lumberjack and falls in love with the boss's daughter, Kyllikki, who scorns his advances. He succeeds in impressing her by his daring journey downriver on a log, but her father, in a reversal of the earlier class barriers, forbids her to marry a lowly worker. He leaves for the city and encounters Ellie in a brothel; he rushes out to a bar, then, consumed by guilt, returns, only to find that she has killed herself. Repenting of his wild ways, he returns home to find that his parents are both dead and confronts Kyllikki's father; realizing that Olaf has thoroughly reformed, the father permits the marriage.

Herr Arnes pengar (*Sir Arne's Treasure,* 1919), the first of Stiller's adaptations from Lagerlöf (and the one that stays closest to her original work), remains one of his most impressive films. The story of three Scottish mercenaries who escape from a Swedish prison and attempt to rob and murder their way back to their homeland was shot partly on location and partly in the studio and manages to incorporate both a realistic struggle of man against a hostile landscape and a mystical element in which dreams and visions accurately foretell the future or reveal the truth about past events. The camerawork and images are continuously striking and inventive, ranging from elaborate tracking shots through the twisting corridors of the prison in the opening scenes, and the fast track that accompanies the soldiers as they flee across the snow after their first act of murder and theft; through the

powerful rhythm of movement and action and the imaginative camera angles of their violent escape from the village; to the final procession of the towns-people across the ice to collect the heroine's body from the ice-bound ship, in a starkly diagonal composition that may have influenced the final scene of Eisenstein's *Ivan the Terrible, Part One.*

This film too received considerable attention abroad, including a somewhat ambiguous tribute from *Variety* when it opened in America two years later. It was "a fine production, well photographed and acted, interest-ing by reason of its difference from native output"; but (alas!) "they are a sad-looking people, these Swedes, with no joy in their faces; . . . The con-clusion must be arrived at that it is not for us." *Moving Picture World* confi-dently recommended the film to "the searcher after novelty coupled with a high order of merit" and declared: "For simplicity of effect coupled with a keen poetic instinct, it is in a class by itself." It ended by exhorting exhibitors to "work up interest in this picture. Tell your patrons that the Scandinavian pictures have been the talk of the town of London for a year and more and that you offer one of the first on this side of the water." Interestingly, however, when the film was revived in New York toward the end of the decade (under the title of *The Three Who Were Doomed*), the *New York Times* found it already old-fashioned and "somewhat incoherent," with its "dramatic high lights . . . frequently apt to inspire ridicule."[47]

Stiller's next film was *Erotikon*, followed by *Johan* (1921)which was based on a novel by another Finnish writer, Juhani Aho, and made good use of some of the same ingredients that had worked so well in *Song of the Scarlet Flower.* There is a climactic journey downriver by boat as the hero's wife flees with the mysterious stranger who has tempted her throughout the film, and this time Stiller filmed the scene with three cameras placed on rafts and accompanying the action on the dangerous journey through the rapids. This achieved an even greater effect of immediacy and involvement than in the earlier film and allowed him to present the characters' reactions in close-up rather than simply following the action in long-shot. The tumul-tuous journey thus becomes a reflection of the characters' fears and pas-sions and ends appropriately as the couple glide safely into calm water. They then take refuge in a hut owned by an old man who has seen all this before ("Every summer another girl," he comments wearily) and eventually helps the husband, Johan, track them down. Though the heroine agrees to leave her lover and return to her humdrum life with Johan, she does so only after confirming that she originally left him of her own free will, thus ensur-ing that he will have to live forever with this bitter knowledge.

$\mathcal{T}$he best of Stiller's historical films, such as *Sir Arne's Treasure*, remain visually
striking and powerful and often influenced later directors. Some of
Eisenstein's compositions in *Ivan the Terrible, Part One* are strikingly similar to
this.

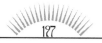

A somewhat similar conflict is found in *Gunnar Hedes saga* (*Gunnar Hede's Saga*, 1922), though here it is pervaded by the mysticism of its source in Selma Lagerlöf's novel. The artistically inclined hero is denied expression of his talents in his repressive home environment and finally leaves to fulfill his dream of emulating his grandfather's achievement in rounding up reindeer in the bleak northern wilderness for sale in the south of Sweden. He is badly injured during a reindeer stampede, however, and in a brilliantly edited and photographed sequence, is dragged endlessly across the countryside by one of the animals. Stiller's use of the moving camera to create a vividly physical effect surpasses even his best achievements in his earlier work. As a result Hede loses his memory and becomes irrationally terrified of contact with any kind of animal: his fears are vividly conveyed in a sequence depicting some of his hallucinations. His sweetheart, an orphan girl brought up by his own family, attempts to restore him to health, but is unsuccessful until, having met up again with her original foster parents (a couple of strolling players who had left her with Hede's family when she was a child), she joins them in playing music outside his window; this prompts him to relive his experience with the reindeer and thus come to terms with it instead of suppressing it. The powerfully realistic scenes of the reindeer stampede are matched by an equally impressive dream sequence in which Ingrid learns of her lover's accident through a vision of an old woman ("The Lady of Grief") who is transporting the injured Hede on a sleigh drawn by bears; the scene literally merges dream and reality by having the sleigh appear inside Ingrid's bedroom before it disappears into the forest.

Stiller's last Swedish film, and the one that brought both him and his star, Greta Garbo, an invitation to work in Hollywood, was *Gösta Berlings saga* (*The Legend of Gösta Berling*, 1923), again based on Selma Lagerlöf. The film was originally released in Sweden in two parts, then condensed into one version, with sound effects, in 1933; an authentic version of the film has recently been reconstituted by the Swedish Film Institute.[48] As it now stands, the first half of the film deals mainly with the psychological and sexual tensions between the three main characters: Gösta Berling, a defrocked priest rejected by his congregation (the part is played by Lars Hanson), and the two women who compete for his affections. A background to this concerns a subplot revolving round the Countess Margarethe and mysterious events in her past for which she must finally atone. The second half contains most of the best-known scenes in the film, including the spectacular burning of the countess's manor and the pursuit of Gösta and Elizabeth (the character played by Garbo) by wolves as they travel by sleigh

across the snow. Together with the fluid editing techniques already displayed in his earlier work, Stiller took particular care with lighting effects in this film and was obviously aware of the potential of the Garbo face, especially in close-up and when it is lit and framed to best advantage.

Though *Gösta Berling's Saga* impressed the MGM representatives in Berlin when it opened there in September 1924, and Stiller and Garbo later met Louis B. Mayer in person to sign the contract that would bring them both to Hollywood,[49] it did not open commercially in the United States until October 1928, long after Garbo had become established as a major Hollywood figure and shortly before Stiller's death. *Variety* had no patience whatever with what was in any case a horrendously shortened and mutilated version of the film: "About par the average Swedish picture in costume . . . a picture only for the sure-seat circle." It blamed the incoherence of the story on the direction and scripting rather than on the cutting which had removed most of the characters' motivations (and of which the reviewer seemed to be unaware), and found time even to sneer at its visual qualities: "Photography is never good, a very general commentary on Swedish film product." The *New York Times* also found the film composed of "hysterical incidents" and concluded that its only interest stemmed from the chance to see Garbo at an early stage of her film career.[50]

Before signing for MGM, however, Stiller had attempted to set up a Swedish-German coproduction that would star Garbo, and, when this project fell through, he agreed to let her appear in G. W. Pabst's *Die Freudlose Gasse* (*The Joyless Street*, 1925). They then returned to Stockholm and set off for America together in June 1925. Alexander Walker suggests that Stiller had second thoughts about working in Hollywood even before leaving and that he tried to provoke MGM into breaking his contract.[51] One question that film historians have never settled satisfactorily is whether MGM wanted Garbo and had to take Stiller as part of the deal, or whether they genuinely wanted both of them, or even (as Pola Negri declared in her memoirs)[52] they really wanted Stiller and took Garbo only when he refused to leave without her. According to Walker, Louis Mayer checked with Sjöström, who was already working for the company in Hollywood, whether Stiller was worth employing and acted on Sjöström's enthusiastic and positive advice.

Whatever the truth may be, the couple were not offered the red-carpet treatment on their arrival that had been accorded to Lubitsch and Sjöström, and no one seemed to have any clear idea at first what to do with them. When things did start to move, it was Garbo who was offered the first chance to make an impact in *The Torrent*, directed by Monta Bell and released early in 1926. Stiller had hoped to direct this but agreed not to stand in the way of an obvious opportunity for Garbo's own advancement, and he was rewarded when, despite the flaws of the film itself, Garbo received ecstatic reviews for her performance. She was immediately given another part in *The Temptress*, and Stiller, who had suggested the Blasco-Ibáñez novel as a subject, was assigned to direct it; after ten days' shooting, however, he was dismissed and replaced by Fred Niblo.

It seems clear that Stiller, who had been accustomed to having his own way while working in Sweden and was used to filming in a largely improvised and apparently chaotic manner, was unable to accept the strict discipline and preplanning that had become normal in the Hollywood studios of the time. He was unhappy with the script that had finally been disgorged by MGM's writers after the usual multiple rewriting process and he tried to change its emphasis during shooting by enhancing Garbo's role and downgrading that of her co-star, Antonio Moreno. This led to fierce quarrels, first with Moreno, and then with the studio executives who tried to sort the matter out. Stiller bitterly resented their interference, and finally Mayer and Irving Thalberg, fresh from the trauma of von Stroheim's *Greed,* made the decision to replace him. Some of the scenes he shot survive in the completed film, but most were reshot by Niblo.[53]

Stiller, naturally enough, blamed this disaster on the inability of MGM to hire someone who presumably knew his business and then leave him alone to work in his own way; valid as this might be in principle, however, it was not, as so many other European directors were to learn to their cost, the manner in which the Hollywood system operated. A more unsympathetic viewpoint lays much of the blame on Stiller himself for not accepting (as Lubitsch and—for a time—Murnau and Sjöström were able to do) that some compromise was necessary between the ideal and the practicable if he was to survive in an industry so very different from that to which he had been accustomed. Walker, for example, describes Stiller as possessing "vanity, ambition, a showy disposition, a talent for seducing or bullying people into doing what he wanted, and an often self-deluding confidence to pretend he had the means to carry out his promises and then intrigue for ways to acquire them"; he adds sardonically that, though these characteristics seemed tailor-made for success in Hollywood, they were undercut by "an incorrigible stubbornness, a tendency to overreach himself, and an arrogance that invited retribution from anyone with the means and disposition to make life difficult for him."[54] It is only fair to add, nevertheless, that if some aspects of his personality may have made it difficult for him to accept the subordinate role allocated to the director by a studio such as MGM, Negri, who worked with him on *Hotel Imperial,* found him "sensitive, patient, gentle,"[55] both as a man and as a director, and he retained the lifelong respect and even devotion of such people as Garbo and Sjöström.

MGM now seemed determined to ignore Stiller as far as possible and were unwilling even to apply for an extension of the work permit that would have allowed him to remain in the United States.[56] Fortunately for him, Erich Pommer, the German producer, who had moved from the UFA studios to Paramount and who knew Stiller's European work well, arranged to borrow him from MGM to direct Negri in *Hotel Imperial.* Eager to show that he could in fact be relied on to work quickly and efficiently (and assisted perhaps by Pommer's organizing talents), Stiller completed the shooting on schedule and with none of the problems that had destroyed *The Temptress.* The film made striking use of the moving camera and was one of the first to employ a permanent "composite set" during shooting: eight connecting rooms and a lobby were constructed and a "flying camera," suspended on rails that ran above the set, was able to follow the action in any direction.[57]

Though *Variety* thought it "just another war picture" whose defects of story outweighed what it acknowledged to be fine direction and camerawork, many other reviewers were highly enthusiastic about the film. *Moving Picture World* declared that it gave Negri her best role in many years and that "the direction of Mauritz Stiller . . . is the outstanding feature. He keeps a positive grip on the development of the story while introducing a number of novel features. . . . He does not indulge in trick shooting merely to inject novelty. He uses it to give greater effect to the scenes." For *Photoplay, Hotel Imperial* placed Stiller "at the forefront of our imported directors."[58] By the time the reviews appeared, however, MGM had already closed their contract with Stiller (in November 1926), leaving him free to sign for Paramount instead.

His work for Paramount in the year before he left America to return to Sweden was plagued by ill health, and it is in fact difficult to sort out the exact chronology of this year from the fragmentary and contradictory evidence which survives.[59] He began work on another film with Negri, *Barbed Wire,* but never completed it and the direction was taken over by Rowland W. Lee. Another film with Negri, however, *The Woman on Trial,* was completed and released within a month of *Barbed Wire,* in October 1927. No prints of this film seem to have survived, but the reviews were

$\mathcal{T}$he European directors were often responsible for introducing technical
innovations into the Hollywood cinema of the 1920s, such as the overhead
rails designed to ensure continuity of movement in the set of Stiller's *Hotel Imperial*.

almost uniformly hostile. The film was a courtroom drama in which Negri played a woman charged with murder; a lengthy flashback establishes her as having sacrificed her own happiness for love and then exploited and mistreated by her husband, and she is finally acquitted. The *New York Times* found Stiller's direction stilted and unimaginative and without "the slightest subtlety"; "the story is dull and the characters are wooden." *Moving Picture World* condemned the film for "uninspired direction of a trite theme" that was "so flatly told that not even the usual interest is achieved," and added that Stiller "shakes out his little bag of tricks," and the "direction is heavy and mechanical." *Variety* found it "thoroughly theatrical and strangely alien in tone and locale," "gushy history," and "laboriously and ponderously unfolded . . . sentimental slush."[60]

Though Walker says that Stiller "was replaced by Lothar Mendes with part-time help from Josef von Sternberg" on *The Street of Sin*, the direction of that film was credited to Stiller on its release in the summer of 1928.[61] The critics did not have much to say in favor of the direction in any case: the *New York Times* found the supposed London setting totally unconvincing and the direction "not especially inspired." Perhaps the unkindest cut was for Stiller, a director previously associated with elegance and good taste, to be freely accused of coarseness, "vulgarity," and dwelling on "disgusting" details. (*Moving Picture World* had already criticized the "glaring bad taste" of a scene in *The Woman on Trial*.)[62]

By this time, however, Stiller was back in Stockholm and his health was failing rapidly. He directed a stage production of *Broadway* starring Gösta Ekman, who had played the role of Faust in Murnau's film. Shortly after this he entered the hospital and died on 28 November 1928. Sjöström, who visited him during his last days, gave a moving account of his last meeting with his friend:

> One day when I came home after being with him for several hours, the nurse at the hospital called me on the phone and told me that Stiller wanted to see me again. He wanted me to come back to him as soon as possible because he had something very important to tell me. I thought he wanted perhaps to talk to me about making his will. He had not made a will—so typical of him. I hurried back to the hospital again and was with him for more than an hour waiting eagerly for what he wanted to tell me. But he only talked about indifferent things. Then the nurse finally came in and said that she could not allow me to stay

longer, she must ask me to leave. But then Stiller suddenly got desperate. He grabbed my arm in despair and would not let me go. "No, no," he cried, "I haven't told him what I must tell him!" The nurse separated us and pushed me towards the door. I tried to quiet and comfort him, saying that he could tell it to me tomorrow. But he got more and more desperate, his face was wet with tears. And he said: "I want to tell you a story for a film, it will be a great film, it is about human beings and you are the only one who can do it." I was so moved I did not know what to say. "Yes, yes, Moje," was all I could stammer, "I will be with you the first thing in the morning and then you will tell me." I left him crying in the arms of the nurse. There was no morning. Next day he was almost unconscious, he tried to talk but although I put my ear close to his mouth I could not make out what he said. And I don't know if he understood what I said. He only kept on staring at me. A day or two later he passed away.[63]

Erotikon and Sexual Comedy

The best of Lubitsch's German comedies look considerably better in retrospect nowadays than most of his epics and costume films, and also provide a stronger link than the latter do with his most characteristic American work. Stiller, however, was given little chance in Hollywood to display his comic talent, and *Hotel Imperial* shows him primarily as a master of technique, extending the interest in fluid and purposeful camera movement and in innovatory editing methods that he had shown in such works as *Sir Arne's Treasure* and *Gunnar Hede's Saga*.[64] His main influence on Hollywood cinema of the period, then, is via *Erotikon* (1920), which Lubitsch certainly knew and which, like the Thomas Graal films, was working toward a blending of cine-comedy and society-comedy that parallels Lubitsch's own experiments in *The Oyster Princess* and *Ich Möchte Kein Mann Sein!*

Cine-comedy, as was argued earlier in the chapter on Lubitsch, involves the use of objects, gestures, facial expressions, gag-refrains, and a pattern of misperception or misreading of visual evidence; social-comedy creates complex plots based on sexual rivalry and jealousy and contains rapid and unexpected switches of emotional tone and sexual allegiance. *Erotikon* possesses all these elements in abundance, together with an insouciant amorality in its ending that Lubitsch himself rarely ever matched.

Lubitsch usually hedges his bets, balancing a woman who initiates sexual encounters and claims the freedom to decide her own destiny with scant regard for the conventions of marriage, against a (usually younger) woman who makes gestures toward a similar freedom but ultimately settles for the apparent security of the marriage relationship. Stiller, however, ends *Erotikon* with Irene, the professor's wife, discarding one lover and happily embracing another, while her husband succumbs to the attractions of his flirtatious young niece.

The film begins with the archetypal absent-minded professor delivering a lecture on the sex life of beetles (who can apparently be polygamous, monogamous, or bigamous, according to species) to an audience of students who are much more interested in their own sex lives and in flirting with Marthe, the professor's niece (another exuberant performance by Karin Molander). The remainder of the film explores these same permutations and potentialities among the human characters, touching on a good many of the possible variants as it proceeds. Later some of the characters spend an evening at the ballet, where they watch a performance that was specially composed for the film and whose theme and personal relationships explicitly parallel much of their own behavior. The ballet is set in a harem, where the Sultan's favorite quarrels with her young lover and has him arrested; she later tries to win back his favor, but he rejects her and she provokes the Sultan into killing him. Within the film, the sculptor Preben, who has fallen in love with Irene, becomes jealous of her ambiguous friendship with Baron Felix and confronts her in a scene whose actions are deliberately designed to recall the climax of the ballet.

These aspects of the film have the literary quality associated with society-comedy, as do the rivalries and intrigues among the main characters. Irene clearly has no interest at all in her husband and, once she has seen him safely off to work, she spends her time ransacking clothes shops (and leaving a trail of devastation behind her as she finds there is nothing that she really wants to buy) or setting off for a flight with Baron Felix in his private plane. Aware of Preben's interest in her, she makes it clear that she is singing for him alone when he is a guest at a party in her house, and she is amused by his obvious jealousy of Baron Felix (her husband, naturally, is totally oblivious to anything that might be going on with either man). The dénouement, however, which has the wife indignantly leaving home when her husband belatedly questions her about her relationship with Preben, and then being reconciled, not with her husband, but with her aspiring lover, is achieved by means of the strategy of visual misperception familiar in cine-comedy and central to so many of Lubitsch's comic effects.

The first character to draw the wrong conclusion from ambiguously presented evidence is Irene, who overhears one of Preben's models buying a fur coat and charging it to Preben's account; shortly after this Preben himself is stimulated to an unwarranted fit of jealousy by seeing Baron Felix accompanying a woman whose face is hidden from view by an umbrella. Jumping to the (incorrect) conclusion that the woman is Irene, he storms to her house and makes a scene and is only convinced of his error much later when he visits the baron's home and finds, not Irene, as he had expected, but the woman for whom he had mistaken her. His misunderstanding, meanwhile, has provided the catalyst for a whole series of plot developments, culminating in Irene's leaving home to return to her "Ma-ma," as the title wittily presents it, offering a verbal supplement to the deliberately stylized gestures with which Irene self-consciously performs her role of the good wife driven beyond endurance by her husband's foolish suspicions. Safely at her mother's, she sorrowfully displays the wedding ring that she now carries in her pocket rather than wears on her finger, but a more genuine regret is stimulated by the sight of a piano and the music that she had earlier played when flirting with Preben.

Objects, clothes, furnishings, gestures, and facial expressions are skillfully used throughout to convey the characters' real feelings and also to hint at their façades. Marthe's change from innocently flirtatious child to sexually provocative woman is conveyed entirely through visual means: left alone in the house while her elders go to the ballet, she lights up a cigarette, stuffs herself with chocolates, and lounges sensuously on a divan in the approved vamp-like manner. Her later experiments in clothing and makeup arouse Irene's jealousy, but, paradoxically, they also pave the way for the "reconciliation" that allows Irene to have Preben while her husband contentedly consoles himself with Marthe. Though Stiller has most of his actors perform with a restraint that was still relatively unusual at this period, a few minor characters, such as one of the professor's academic colleagues, display the deliberately grotesque appearance and physical actions associated with the earlier stages of cine-comedy.

Although Lubitsch went on to refine these techniques even further in his American films (keeping in mind that the comedies he was making in Germany in 1919–20 were working along similar lines), it is obvious that Stiller had as much to teach Lubitsch as Chaplin had in *A Woman of Paris,*

*S*tiller's *Erotikon*—made before *The Marriage Circle*—displays through visual subtlety, gesture, glances, and innuendo the complexities of a triangular relationship, in a style more commonly associated with Lubitsch alone.

and that, in 1920 at any rate, his films were probably more advanced and sophisticated. Circumstances, however, worked in favor of Lubitsch rather than Stiller, and the latter never had another opportunity to show whether he could continue to compete with his better-known rival.

    The subsequent development in America of this type of sexual comedy derived directly from Lubitsch and his many followers and imitators in the late 1920s and early 1930s. Among the most notable of these were Harry D'Abbadie D'Arrast, Monta Bell and Mal St. Clair, but Jacques Feyder's neglected *Daybreak* (1931) provides as good an example as any of the way in which Lubitsch's methods had become the accepted norm around which comedy based on sexual themes was constructed. Though it is a sound film, and thus somewhat outside the limits observed in this book, it illustrates the

American work of another talented European filmmaker who is often too easily assumed to have produced little of interest during his brief stay in Hollywood.[65]

Daybreak has the Central European setting and military characters found in much of Lubitsch's work at this time; it has scenes set quite frankly in a brothel (shortly before the Production Code would put an end to anything so shamelessly explicit); and, though it has a more conventional ending than Lubitsch would probably have provided, it offers a heroine who knows her own mind and allows union with the hero on her terms rather than his. Kasda (played by Ramon Novarro) begins as a thoughtless, pleasure-loving lieutenant, whose response to the news that a fellow officer has just shot himself because he cannot pay a debt of honor is to offer him a respectful toast. He becomes attracted to a young woman, Laura, who teaches music lessons for a living, and forces his attentions on her, going so far as to intrude into the house where she works, pretending to be her cousin. She finally succumbs to his charms and allows him to take her to a wine garden and then home for the night. Being more used to casual encounters of this kind than she, he tactlessly offers her money over breakfast the next morning, and, when he tries to see her again, she tells him indignantly that she can sell herself for a better price elsewhere. In order to provoke his jealousy, she attaches herself to the most obnoxious of his army comrades and accompanies this man to the casino, where Kasda is trying to win money to pay off a friend's debts. He ends up owing money to Laura's escort instead, and, in a deliberate reprise of the earlier breakfast scene, she offers him money, telling him that their previous encounter had been as emotionally meaningless to her as it had obviously been to him. Her cynicism is of course assumed and, after Kasda has refused his uncle's offer to pay off his debts if he will marry a wealthy young woman of his uncle's choice, the two are reunited, with Kasda resigning his commission in order to marry her.

The film has the elegance, the charm, the visual and verbal wit, and the smooth and fluid camerawork that are commonly associated with Lubitsch's work at this period. If it ultimately lacks Lubitsch's ability to suggest more than is revealed and to offer at least an ambiguous challenge to accepted moral codes, that is perhaps merely a reminder that by 1930 the essence of Lubitsch's appeal had become inimitable, though its surface manifestations had become the guidelines to which others, almost instinctively, adhered.

"They are all doing circus pictures now"

Together with *Passion, The Cabinet of Dr. Caligari,* and *The Last Laugh, Variété (Variety,* 1925), directed by Dupont, was one of the small number of foreign films to enjoy a degree of commercial success, as well as critical esteem, in the United States.[66] The film was originally scheduled to be directed by Murnau, but Erich Pommer, head of the UFA studios, assigned him to *Faust* instead. Interestingly enough, it was based on a novel by Felix Hollaender that had already been used as the subject for two Danish films, one of them titled *4 Devils;* Murnau's later American film of the same name also draws on this material. Most critics give the credit for *Variety*'s visual daring to Pommer and the cameraman Karl Freund (fresh from his triumph with the moving camera in *The Last Laugh*) rather than to Dupont, who wanted to use more conventional techniques. Freund and Pommer apparently insisted that they begin by shooting the scenes both their way and Dupont's way and, when the director saw the results, he agreed to adopt their methods.[67]

American critics and audiences were particularly impressed by the way in which the psychological conflicts and jealousies of the characters were conveyed by purely visual means, by the acting of Emil Jannings (who was himself lured to Hollywood shortly afterwards), and by some of the spectacular tours de force of camerawork and visual style. The story is told in flashback as the character played by Jannings is released from prison after serving a sentence for murder: a trapeze artist in a second-rate circus, he had abandoned his wife overnight for a young gypsy girl and had later formed a partnership with a much more famous artist to perform at the Berlin Wintergarden Theatre. Artinelli and the young woman begin an affair to which her lover remains oblivious, until an outsider points it out to him. He imagines taking his revenge by deliberately letting Artinelli fall at the high point of their act, when his blindfolded rival is wholly dependent on him to catch him; he denies himself this satisfaction, however, and instead confronts him after a performance, forces him to kneel and beg for forgiveness, and then stabs him.

The scenes of the trapeze acts themselves (in which all three principals were naturally doubled by professional performers), and especially the climactic one in which the fantasy of revenge is graphically visualized, first through the eyes of the (unnamed) character played by Jannings, and then from the (imagined) viewpoint of Artinelli as he plunges helplessly to his "death," aroused great excitement at the time and are still gripping and effective today. Freund's camera sways back and forth on the trapeze, tak-

ing the place of the performer and sees what he sees, and finally hurtles sickeningly downward toward the spectators as the imagined fall takes place. It could be argued, however, that in comparison with the use made by Murnau and Freund of the subjective camera in *The Last Laugh,* with its subtle creation of the porter's pride and vanity, as well as his pathetic deflation, these scenes exist largely to elicit a gasp of awe from the audience and have little significance beyond this. The overall atmosphere of decadence and moral ugliness is powerfully conveyed, as is the overt and sleazy sexuality of the young woman and her relationship with her protector.

The circus, nightclub, or music hall as a setting for a drama of sexual tension and betrayal, though it can hardly be dignified with the title of a "genre," was a popular and recurring subject in American cinema, especially in the years that followed the release of *Variety.* Together with dependable subject matter, it offered the opportunity for unusual and spectacular visual effects and allowed for the introduction of bizarre and exotic methods of settling sexual accounts at the conclusion (such as the released lion in *He Who Gets Slapped*). Sjöström's film, which actually preceded *Variety,* has already been discussed in some detail earlier: though his visual sobriety eschews such possible devices as placing the camera on horseback to present the viewpoint of the heroine as she carries out her performance, it shares some formulaic plot elements with most of the other films of its type, including Chaplin's *The Circus* (1928). Among these are the hero's long-suffering and unspoken devotion to a young female artist who is brutalized and/or sexually sought after by a male who controls both her personal and professional life;[68] the hero's attempts to protect her, ineffectual at first but finally meeting with success; and the ironic twist whereby he loses (or surrenders) the heroine to a younger rival within the circus troupe.

If Lotte Eisner's summary of *4 Devils* is correct, Murnau had no hesitation about putting his camera on horseback and showing the circus audience as if through the horse's eyes rather than the rider's.[69] His *4 Devils* combine bareback riding and trapeze artistry, and the sexual threat comes from a source both outside the group and outside the circus world itself. Fritz is in love with Aimée,[70] who is also his partner in the trapeze act, but is seduced by a woman who takes a box close to the ringside and makes her interest in him unmistakably obvious. Aimée suffers patiently for a time, then pleads unsuccessfully with her rival; Fritz meanwhile alternately succumbs to the vamp's charms and makes futile attempts to free himself from her clutches and return to Aimée. In the film's climax, Aimée deliberately allows Fritz and herself to fall to their deaths, their bodies clutched tightly together in a last embrace. Murnau seems to have taken full advantage of the opportunities for camera mobility provided by the subject and to have deliberately competed with *Variety* in showing the circus audience from the perspective of the trapeze artists, and the performers approaching and receding from each other as if through their own eyes; as well as filming the final plunge towards death as if the camera were falling with Aimée.

Though *Moving Picture World* felt that Christensen's *The Devil's Circus* "differs widely from the usual circus story," the film in fact has many elements in common with *He Who Gets Slapped* and *Variety*, both of which preceded it, and *4 Devils*, which came afterward. Carl, an ex-convict just released from prison, meets up with Mary, an innocent country girl looking for work in a circus. He intends at first to seduce her, then is swayed by his better feelings and decides to help her.[71] He finds her a job at the circus, but is then arrested once more when he attempts a robbery with the aim of securing enough money for them to marry.

Deprived of his protection, Mary is accosted by the brutal lion tamer Hugo; when she rejects his advances he responds by raping her. Hugo's mistress Yonna is incensed by his interest in Mary and plots revenge on her. Mary has become a trapeze artist whose performance is carried out while the lions are loose in their enclosure directly below her; one night Yonna cuts the rope which supports her, sending Mary plunging among the lions, where she is badly mauled before she can be rescued. The war intervenes, and Mary, now crippled, is next seen selling puppets in the street; Carl, released from prison, meets her again and seeks vengeance on Hugo. Fate (or God—the opening and ending of the film are excessively pious and filled with religious exhortations in the titles and the dialogue) has taken a hand, however, and Hugo has gone blind and exists only on the money earned by Yonna through prostitution. Carl concludes that Hugo has been punished already, and the film ends with Mary able to walk once more.

The standard elements of the circus film are all present here: a vulnerable heroine, sexual jealousy, and a climactic moment in which the circus props (here combining both lions and a trapeze act) are used to settle accounts with sexual rivals. Christensen films the trapeze performance, not with the moving camera of Dupont and (presumably) Murnau, but with effective use of high and low angles that create a sense of space and perspective: Mary is seen from far below, as a tiny figure balanced precariously above the ring; then, from her viewpoint, we see the space beneath her, with the prowling lions reduced to almost invisible specks. Her fall is shown from above and is followed by shots of the terrified spectators milling around,

*C*hristensen's first American film, *The Devil's Circus*, brings social realism and melodrama into somewhat uneasy alliance. The realism is probably the more convincing.

....

while Hugo fights to drive the lions away from Mary's body: "Oh boy, what a wallop," as *Moving Picture World* enthused over this particular scene.

Paul Fejös's *Broadway*, though it does not take place in a circus setting, also makes effective use of the potential for imaginative and striking camerawork that the circus film had been quick to exploit. The huge and elaborate nightclub set allowed him maximum opportunity for camera mobility, and it is this, rather than the somewhat anemic plot and characterization, that remains the major interest of the film today. The film combines two plot strands: a making-it-to-the-big-time show business theme, dealing with the dancer Roy and his partner and girlfriend Billie; and a gangster story, revolving round the activities of a gang of bootleggers who frequent the nightclub. The film was released as both a silent and a talkie, and Fejös solved the obvious paradox of how to film a "silent musical" by shooting and editing in such a way that the musical numbers and the conversations among the gangsters in the audience could be seen as alternately foreground or background, depending on whether the sound or silent version was being watched.[72]

Mohr, Fejös's cameraman on the film, confirmed in the interview with *Film Comment* that the possibilities for technical innovation became for both of them, the major interest of the film: "We were trying to outdo Dupont on his VARIETY. And that was the purpose, the idea of the thing."[73] After an introduction depicting Broadway at night, full of multiple superimpositions of streets, nightclubs, neon signs, dancers, and a huge blowup of what the *Variety* reviewer identified as "Demon Rum" looming, like Murnau's Faust, over everything, the first full shot of the Paradise Club appears, with the camera craning up and over the huge set before tracking through the corridors backstage with the manager. Most of the musical sequences begin with an overhead shot of the whole scene, tracking slowly in and down to medium long-shot for the dancing of the chorus and medium close-up for the singing of Roy and his partner. In those close shots where accurate synchronization of songs and lip movements is important, the camera is, of necessity, kept static; but, in general, Fejös's combination of music and dancing with extensive and elaborately swooping movements of the camera is quite extraordinary for the period. At the end of these set pieces, the camera usually moves up and out from the performers again, restoring the overall viewpoint from which it began.

Often, too, during these scenes, the camera will indulge in sweeping pans of the audience, moving both sideways and up and down to pick out details of the drunken celebrations at the various tables and in the boxes. In the last reel, filmed in Technicolor[74] a shot of this kind is performed with dizzying speed, as the camera rushes rapidly round the faces with almost whip-pan effect. As a final example of Fejös's and Mohr's virtuosity, there is the rather gratuitous, but nevertheless spectacular, shot that begins with the cleaning women finishing their night's work, cranes back and upwards to long-shot, proceeds to a 360 degree pan of the deserted stage setting, moves back down again to the cleaners, then tracks away from them to prepare the way for the entry of the main characters. If Fejös had been allowed to continue working in Hollywood with even a modicum of creative freedom, he would surely now be ranked with Lubitsch and Mamoulian as one of the major innovators of the sound period.

Thrillers and comedy-thrillers

Mohr's suggestion that many filmmakers of the late 1920s were consciously competing with *Variety* by attempting unusual and bravura camerawork is relevant to a discussion of Fejös's *The Last Performance,* which seems to borrow directly from Dupont's film in the structure of its plot. It takes place mostly within a vaudeville setting and has the now-familiar pattern of the circus film: the illusionist Erik the Great is sexually interested in his innocent young assistant, Julie, and becomes obsessively jealous when she falls in love with a newly hired helper, Mark. He tries to frame Mark for the murder of his chief assistant, Buffo, by altering the props of his main stage act (in which swords are plunged into a chest from all sides, with the man or woman inside eventually emerging miraculously unscathed), so that Buffo, inside the chest, is not allowed to escape in the normal way and is killed. The film is classified as a "thriller" here for convenience, in that it contains elements of mystery, menace, and suspicion, and ends with a courtroom scene in which Mark, on trial for the murder, is saved only by Erik's last-minute confession of his own guilt.

The film opens with a quick series of dissolves that takes us inside the theater where Erik, a magician and hypnotist, is about to perform on stage; multiple images of the legs of chorus girls and the faces of spectators flash across the screen; and another series of rapid dissolves shows the preparations for raising the curtain before Erik himself appears on stage, the lighting throwing his shadow, hugely enlarged, on the backcloth. He demonstrates his hypnotic power over Julie and then transfers his attention to the audience in the theater, the camera swinging in towards their faces

*T*he many "faces" of Conrad Veidt in Fejös's *The Last Performance*.

and out again in shots that Mohr, in true *Variety* style, apparently filmed while sitting on a trapeze.[75] Swirling images of the city follow, with Erik's face superimposed to indicate his megalomania and lust for dominance.

Interesting visual effects abound elsewhere in the film: Masks hanging on the dressing-room walls are used in juxtaposition to the faces of both Erik and Buffo to suggest their distorted emotions and the hypocrisy of their professions of friendship to Julie and Mark; and a powerfully effective use of shadows occurs when Erik, planning to announce his engagement to Julie, comes across Mark and Julie together. His huge shadow is seen dominating and dwarfing them, then shrinking rapidly as he walks away and then unexpectedly reappears, life-size, beside them. The shot in which Buffo's body is discovered in the chest was achieved by means of an elaborate system of overhead cables that allowed the camera to swing in rapidly from long-shot to extreme close-up.[76] Mohr created similarly complex visual effects for Leni's *The Last Warning*, which shares with Fejös's film a theatrical setting and an opening in which multiple superimpositions of dancers, singers, faces, and Broadway itself establish the visual complexity which is to dominate the entire work. Leni's film is more obviously a thriller, however, with an apparent murder in the opening scene, followed by the mysterious disappearance of the body. The theater is closed for some years, then reopens with the manager intending to perform the play that had been interrupted by the murder, using the survivors of the original cast. What appears to be the ghost of the murdered actor begins to interfere in the preparations: mysterious warnings appear in the most unlikely places (including a page of the play's script), characters vanish suddenly through trapdoors and then reappear, and the stage props take on an apparently murderous life of their own, attempting to crush or impale the actors at any opportunity. In accordance with what was to become a tradition in films of this type, many of these happenings are never satisfactorily accounted for in the obligatory rationalizing explanation that ends the film: mystery films (which cannot be checked back page by page as a book can) seem to be allowed to create impressive local effects that intensify the atmosphere of omnipresent menace but could not logically, or even physically, ever have happened, provided that the overall pattern of action and motivation is neatly enough tied together by the end.

Stage props are used to expose the real criminal at the climax, when the sets are suddenly raised to reveal his activities; this is followed by a wild chase all over the theater in which Leni and Mohr handle the camera with the utmost possible freedom, culminating in a scene in which the camera swings on a rope with the villain from one part of the theater to another. Along the way, Leni revels in the shadows, cobwebs, tilted angles, subtly distorted perspectives, ominously confined spaces, and clutching hands that had by now become his trademark.

All these had been similarly indulged in his earlier *The Cat and the Canary* (1927), which enjoyed immense popular success and (rather as *Stagecoach* was to do a decade later for the Western) laid down the ground rules that the comedy-mystery and the "Old Dark House" films were to follow for many years to come. The film was adapted from a stage success, many of whose devices had been "prolifically copied," in plays and films already, as the *Variety* review was quick to point out; it was generally agreed, however, that Leni had done something distinctive and novel with what was by now familiar material.

*T*he curtain falls on an unexpectedly real murder in Leni's *The Last Warning*.

As with *The Last Warning*, subtlety of characterization and even plausibility of detail are subordinated to the creation of mood and atmosphere through lighting, camerawork, and setting. The plot gathers together a group of characters for the reading of a will: the inheritance will go to Annabelle, the film's heroine (played by Laura La Plante), but only if she can prove her total sanity to a psychiatrist. If she cannot do this, another member of the family, who is named in a sealed envelope held by the lawyer, will inherit. Everyone, then, has a motive for trying to drive Annabelle insane, and the film systematically shifts suspicion from one character to another (including the person who may or may not be a doctor who arrives half-way through and immediately starts to act in an obviously sinister manner), until the real villain is unmasked. The pattern once again involves certain local implausibilities, designed to make innocent characters behave at least once in an ambiguous or threatening manner, or creating terrifying incidents whose rationale is conveniently left unaccounted for in the audience's relief at having the true source of the danger identified at the conclusion. Whether played as straight drama, as in Robert Siodmak's *The Spiral Staircase* almost twenty years later, or with the admixture of comic incidents and deliberately grotesque characters employed by Leni, the formula proved remarkably durable and provided a reliable source of income for Universal Studios in particular for the next two decades.

Leni's visual style too, suitably modified and adapted to post–Second World War themes, was to be a major link between the visual richness and daring of the finest works of the late silent era and the films noirs of Siodmak and others in the 1940s. Much more than either Lubitsch or Murnau, Leni assimilated the extravagant visual effects of his own *Waxworks* and similar expressionist works of German cinema into a form acceptable to an American public; they lay relatively fallow throughout the 1930s, but were there to be drawn on once again from *Citizen Kane* onward.

The opening shot of the old dark house with its jagged towers dissolves to an interior where a collection of bottles mirror the shapes of the towers. The cat imagery which will run through the film, associated especially with the apparent maniac who seems to be the cause of all the mayhem, appears in a superimposed shot of huge cats clawing at a tiny human figure. The old man makes his will, and twenty years later we see his potential inheritors arrive. The camera moves through the long corridors of the house taking the subjective viewpoint of one of the characters, billowing drapes reaching out to impede its passage. Shots are lit only by a wavering flashlight as, once again from a subjective viewpoint, a figure opens a safe. Cobwebs shroud door handles, a moth is found in the safe, a clock that has not been wound in twenty years suddenly strikes. The lawyer's mouth is shown in extreme close-up as he reads the will, and the disappointment of one of his listeners when the legatee is named is shown through the visual distortion of her features. Characters are viewed through the backs of chairs as if behind bars, and when one of them mentions the word "death," a skull is superimposed on the top right-hand corner of the frame. Claw-like hands reach out and clutch at their victims or seize objects that might serve as clues to the villain's identity. A wall panel is drawn aside and the lawyer's body topples forward, directly toward the camera. Everywhere the lighting is mysterious and sinister, concealing as much as it reveals; low camera-angles distort faces and bodies, making the most innocent gesture and movement an object of suspicion; everywhere the camera swoops and glides and probes.

Christensen's films for First National and Warner Brothers in the late 1920s seem to have followed the successful formula of mingling comedy and terror found in *The Cat and the Canary*. The only one of these that has survived, *Seven Footprints to Satan* (1929), is less accomplished than Leni's best work, but has its moments of interest none the less. As with *The Last Warning*, an explanation at the end reveals that the seemingly supernatural and inexplicable events have all been manipulated by one of the characters—in this case the hero's uncle, who wishes to demonstrate that his timid, bumbling, bespectacled nephew (played by Creighton Hale as an exaggerated version of his very similar role in *The Cat and the Canary*) is totally unsuited to carry out the expedition to the African jungle that he is planning. This involves staging an apparent kidnap and then stranding the nephew in a dark and sinister house where a whole series of often deliberately grotesque characters take turns to threaten, bewilder, and terrify him, and to inundate him with cryptic and mysterious messages. The absurd plot makes little sense, and the perfunctory explanation at the end can be accepted only if the viewer is prepared to believe that an elaborately staged deception of this kind, involving a multitude of costumes and disguises, split-second timing, and a sophisticated mechanical apparatus to carry it all out could have been set up at virtually a moment's notice to teach the hero his lesson. Though the device is admittedly within the boundaries of what could be accepted as screen "realism" in the period, Christensen seems at one point to stress the artificiality of the proceedings with a tilt from the lower floor of the house to the upper that makes it blatantly obvious that the house is part of a studio set. Elsewhere the usual shadows, tilted angles, dark corridors, and closed doors behind which unknown dangers are lurking, place the film firmly within a genre to which directors with a European background made the most striking and lasting contribution.

Costume films: ancient and modern

Leni's *The Man Who Laughs* (1928) came in the wake of Universal's successful adaptation of a better-known book by Victor Hugo, *The Hunchback of Notre Dame*. The film is set in England in the late seventeenth and early eighteenth centuries and its complicated plot has Conrad Veidt as Gwynplaine, the heir to an earldom who is deliberately disfigured as a child by order of James II and left to grow up as a freak in a London carnival. He falls in love with a blind girl, who was also abandoned as a child, but, dur-

*C*hristensen's *Seven Footprints to Satan* (above), like Leni's *The Cat and the Canary* (left), revels in the disguises and the visual exoticism of the comedy-thriller format.

....

ing the reign of Queen Anne, his true identity is discovered and the queen, wanting to punish one of her favorites who has fallen out of favor, orders her to marry him. The film as a whole shares the vaguely populist sentiments found whenever Hollywood can safely distance political disputes to a remote and unthreatening past: the court and the nobility are corrupt, scheming, promiscuous, cruel, and selfish; while the poor are, for the most part, picturesquely squalid, grotesque, and comical, though they rally round the persecuted hero at the end to thwart the soldiers who are pursuing him and give him the chance to escape to safety. As with Lubitsch's German costume films, however (whose very similar assumptions helped to account for their popularity in the United States), the focus is on the fate of a few individuals rather than on any serious discussion of social inequalities and injustices, and the fulfillment or destruction of a love relationship becomes more important than any political crisis.

Leni handles the two contrasting worlds of court and fairground effectively throughout. Among the bored, languid aristocrats, the Duchess Josiana displays a provocative, if sometimes rather perverse, erotic energy, mingling in disguise with the crowds at the fairground, or reclining seductively on her bed to receive the freakish Gwynplaine in a pose and a costume of black lace that make her look startlingly contemporary. The low-life scenes, by contrast, are full of vigor and movement, and are marked by the inventive and unusual camerawork that is generally associated with the circus fairground and vaudeville settings in the films discussed earlier. At one point the camera surveys the fairground from a seat in a turning Ferris wheel, and Gwynplaine's escape after being publicly humiliated in the House of Lords has him, and the camera, resorting to feats of acrobatic skill to evade his pursuers.

Like the hero of Sjöström's *He Who Gets Slapped*, Gwynplaine (though not by his own choice) is constantly exposed to public scorn and ridicule, and Veidt's performance skillfully plays off the pain and torment conveyed by his eyes against the perpetual and hideous grin carved on his mouth, or uses the motif of the hand touching or attempting to conceal the mouth as a vehicle for a whole range of expressions and emotions. One particularly powerful scene shows Gwynplaine and an equally horrific-looking figure standing side by side on the stage; his companion steadily removes his makeup to reveal his normal features, while Gwynplaine, seen in anguished close-up beside him, can never achieve the same release. Scenes like this compensate fully for the rather banal ending of the film, in which Gwynplaine and Dea, the blind girl, escape to safety after, as *Variety* scornfully put it, "one of those scenes where Rin-Tin-Tin gets his man" and the villainous court jester who has been responsible for most of the hero's misfortunes throughout engages in a life-and-death struggle with what is only too plainly a stuffed dog.

Films like *The Man Who Laughs*, *Passion*, and *Deception* provide a generally unsympathetic picture of a privileged court and aristocracy (a

*C*onrad Veidt's grotesque makeup hides a vulnerable heart in Leni's *The Man Who Laughs*.

social system which Americans could congratulate themselves on having escaped) and contrast this with an oppressed lower class that is used mainly to provide a setting for the love interest but can become menacing and terrifying when it rises up against its oppressors (however justifiable, in the abstract, its grievances may be). When it came to dealing with the same basic plot in a more modern setting, such as the Russian Revolution, however, Hollywood became even more ambivalent than usual. Bolshevism very quickly became associated in the American popular mind with chaos, disorder, subversion, and cruelty of all kinds, and the sturdily "democratic" perspective found in a film like Leni's was no longer quite so easy to maintain. Christensen's *Mockery* (1927), which, while being no masterpiece, is not quite as negligible as contemporary reviews proclaimed it to be, demonstrates very clearly the problems which arose when it could be safely agreed

that the upper class had become corrupt and self-seeking, but the alternative presented was believed to be, if anything, even worse.

Mockery, like most American historical films, tries to solve these difficulties by identifying political struggles with sexual tensions: in this case, the constant threat of rape faced by the Countess Tatiana throughout the film. As in *The Man Who Laughs,* there is a beauty-and-the-beast subtheme in which the physically repulsive and mentally dull peasant played by Lon Chaney displays, an initial animal-like devotion to her, then an equally animal-like lust, and finally a self-sacrificing protectiveness once more.

The meandering plot can be roughly schematized as follows. The film opens with the countess disguised as a peasant on a mission to collect information for the Whites in war-ravaged territory occupied by the Reds. She persuades the peasant Sergei to help her by giving him food and tells him to pretend to be her husband when they reach a checkpoint. They take shelter for the night in a hut, where Sergei saves her from the unwelcome advances of another peasant, and are later discovered by a Bolshevik detachment; Sergei persists in his claim that the disguised countess is his wife and refuses to betray her. He is brutally whipped in a vain attempt to make him speak. Some White soldiers arrive and drive the Reds away, and the injured Sergei is taken to the hospital. So far, the meaning is fairly clear-cut: Reds are bad and Whites are good, and an ignorant peasant like Sergei is better off trusting to the nobility than taking the side of the revolutionaries.

In town the countess returns to her normal status and resumes her life of balls and party-going. The White officer Captain Dmitri starts to court her, and she willingly responds, meantime snubbing Sergei and relegating him to the rank of one of her servants. Envious, hurt, and bewildered, Sergei is easy prey for a discontented demagogue among the servants, who tries to gain his support for the revolution. The countess is now shown to be snobbish and ungrateful (unattractive qualities in American eyes), but the motives for discontent among the lower classes are equally unworthy and stem from greed and envy rather than a genuine idealism.

The White soldiers leave town, and the servants and lower classes become increasingly bold and unruly, neglecting their duties, raiding the wine cellars, and even accosting and robbing the countess in broad daylight in the open street. Set against this, however, are scenes of the idle and bloated rich, who are seen (literally) eating cake, oblivious to the dangers as the poor prepare to take their revenge against them. The Reds invade and occupy the town, and Sergei takes advantage of the fighting to lock his fellow servants in a cellar and then tries to force himself on the countess, chas-

*L*on Chaney, as the dull-witted peasant of Christensen's *Mockery*, plots revenge on the oblivious and self-indulgent bourgeoisie.

ing her through the empty house. She is saved by a White officer, and Sergei is about to be shot along with some of the other revolutionaries when the sight of the scars left on his body by the whip reminds the countess of his earlier services to her, and she asks for him to be pardoned. The servants (who are presented simply as cowards, concerned above all with saving their own skins) are released from the cellar; when the officer leaves, some of them seize the opportunity to attack the countess and once again she is saved from sexual assault by the repentant Sergei. He is wounded in the struggle, however, and dies, which conveniently solves any further problems as to how the countess, who could obviously never marry him, can reward him adequately for his devotion this time.

Like so many other American films that touch on class, racial, and political conflicts, from *Birth of a Nation* onward, *Mockery* cannot bring

H̸otel Imperial was the only film that Stiller was able to complete, to his own satisfaction, in the United States. Pola Negri, as the maid, offers her assistance to the fugitive lieutenant (James Hall).

itself actually to support revolutionary activity, even if the logic of the plot seems to demand this. The rich, it suggests, deserve to be given a few shocks, to put them in their place a little and make them aware that suffering and misery exist elsewhere; the lower classes, however, should never attempt to take the law into their own hands and redress social injustices on their own initiative. They will fall easy victims to their own greed, lust, and gullibility, and will need to be rescued from their own worst impulses by an enlightened upper class that has learned its lesson and will treat them more justly in future. The whole message is displaced into a plot that equates revolution with rape and, like Griffith's Reconstruction scenes, proclaims that decent women will never be safe if the under-classes are allowed to reverse the natural order of things, and refuse to recognize that their interests are best served by accepting the wise leadership of their betters.

Stiller's *Hotel Imperial* is set a couple of years before the Russian Revolution, in 1915, and deals with a war-time incident during the fighting between the Austrian and Russian forces. Negri plays a hotel chambermaid, Anna, who shelters an Austrian officer, Paul, who has been separated from his detachment in Austrian territory that is occupied by the Russians. Although the hotel cook wants to hand him over to the Russians, Anna has him disguised as a waiter and, when he kills a Russian spy to prevent him reporting vital information, she protects him once more by claiming that he was in her bedroom at the time of the shooting. This leads to her public humiliation at the hands of the Russian general, who had earlier made advances to her and whose gifts of clothing and jewelry she had, after some initial resistance, finally accepted. When the Austrians re-occupy the town, however, Paul is decorated for his services and he and Anna are married.

As *Moving Picture World* observed, "the war serves as a background for intimate melodrama" and there is little of the overt attention that is paid to political conflict in *Mockery*. It is interesting, nevertheless, that it is the Russians, who in 1915 were fighting on the "right" side, who are presented as the enemy, while the film's sympathies are very clearly with the Austrians. Although America was still neutral in 1915 and might at the period have maintained a relatively objective viewpoint toward both nations, the film clearly reflects the mentality of the time of its release, in which the Russians were more to be feared than the Austrians (or, for that matter, the Germans).[77] The bias is made most explicit in the contrast, first between Paul and the Russian general, and then between the Russian and Austrian generals at the end. Paul is brave, dashing, patriotic, and romantic; the Russian general is gross, obese, lecherous, and more interested in pleasure than in carrying out his military duties. The Austrian general, who appears briefly in the final scenes, is a slim, elderly, dignified father figure, who gives his blessing to the couple's marriage.

Much of the contemporary praise of the film was lavished on its technical skill, and Stiller demonstrates his mastery both of editing and of innovative camerawork. The carefully constructed hotel set, as has been mentioned earlier, allowed him to move the camera rapidly and smoothly from one area of the hotel to another, or from interior to exterior: two typical examples are a swift track away from the proclamation announcing the Russian occupation of the town, followed by a pan that accompanies the arrival of the Russian general and his entourage; and an elaborate overhead shot from Paul's point of view that signals the arrival of the Russian spy and establishes his significance. Earlier in the film a complex montage of horses, battles, flames, and marching soldiers is superimposed on the exhausted and restlessly dreaming Paul, and this merges, as he wakes, with shots of the military band accompanying the Russian troops as they arrive in town.

Stiller, like Murnau in *Sunrise* and Leni and Christensen in the films just discussed, had learned by now that American taste demanded that even the most intense drama must have moments of comic relief inserted at regular intervals, and he employs the standard method of using deliberately grotesque minor characters for this purpose: the old porter at the hotel, or a soldier who peeks through a keyhole at the general's first attentions to Anna, and is then kicked in the pants by one of his comrades. Contemporary reports agreed that Stiller was trying very hard to "redeem" himself with this film, and he managed to produce an acceptable mixture of American content (romance, suspense, comedy, and a happy ending); an exotic but not too controversial setting that serves as background for a story focusing on personal relationships; and the dash of European technique that by 1928 was all that was really expected, or even tolerated, in the way of novelty from a foreign director.

Ordinary people: Fejös's *Lonesome*

The films by Stiller, Leni, and Christensen discussed so far all conform to the accepted pattern of American entertainment cinema in that they provide an alternative to the mundane reality experienced and lived through by the vast majority of the members of their audience. The circus and vaudeville films present dramas of hatred, revenge, sexual jealousy, and murder in settings where the characters risk their lives in trapeze acts, and in illusionists' boxes that are then run through with swords; they are also in danger of being consumed by lions. Costume and historical films transport us in space or time to royal courts and palaces, to ballrooms filled with elegant soldiers and beautiful ladies, or to the perils of the battlefield. The thriller and comedy-thriller offer murder, suspense, mystery, and flirtation with the eerie, the supernatural, and the unexplained. Even the sexual comedy, potentially the closest to everyday experience in its subject matter of marital conflict and betrayal, is distanced in the hands of Stiller and Lubitsch into an

o

*P*aul Fejös's style could be elaborate and grandiose, as in *Broadway*, or small-scale and intimate, as in this shot toward the end of *Lonesome*.

upper class world of wealth and privilege in which the characters have the leisure and the money with which to conduct their amorous intrigues; they are also far more handsome, elegant, beautiful, witty, and well dressed than most of the cinema audience can ever hope to be.

Murnau, in *Sunrise* and *City Girl*, and Sjöstöm in *The Wind*, provide partial exceptions to this, to the extent at least that they deal with characters whose social status and everyday living conditions approximate much more closely the reality of the average spectator. Yet *Sunrise* has an attempted murder and a spectacular storm on the lake; *City Girl* puts its newly-married heroine almost immediately into a situation where she has to cope with both an exceptionally hostile father-in-law and a would-be seducer; and the heroine of *The Wind* experiences an attempted rape, the killing of a man in self-defense, and a bout of madness. Of the films of the period, only King Vidor's *The Crowd* is comparable to *Lonesome* in its concern for characters who are average and unexceptional in every respect and who live, dress, work, and amuse themselves in ways that would be recognizable to the vast majority of the spectators. Certainly the *style* of the film is far from mundane and is very different from the "invisibility" sought by such later neorealists as the early Roberto Rossellini and Vittorio De Sica; while the plot works throughout by means of explicit parallels and repetitions rather than seeking the effect of random and insignificant incident found in films like *Bicycle Thieves* and *Umberto D.* The parallels, however, instead of emphasizing the possible artificiality of the situation, serve to create the sense of how *typical* the characters are and how normal are the circumstances of their lives.[78]

Jim and Mary have almost aggressively average names; live next door to each other (though they do not realize this until the end of the film) in an ordinary apartment block in New York; travel to work in crowded and uncomfortable subway trains; are employed in the same factory, he punching out razor blades on an assembly line all day, and she coping with an endless barrage of complaints and inquiries as a switchboard operator; are both single and lonely; and end up seeking relaxation and escape at the Coney Island fairground. The film follows them through the events of a typical day in parallel scenes from the time they get up to the time they encounter one another for the first time on a bus going to the fairground. Chance and accident keep them apart a little longer, but they finally meet again and spend the remainder of their time at the fair together, until, in the confusion that follows a minor fire on a roller-coaster car, they are separated once more. Though they search for each other, they are unsuccessful and, as neither knows more than the other's first name, they believe they have lost each other for good. On returning home, however, they discover that they have been neighbors all along.

The visual and structural complexity of the film works, paradoxically, to establish the sense of normal, everyday activity that it creates. The multiple paralleling of the characters' experiences makes their final reunion seem inevitable, and the visual and aural density that is achieved in many scenes by several layers of superimposition and by a barrage of the noises associated with urban life, creates a strong sense of the confusion and stress of city living.[79] Without simultaneously boring the audience, Fejös conveys the tedium and monotony of the jobs that the characters perform: their experiences, frustrations, and dreams can be shared by almost any member of the audience, and yet the dance hall scene at the fairground, in which the background fades away to leave the couple literally in a world of their own, dancing on the clouds with a yellow half-moon (hand-tinted in the original prints) below them, suggests the uniqueness as well as the typicality of their lives.

The ending brings the lovers together again, and the final close-up of their embrace (as with the similar ending of *Sunrise*) performs the ritual function of suggesting that love will ultimately triumph over all obstacles. Yet, as with Murnau's film, the tensions explored earlier remain significant and act to undercut the sense that all the characters' difficulties have been overcome. In *Sunrise* the husband's attempt to strangle the Woman of the City shows him just as capable of resorting to irrational violence to solve his problems as he was at the beginning; in *Lonesome* the basic social conditions that Jim and Mary have to face remain unchanged, even if their personal happiness is assured. The anonymity of city life (portrayed even more powerfully in this film than in King Vidor's virtually contemporaneous *The Crowd*) will still surround them, and Jim, if not Mary, will have to return to the repetitive, monotonous, soul-destroying job that has to be performed if the couple's basic needs of food and shelter are to be supplied.

Like *The Crowd* and *Sunrise, Lonesome* was more of a critical than a popular success, and it suffered also from the misfortune of appearing at a time when silent films, no matter how high their quality, were largely overlooked in the rush to exploit or experience the novelty of the talking picture. It demonstrates, nevertheless, the freshness of vision with which an outsider could view an aspect of America so taken for granted by most native-born directors that it never occurred to them to explore it: in Fejös's eyes, the mundane becomes marvelous and the commonplace becomes unique.

Conclusion: "The Conclusion Must Be Arrived At That It Is Not for Us"

For a period of not more than three or four years in the early 1920s there seemed a distinct possibility that European films and filmmakers might radically alter the viewing habits and tastes of the American public. Although films like *Passion, The Cabinet of Dr. Caligari* and *The Last Laugh* broke few box-office records, they attracted considerable public attention and discussion, and critics at the time speculated freely that the challenge of foreign films might force the native cinema to become more "adult," more "mature," more "artistic," more "real." The fact that the barrier of language was more easily overcome in silent than in sound films also contributed to the potential threat to the standard American product, and Hollywood saw the problem as being real enough to demand effective countermeasures.

While the main intention of the industry itself was primarily to defuse the danger by having the more talented of its foreign rivals safely under its own control, the optimists among the critics continued to hope that the newcomers could infuse into American cinema some of the virtues of their previous films and possibly lead that cinema into new and hitherto unexplored directions. Some of the initial films—*The Marriage Circle, Sunrise, Name the Man*—seemed to encourage this speculation; yet even with *Sunrise* a backlash against films that were "artistic" rather than "popular" had begun to make itself felt. The studios, after giving their new acquisitions a relatively free hand to begin with, became alarmed at the unexpectedly meager financial returns and began to resist—not so much stylistic innovations, which had become virtually a trademark of the foreign directors—as subject matter that was considered too bleak, too downbeat, too pessimistic, or too negative. Meanwhile those critics who identified themselves most strongly with mass tastes were reflecting the increasingly strident nationalism of the country as a whole in demanding that films display the truly "American" qualities of wholesome, optimistic, popular entertainment instead of dabbling in the "morbid," "depressing," "ugly" side of life favored by too many of the European imports. Squeezed between an industry concerned primarily with maximum financial profit, and an audience encouraged by a growing number of critics to continue to equate "entertainment" in film with mindless escapism and to resent as "un-American" anything that ventured to diverge from this, there was little hope that people like Sjöström or Murnau could continue to work with the intensity and commitment that their temperaments demanded.

The 1920s probably offered the last opportunity for American cinema to strike some kind of positive balance between the claims of "art" and the claims of "entertainment."[1] The coming of sound merely confirmed the decision that had been reached a few years earlier by consolidating the distinction between "art" (i.e., foreign-language) films and "popular" (i.e., American) ones and giving it an economic justification either in the expense involved in dubbing foreign films or in the reluctance of audiences to patronize films with subtitles. There is no point, at this late date and with the very real achievements of the best of Hollywood cinema before us, in questioning whether the choice was the correct one or not; it has meant, however, that Hollywood has never offered scope for the emergence of a Robert Bresson, an Eric Rohmer, a Werner Herzog, or an Ingmar Bergman, and no doubt never will—though it will continue to attempt to lure these and similar figures into its ambiguous embrace.

Brian Attebery, in seeking to account for the American resistance to, and distrust of, fantasy in literature, has attributed this to a distinctive orientation in the American mind that he sums up as follows:

> Our folk songs, stories and beliefs, especially our beliefs, portray a population increasingly pragmatic and impatient, interested mostly in the here and now, susceptible to sentimentality, but only if convinced that its tears are being jerked by real events. If the dark vision of the Puritans still haunts us in our midnight dreams, that is all the more reason for scoffing in the daylight. Most of our popular literature falls into the same pattern: indeed, the line is thin between the broadside ballad and the newspaper eulogy, or the oral and written tall tale. Both kinds of narrative, folk and popular, have shaped American habits of expectation and belief and have created a serious problem for the artist . . . who wishes to reach beyond practical concerns and the limits of daily existence.[2]

o

Whether one accepts this particular definition or not (and it seems to me to shed considerable light on American popular cinema as well as literature), it seems clear that there is a strong and persisting current of American thought, largely unconscious yet often specifically articulated, that sees the tastes and values resulting from the particular circumstances of the nation's development as having a universal and self-evident validity. These values, which can be traced in the political sphere as much as in film and literature, have been incorporated into the mainstream of American cinema and then imposed, by virtue of Hollywood's economic predominance, on most of the rest of the world. It is so widely taken for granted that only Hollywood possesses the secret of creating genuine popular entertainment that—to take only one example—television programs like *Absolutely Fabulous* or *Prime Suspect,* which offer no language barrier and have proved enormously popular in Britain, are nevertheless denied prime-time exposure on network television and are either shunted off to the Public Broadcasting Service (TV's equivalent of the art-house ghetto) or are remade for American audiences with anything unsettlingly "strange" or "foreign" eliminated from them. The mentality behind this stems from a belief in America's cultural supremacy and in Hollywood's monopoly of the correct know-how and expertise necessary for successful filmmaking that was challenged briefly in the 1920s by some of the people discussed in this book; after a moment of self-doubt and self-questioning, the challenge was met head-on and comprehensively, and apparently permanently, overcome.

Appendix A
"Masters of the Motion Picture"

by Matthew Josephson

From *Motion Picture Classic* (August 1926), 24–25, 66

> *Mr Josephson is a well-known young radical writer, who has been taking a profound interest in motion pictures. He has written interestingly and authoritatively on the screen's greatest achievements. This is the second of the series of Masters of the Motion Picture, in which he gives a critical discussion of the screen's advance.*

In the modern period of the movies, the films of Messrs. Lubitsch, Chaplin, Stroheim, Vidor, Cruze, have developed a complete character of their own as an art, instead of being a mawkish rendering of cheap theatrical successes in photos.

The eye is struck first by the immense improvement in the quality of the camera work, the cleanness of line, the absence of waste detail. All of them manipulate their groups, their sets, as well as the light they spill over the scene, to get a balance, a form that keeps your eye unswervingly on the things that count most.

Not only have they learned to *paint* with the camera, but also to *suggest*, by the interplay of sequences, by the terrific power of concentration in a close-up, by the shrewd angles they catch, almost a new understanding of life. The modern film, in short, becomes an instrument fit for artists to express the highest flights of their imaginations, their most delicate and subtle fancies.

That Masterpiece Again

The one film out of this rich period which you have doubtless heard critics refer to more than any other is "The Last Laugh." It is a German picture, directed by F. W. Murnau, with the great Jannings in the central role.

There is virtually no plot at all, no love interest, no sensationalism of any kind. What is the merit of this picture, which failing, as it did, to become a popular success, appealed to insiders, critics, artists, column conductors, everywhere as most nearly approaching the ideal of perfection?

"The Last Laugh" gave us the unique feeling of looking into the interior of a man's life thru some wholly unaccountable peer-hole. We not only watched this man's expressions and movements, we watched the states of his soul. Jannings, who is possessed with some divine understanding of his business, seemed to know more about how to make his whole body expressive than most of the other film folks put together.

The picture forms simply the inside history of a crisis in the life of an old hotel porter who is demoted because of senility to a still more servile occupation, that of lavatory-attendant! And because of the simplicity of his material, because he didn't have to bother with the details of some silly plot, the director was able to bear down upon the pure creation of his character and his awful fix thru cinema technique alone. It is one thing to interest you with pictures of pirate ships, knights-at-arms, society gals. It is another to make you feel with the pride, the hope, the passions of an old derelict like this. Within the hour you have a sustained motion picture which thru its overtone hands over to you his whole code of living. This idiotic old creature is interpreted with as much *éclat,* sympathy, intimacy and frankness, as let us say, Chaplin interprets Chaplin.

Perfect Technique

The background, the group of characters, the labor which fills this life are all drawn with a tremendous effort at reality. There are no subtitles at all to interrupt the mood of understanding into which you are thrown. The pictures as Murnau compose them put the stuffy and artificial-looking studio sets of his expressionistic colleagues to shame. He uses every trick of the modern cinema that will help him trap an idea, an effect, and hurls it at you.

For instance, there is a daring full-length flash of a revolving hotel-door, which with its glassy glitter and whirl recurs in the sequence of the film like a refrain, a dominant motive in music, setting off the whole idea of this proud and cruel hotel. Or, there is a wedding feast in which the camera, itself, seems to go drunk with wine and contentment and, wandering about the meager North Berlin interiors, drops into a brass instrument and brazens out to you the very music of the occasion in a few inspiring mechanical close-ups.

All the "stunts" and tricks of the director followed his material with absolute faithfulness. They did not stick out like useless fandangles, as in "Caligari." All the shades of joy, grief, desperation, came to you thru the insidious overtones that caught you in their spell.

After all, the secret of any great art is to create in us the illusion of absolute understanding and sympathy with the experiences the artist expresses; thus, to make us forget ourselves, and think only that we are living thru these experiences and that they are just as momentous or tragic as they seem to be to the artist.

Otherwise, the moving picture camera arena seems to be divided for the moment into two camps. One is trying to bring the beauties of painting, the thoughtfulness of good literature and drama and music into the cinema. The other camp, develops out of the movies themselves, and especially the slapstick movies. They want to get over the effect of motion, its humor, its vertigo, its hypnotic thrill and drive. We shall come back to these later.

In the Lubitsch Manner

The films of Ernst Lubitsch place him practically as a leader of the first group. Again, they do not always pay, but they make him the envy of fellow directors. Their recent successful revival in New York before a serious film following by the International Film Guild shows how much good there is in Lubitsch's Collected Works.

Anyone with half an eye can see that he excels in imagination, delicacy, wit, taste. He has the spirit of the artist, and he bring this to his work in the movies. He has been a profound student of this new art, and like certain other of our late enemies, he has, we gallantly admit, all the cinema tricks at his finger tips.

From his early successes in Germany with historical films such as "Passion," which gave us a plausible and bewitching Dubarry in Pola Negri, Herr Lubitsch was driven to light social comedy by the severe strictures of the box-office.

So far as I know, we had never seen historical characters so appropriately and delightfully gotten up, nor scenes of such regal splendor and licentiousness *à la Louis Quinze* so accurately and tastefully pictured. The action moves deliberately thru the sequences, which show us all the agreeable wickedness of *Louis's* court at Versailles, then rushes to the miserable death of *Mme. Dubarry's* great patron and the gathering storm of the French Revolution. This last affair turns out to be a melodramatic hurly-burly, and for convenience's sake is pushed back—some twenty years in history.

Amid this historical business Lubitsch found the most adaptable material for his imagination. He worked for grandiose pictorial composition, and for human types that fitted as plausibly into his setting as the period furniture. Against this, he would throw sudden, hideous contrasts of misery and poverty.

In short, we have something here that we can honestly feast our eyes upon. Glittering chandeliers, mirrors, decorated wall-spaces, savagely drawn faces (that seem to come out of the paintings of Daubigny), whose interesting wrinkles and crow's-feet give us much food for thought. Furthermore, he never insults the understanding. Here, since we are all grown-ups, a courtesan is a courtesan; a pander is a pander. We are made to feel the reality of these genre portraits despite their romantic background.

The Art of Satire

Lubitsch's social satires, such as "The Marriage Circle" and "Kiss Me Again," force themselves even more easily into the category of masterpieces.

There is less glitter to dazzle your eyes. The nature of these films is simpler as the highest art is nearly always the simplest. While dealing with more trivial moods, "Kiss Me Again," for instance, is created out of much characteristic movie "business." There is a sequence running several thousand feet in which the husband and wife, Monte Blue and Marie Prevost, discuss with their lawyer the most sensible method of getting their divorce. The pantomime here is tremendously funny without having any of the dynamic farce of the Harold Lloyd buffoonery. The face, hands, body of Monte Blue suddenly become an instrument that flickers before the camera lens with infinite fantasy. The film offers a brilliant psychological portrait of these frivolous but extremely human characters.

Instead of being panoramic like Griffith, who gives you a great sweep of thousands of men and horses over a span of years, Lubitsch is analytical, and prefers to film a few highly concentrated moments which have the imaginative fill up of any highly distilled beverage. It all has the effect sometimes of certain dreams in which events unfold themselves with an unearthly clarity, so that every detail of a room, of a person's speech, is imprinted on your mind.

"*To see eternity in a grain of sand . . .* " said the poet, Blake. And Lubitsch can see and show us eternal truths in a casual gesture, or the oscillations of Mr. Menjou's eyebrows.

Lubitsch's great stunt is that he gets all these effects with such simple means, with such *reasonable* material; like the framework of the old domestic triangle. He is so intelligent and competent as he moves from one bit of business to another that he makes pantomime, which is too often mere dumb show, have a much greater range of meaning.

There is one side of these films that I object to, however; the overtone of cynicism. Granting that sometimes the fate of an empire rests upon the proportions of a naughty woman's nose or hips, I still feel that this is not the whole story. Nine times out of ten the greatest victories are simply won by sweat, gameness, suffering. Technically, Lubitsch touches the deepest tones of his instrument; emotionally he scratches only the surface of life.

Appendix B
"Film Imagery: Seastrom"

by Robert Herring

From *Close-Up*, 4, no. 1 (1929), 14–27

You do not mean a view when you say "landscape." You do not mean a cleft in rocks, you do not mean a tree, but rocks themselves and trees. Woods even more than valleys (not so much one valley) rather than rocks. And if there are clefts, it is so that the rocks will stand out the more, because of the difference in their aspect the gash will cause, breaking up the light. And if there are rocks, it is so that the valley will stand out the more.

You cannot play tricks with a landscape, any more than you can "fold a flood and put it in a drawer." You cannot make it a Balkan kingdom or the edge of the world. It isn't detached, it relates always to something bigger. A man who likes landscape and is at his best in dealing with it is not a man who likes tricks. He likes it for its sweep, and though he can, of course, choose it, he cannot just make it a background. He can choose which he will have, but he cannot choose what it will be. It is that already, even though what it is depends on his having chosen it. There is a sweep about the word: "horizon" leaps to mind at once. There is a sweep about Seastrom. The names of many of his films show their elemental characteristics . . . *L'epreuve du Feu, Vaisseau Tragique, Charrette Fantôme, The Wind.* (I quote from the books and countries, English and French, in which I found them. If you saw *Les Proscrits* at the Ciné Latin last spring, you think of it as that, without bothering to give it yet another foreign title in English, and I can't help that).

Similarly, when it comes to people, a landscape-man will deal with people in the larger emotions. The rocks and trees and the horizons of their characters more than the flowers in the crannies and the rabbit-warrens in the roots. But because he deals with the flood, he will deal also with any attempts to put it in a drawer, and continuing the bad habit of quoting, he will do so by relating not only the wind but the cedar floor to it. The eddies of the current may not interest him, but the depths will.

This is not specially Seastom's, and what is Seastrom's is the lyricism which makes his landscapes lyrical landscapes. It is a Scandinavian quality, and finds itself in the films of Brunius, of the regretted Stiller (especially in *Arne's Treasure*), and even in Molander's *Marriage* there was more in the background, more pervasive influence, in consequence more many-sidedness in one side than in American, German and most French films. And *Marriage* was late, not of the good period, not even a good film. But the apprehension was there. The only American films in which you get this landscape coming into its own are the Westerns. Here the earth has life. It is not for nothing that clouds of dust follow the flying hooves; the earth is exerting its parentage. The men are not rooted, but they are still related . . . earth is there, itself, alone in American films. Reality, of course. The Westerns are the nearest America has to an equivalent of the reality of the Russian films, and the reality comes from the fact that in these cowboy stories, fights with floods and fire and struggles to live, America is dealing with something of her own she knows about and not trying to pass off a life she has grafted on to herself. These *were* struggles to live.

And so are the stories of which the Swedes make their films. They are sagas, if that word helps you at all. Stories of men who had to live, had to get a living from an earth that provoked that necessity. Swedish films deal at once, simply, with the living and the earth. They're bound up. There is no saying "this will look better in a mountain background," no going on location to the South Seas or building a studio sandstorm—mentally, at any rate. The mountains, as I once before observed, aren't a background. The people are offshoots of them, another form of life. Look at the Swedish films you know. What you think of is the dragging of the chest across the SNOW in *Arne's Treasure*, the REINDEER stampeding in *Herrenhofsage*, the TORRENT in *Les Proscrits*, the wolves across the SNOW in *Gosta Berling*. Sweeps of country which, as Moussinac says, become "un des éléments actifs du conte." And because of the expanse, there is the natural result that the human life in it is much more intimate, firm and close-knit. Out of protection. It has not been conserved, concentrated. It has to offer compactness for "the great common task, the preservation of mankind against the supremacy of nature." Which is its parent. Against which it rebels. So along with the capacity to deal with expanses, and lyrically in the case of Seastrom, there is also the ability to show ordinary, domestic hedged-in life with extraordinary grace and intimacy. Power—and also delicacy. This is because the living is bound up with general life. When Seastrom made *The Tower of Lies* in Hollywood and his landscapes were reduced to softened orchards, and smooth hills, life in the house was still as living, still almost as Swedish, in the way details exteriorised the main theme as much as ever, even though to my taste the theme was poor.

He has made a great number of films, including *He Who Gets Slapped*, *Name the Man*, and *Confessions of a Queen*, in America; but it is unfair to judge him too much by his American productions, his talent is clearly folded in a drawer here, and the most we can do is to look for some hints in them of what his Swedish films have shown us. The chief of these is that his mental landscapes are large, elemental—conflicts. In *Les Proscrits*, in the (American) *Scarlet Letter*, people are against the community in which they live, solely because of their finding themselves in it. His people are trying to stand up against the storm, and the film resolves itself into whether, in face of the storm, they will bend or break, oak or willow. A slight cynicism limits their endeavour to these two alternatives. If you succeed, you compromise, with the corollary that if you compromise you don't succeed for long. You grow tired of that kind of success you are having.

In *The Tower of Lies*, a woman came back, "soiled," from the city. Where did she get those clothes? But though the home and the village and the community were against her, her old uncle (I think it was) had to be spared, She was his beautiful white queen, or something like it, and the myth he had of her must be kept. And it was this or nothing, But the village stormed and stormed, the storm grew; one could only bow to it—the girl left, went back to the city, and the old man, rushing down to the quay, following the boat with his eyes, and all of him in his eyes, ran over the end of the pier. He drowned, but the myth was kept. I am not sure if anyone told him the girl was a whore, but I am sure that if they did, he denied it. In any case, my point is illustrated. If he had discovered, he would have died of a broken heart. It wasn't, forgive me for saying as if I were a movie star being interviewed, death that mattered, but the keeping of an idea. So Swedish, I venture to think that here was a theme as universal as that of *Sunrise*, though when I saw the film under the title of *The Emperor of Portugalia* at the Film Society, it is true that I was not affected by the ending to anything but quiet laughter. It did not get away with it because the actual whole cumulation of the film had been *simplesse* instead of the intended simplicity to my perhaps more sophisticated mind. There is a certain *naïveté* about fundamentals in these Scandinavian films which is always a stumbling-block, but it should not be allowed to hide the terrific sincerity of their makers.

In the film which was generally released in London in October, there was Lillian Gish against *The Wind*. Against a destructive force. Against the type of life it produced, the type of men the life produced, and the woman she would be if she stayed, married to one of the men. The storm in her mind is produced by the storm of the wind. Inner and outer conflict, the outer in this case serving to throw up the inner. Like a chord or a subsidiary colour, an image. The wind is an image, the fields of snow are images, the roads and woods of *The Scarlet Letter* are images. Landscape is image in Seastrom.

All being set, consider then his imagery. But all being set, be careful not to jolt it. The landscape is not only a mauve to throw up a blue. It is a darker blue itself. It is of the same colour, it is the same mood, as that colour or mood it brings into prominence. What I said of *The Wind* shows this. Wind causes the psychological stress, but that stress is in terms of wind. It is in this, though it is used rationally, as psychological as Dr. Sachs showed the beetle to be in *Mother*, and *that* was used psychologically. Seastrom's landscapes *are* used psychologically, but they connect logically. They could never be mistaken for "visual subtitles" as the spring shots in *Mother* have been.

He achieves this by a very subtle adjustment between conception and execution. In the first place, he sees the wind, or some other element or surrounding, as responsible for the states of mind of his characters. BUT, the characters having been treated as influenced by these, these things in turn have to be treated to relate to the people's minds, in order to bring it all out. In order to express what they are, Seastrom makes them be something else. But they have to be themselves too. And because of this, because they are fact it is not always seen that they are image too. They have to partake of something of what they have caused for us to see that the results visible in the people were latent in them. In fact, "there is a blending of the two sets of images, the apparent and the real."

There is a scene in *The Scarlet Letter* where Hester and her lover are lying in a dell. "The feeling of threatened and short-lived peace so evident in this Seastrom landscape is built up by a number of small touches; rocks, sharp flags pricking up at the lovers, who are themselves at the edge of the water, and a background whose roots and undergrowth call to mind the conventions which have the lovers in their grasp" (Herring, *Films of the Year, 1927–1928*). That was thought fanciful at the time. We may have progressed since then, but in any case there is this instance from *The Wind*. Lars Hansen, who has married Gish, has tried to kiss her. She has registered loathing, after he has won, with a new and sudden expression that completely renovates the incident (Seastrom nearly always gets the unsuspected out of his casts.) He flings out of the room, and she, shut up, with the wind outside, starts pacing up and down. Hansen, outside, strides about. Gish is facing things and both are working something out. We only see the boards of the floor and the feet. But the boards seem to matter most. They are not quite alike, because they are run in different directions, the angle is different, so, through noticing this, we get the fact that they are both boards much more. They are there, impassively, while the feet walk about and work things out above them. Gish, of course, knows it can't go on much longer, she is, after all, married to the man, and the man is damned if he sees why it should go on much longer, since she is, after all, married to him, and what is marriage for? He took her in a mug of cocoa when she arrived. The cup lies on his floor. The hopes he had, the kindness he was prepared to pay her. Here, drink this, I made it myself. The cup lies on the floor. Of course, he kicks it. The alternating rhythms on the still floor are broken. The act follows the mental decision and preparation for what he has decided. He goes into her room, through a door, onto another set of boards. We scarcely notice that he has left his room, because the continuity of the action has been set up in our minds by the boards. The feet meet, Gish's draw back. Well, how important the floor has been.

I mentioned the intimacy of Seastrom in home scenes. The birth of the calf was not good in *The Tower of Lies*, but in this newer film, Gish is at work with the people she lives with, and the woman is ripping a carcass. Everyday stuff. But watch the way Gish draws her skirts as she passes the carcass to fetch an iron. You find that for the first time in weeks at a London cinema, you have a state of mind pure before you. Gish, of course, moves beautifully, even under Fred Niblo's direction in *The Enemy*, and Seastrom, of course, understands motion and the waves of motion, notice the way the dance stopped, and the floor emptied and the people swept down to the cellar in *The Wind*, while one or two waited on the empty floor busy barricading the door and the typhoon hung over the town outside—to return, more or less literally, to the mutton; when the children came home, they ran to Gish, and the mother was left with blood on her hands and the knife; she put it down but it made no difference. The children were instinctively repelled, and no one knew it but she and them. When her husband came home, she smeared the blood away, but he greeted Gish over his wife's shoulder, and she was jealous, and the carcass hung there. She could not help having to slice and scrape it. But the children turned from her, from the blood and knife part of her.

Very simple. Three images and only small incidents. They were allowed to be small, they were not in the least Germanic, not Lupu-Pick-*Wild Duck*-ish. They were not piled up till by their accumulation they became significant, as do the incidents in Czinner films. They were rather the turning over of the whole which reveals these facets as it turns. You tell a whale by the water it spurts, yet there is water all round. It isn't the whale that makes Whale evident, but the water it has taken in from the surroundings and then spurts up.

When Gish is alone in the house, there is another instance of the peculiarly simple and potent use Seastrom makes of his imagery. Turning it over as if he were looking at it and would be very surprised but quite pleased if you noticed it too. The wind comes. It breaks a window pane. She stuffs a coat in. She makes things fast. The shelves sway. A lamp is knocked over, it sets fire to the tablecloth. These are little things, results of the wind. To put it out she has to take the coat out of the pane. Then the wind comes in again. All this is actual, but it is one of those rare occasions when actual representation gives us state of mind more clearly than purely psychological interpretation would. Tricks, dissolves, all that. Here, we follow her, we run around, doing hopelessly small things against the wind, wondering how long it will be before the shelves fall, wishing the dog would stop barking, till we are terribly in the girl's state of mind. But in *Manhattan Cocktail*, a nice light film, a girl is told that 5,000 dollars will bail her young lover out. She walks down the street and, of course, sees everything in terms of that sum. It beats in on her brain. Dorothy Arzner, usually intelligent, uses tricks so that the figures swim before her eyes. This is all right once, but we do not want them to merge on every fur coat, every pearl collar she passes. We are there before, that is it. Seastrom knows this, and the windstorm is done by actuality, the room just sways a bit, that is all. At the same time, since this is not an appreciation of Seastrom, he is never very interested in tricks. There was good technique in *Charrette Fantôme*, but *The Divine Woman* shows very little use of recent improvements, which I use deliberately, because if you have a firm conception, *truquages* will not hurt it, and it is foolish not to avail yourself of anything that will get you there most cleanly. Now, Seastrom uses old tricks, but not new ones. Now he is quite capable of outdated clumsy visions in *The Divine Woman* and emphasises the new lover treading on the cap of a former that has fallen to the floor. In *The Wind*, Gish was against Nature. In *The Divine Woman*, what is Garbo against? Her own nature? You have to consider. It is true that you see most of a Swedish film after you have seen it. You see then something different, something underlying. Whereas in Eisenstein or Preobrashenskaja, you see more intensely. You hold in your hand what you had grasped before with the Russians. The first thing that you get from consideration of *The Divine Woman* is cynicism. At first it has seemed an ordinary film (and it never becomes a very extraordinary one) of a girl who loved a soldier, became an actress; became the mistress of a producer to go on being an actress; and gave up being both in order to settle down with the soldier. But simply because Seastrom has earned respect, you look more closely, and that rewards you. For one thing, there is the shape, as I tried to show in giving the plot. Then, the way the girl got what she wanted, and, as the action swung between actress and love, the director's emphasis swung between "divine" and "woman." Was it by mistake that the divinity was so very tinsel? Then again, it was remarkable that for once Seastrom was so little occupied with his background. The stage, furs, flowers, receptions . . . you would have thought all this would have been seized on. God knows, it has been often enough.

Well, the furs and the chrysanthemums are there, but they're not insisted on, not even stressed dramatically, certainly not relished visually. They ARE background. Miss Arzner brings her backstages to life, but here Seastrom suddenly concentrates on the woman. He concentrates on the effect of the furs and flowers on the woman. In his old habit, but it is not in his habit to show only the woman. I do not think this is because the woman is Garbo, a star, because Garbo is handled much less as a star than she has been in America. He is not too impressed by her importance or her beauty, which is good for all of us, and Garbo becomes amusing, and gets laughs as a laundry-girl and does Bébé Daniels' stuff. None of this is because this is a picture Seastrom did not bother about. When the great actress breaks down she cries, "I can't go on. Oh, God, I'm done for. I hate it all!" And in all the numbers of times we have seen an actress break down on the screen, we have never heard one say quite this. It may not have been Seastrom's, but the way it fitted into the spirit of the picture, and the fact that there was a spirit, was Seastrom's. A logical sequence; consider the placing of the "I hate it all," at the end. Realising *why* she is done for. One is done for if one hates it. Swedish and Seastrom. The best things in life are free; that is flung at us in most films, what would Queen Pickford have had for a motto without it? But here they are free, they are the best because one has paid for the worse things.

The director felt cramped with this story and its setting, especially, why not? the setting. So he took the most elemental thing, the woman, and did what he could. I have dealt with it like this, because it will be possible to see it in England (think of that!), and it may seem a contradiction of what I said about landscape and background.

Naturally, there is not very much imagery in it. Plenty of symbols. The most clear image is the soldier's cap, which runs through. It is through his first dropping it that he met Garbo, and when he is arrested it is left behind. It is an image, different from the clothes he steals for her while she is trying on better ones at the theatre. There are more symbols than images because the film progresses dramatically, but the use of the cap has interest, because as an image it links past and present, and the past scenes in a film are the horizon. The cup in *The Wind* did the same. It was on the floor from another scene, which it led back to. It took the place of that scene and held it visible while another one went on. Seastrom's images do this. They carry on. They represent the whole while a larger part of it than themselves is filling the attention. Stones in the foreground, rolled down from the rocks at the back. They show the scale, and however dramatically important, they remain in themselves small. His imagery rarely has close-ups. It has to be looked for. It is part of the atmosphere, the unemphasised, limpid, clear air we breathe, whose effects we feel after. There is nothing startling about it. It is either the whole background, or a feature in the foreground that relates back to it.

His films progress dramatically, which is the thing that prevents him from ranking among the few. The thing that prevents Swedish films from being, save in part, among the few great films. Seastrom's outlook is primarily dramatic. Swedish films are primarily dramatic. Their use, and the use they make, of stories shows this. "Leur films restent des contes populaires auxquels le metteur en scène a communiqué une part d'émotion personelle et assez largement humaine pour que nous ne la subission pas impunemént. Une telle formule ne repond, certes, pas aux fins vraies et idéales du cinéma, mais elle n'en est pas moins une des premières formules *complètes*" (Moussinac; *Naissance du Cinéma.*) [Spelling as in original.]

But it is because they are Swedish that they have "atteint à un lyrisme large, inconnu jusqu'alors a l'écran, si ce n'est pas dans quelques films d'Ince: calme tragique, sérénité noble et puissante de quelques scènes . . . des *Proscrits* . . . Je ne sais rien de comparable a l'intimité de leurs intérieurs 'reconstitués' avec une simplicité étonnante. Il n'y a presque rien et tout y est . . . Ils ne craignent pas d'éliminer impitoyablement tout ce qui pourrait encombrer l'action et nuirait à l'ensemble."

This lyricism, this force of "nuances du sentiment exteriorisé par une geste ou la lumière d'un regard," this broad landscape, these torrents that sting so, this air that cuts—all this make up their gift to the screen, bringing these things to us as they are, giving them their importance. The Swedish cinema may not be true, pure cinema; but the cinema there is in them is pure, and their own, which is why they breathe a nobility unlike any other films' nobility—the spectacle, to quote Freud, "that men can offer when in the face of an elemental catastrophe they awake from their muddle and confusion, forget all their internal difficulties and animosities, and remember the great common task, the preservation of mankind against the supremacy of nature."

Appendix C
Biographical Summaries

Ernst Lubitsch

Lubitsch was born in Berlin on 28 January 1892. His father owned a small clothing store, and though the young Lubitsch, like Murnau, displayed an early interest in the theater, he was made to enter the family business when he left school at the age of sixteen. He persisted with his acting ambitions, however, and was accepted into the Max Reinhardt company in 1911. He worked there for seven years, usually in relatively minor comic roles, and combined this with first acting in, then writing and directing, comic films that often had their setting in the Jewish garment business of his own childhood. The most successful of these starred the actress Ossi Oswalda.

His first dramatic feature, *Die Augen der Mumie Ma* (1918), starred the Polish actress Pola Negri, who had also worked for the Reinhardt company. She later starred in *Carmen* (1918) and *Madame Dubarry* (1919) which, under the title *Passion,* was the first German film to be shown in the United States after the war, breaching the official blockade that had been imposed on their importation. Its success was followed up, though not to the same extent, by *Sumurn* (*One Arabian Night,* 1920) and *Anna Boleyn* (*Deception,* 1920). Meanwhile Lubitsch continued to make such comedies as *Die Austernprinzessin* (*The Oyster Princess,* 1919) and *Die Bergkatze* (*The Mountain Cat,* 1921), though these, unlike his costume films, were rarely acquired for U.S. distribution. In 1921 he formed the EFA production company, in association with Adolph Zukor's Famous Players Corporation, and visited the United States at the end of that year to discuss the possibility of making a film there. Though he received a friendly reception in most quarters, some hostile letters and phone calls led him to return to Germany earlier than he had planned. When Famous Players withdrew from EFA in 1922, they offered Lubitsch a contract to work in America; but when he went there in December 1922, it was specifically at the invitation of Mary Pickford, and he directed her in *Rosita* in 1923.

His contract with Famous Players (who had loaned him to Pickford) was cancelled by mutual agreement in June 1923, and plans to make another film with Pickford came to nothing. He signed instead a four-year contract with Warner Brothers, and his first film for them, *The Marriage Circle* (1924), established him as a master of the sophisticated sexual comedy with which he was to be primarily associated for the remainder of his career. Other films for Warners included *Lady Windermere's Fan* (1925) and *So This is Paris* (1926). By 1926 several companies were competing for his services and he finally signed for Paramount in 1928. He enjoyed considerable success there with his first sound films, *The Love Parade* (1929) and *Monte Carlo* (1930), both musical comedies that were stylish, witty, and technically innovative.

After a brief interlude as supervising director of Paramount's short-lived attempt to operate a studio on Long Island, Lubitsch returned to Hollywood, where he made the only serious drama of his later American career, *Broken Lullaby* (also known as *The Man I Killed* [1931]), which was a commercial failure. This was followed by a remake of *The Marriage Circle*, entitled *One Hour With You* (1932), starring Jeannette MacDonald and Maurice Chevalier. After signing a new contract with Paramount in March 1932, he made *Trouble in Paradise* (1932) and *Design for Living* (1933). In 1935 he was made head of production at Paramount, but he held this post for barely a year before returning to directing. After making *Angel* (1937) and *Bluebeard's Eighth Wife* (1938), he ended his association with Paramount, who were reportedly unhappy that his films for them had rarely been major commercial successes. Lubitsch then set up two independent production arrangements, out of which came such films as *Shop Around the Corner* (1940), *Ninotchka* (1939), and *To Be or Not to Be* (1942), before taking up a contract with 20th Century-Fox in 1942. He suffered a heart attack shortly after completing *Heaven Can Wait* (1943), but returned to work early in 1944, serving as producer on two other films as well as directing *Cluny Brown* (1946). While working on *That Lady in Ermine* (1947) he suffered another heart attack and died on 30 November 1947, at the age of fifty-five. The film was completed by Otto Preminger.

F. W. Murnau

Murnau was born Friedrich Wilhelm Plumpe in Bielefeld on 28 December 1888; he took the name Murnau at an early stage of an acting and theatrical career that was begun against his father's wishes. At the time of his birth his father was a prosperous manufacturer; but he later suffered business losses and the family had to adopt a more modest style of life. Murnau was fascinated by both literature and the stage from an early age and began to act in a Berlin theatre while he was studying philology at the university there. He later studied art history and literature at the University of Heidelberg, but seems not to have completed work for his degree at either institution. His acting brought him into contact with Max

Reinhardt, who offered him a place at his theater school, and he worked there until the outbreak of the First World War. During the war he served with distinction in both the infantry and the air force.

In 1919 he decided to go into filmmaking, along with several former colleagues from the Reinhardt school, and directed his first film, *Der Knabe in Blau*. As is the case with most of his early work, no prints of this film survive today, and the earliest of which a copy exists is *Der Gang in die Nacht* (1920). By 1924 he had established himself as one of the leading German directors and had built up fruitful working relationships with such regular collaborators as the scriptwriter Carl Mayer, the set designers Rochus Gliese, Robert Herlth and Walter Röhrig, and the cameraman Karl Freund. *Der Letzte Mann (The Last Laugh*, 1924) was his first major international success, and it brought him an invitation from the Fox Film Corporation to work in the United States. Before leaving for America in July 1926, he completed two other films in Germany, *Tartüff* (1925) and *Faust* (1926).

His first American film, *Sunrise*, was critically acclaimed, and achieved a moderate, though not spectacular, box-office success. No print of *4 Devils* (1928) is known to exist today, and *Our Daily Bread* was extensively tampered with by the studio, against Murnau's wishes, before being released under the title *City Girl* (1929). In an attempt to regain a degree of creative independence, Murnau went into partnership with the documentary film maker Robert Flaherty to finance and produce *Tabu* (1929), which was shot on location in the South Seas. A week before the New York premiere of the film, on 11 March 1931, Murnau was killed in a car accident. His body was transported to Berlin, and he was buried in Berlin at a service attended by, among others, Emil Jannings, Carl Mayer, Erich Pommer, and Fritz Lang.

Victor Sjöström

Sjöström was born on 20 September 1879 in the Swedish province of Värmland. When he was barely six months old, his father emigrated to America, and his mother followed him, with Victor and his sister, at the end of 1880. His mother had been an actress before her marriage, but during the early years in New York she had to take in lodgers to help make ends meet. Though Victor was very close to her as a child, he was separated from her when his father left her to move in with another woman (whom he later married) in 1886. Relations between Victor and this woman became so bad that he was eventually sent back to Sweden in 1893 to live with his aunt in Uppsala. Though the father had built up a prosperous business in New York, he eventually went bankrupt; and his actions and their consequences seem to have had a profound effect on his son.

While he was at school in Uppsala, Sjöström became interested first in the circus and then in the theater and began to involve himself in amateur theatrical productions. When his father returned to Sweden in 1895, Sjöström left school and went to live with his father and stepmother in Stockholm; but once again personal conflicts forced him to move out and live with friends instead. He worked for a time in a lumberyard, but on his father's death in May 1896, he felt free to pursue his theatrical ambitions on a more professional level. He managed to find work with a company that was about to make a tour of Finland, and spent the next sixteen years, until 1912, as a touring player, visiting almost every part of Sweden. In 1900 he married his first wife, the actress Alexandra Stjagoff, but they separated around 1906 and were divorced in 1912. His theatrical work during this period took him occasionally to such places as London and Berlin, and he visited relatives in America in 1905.

His theater work had come to involve direction as well as acting, including a very well-received production of *A Midsummer Night's Dream* in 1912. Though he was to continue making guest appearances on the stage until 1921, he transferred his main interest to the cinema when he joined the Svenska Bio company in the summer of 1913. He worked as much as an actor as a director in his early film career, both in his own films and in those of Stiller in particular, and was to appear in the leading roles of several of his own most important films, including *The Outlaw and His Wife* and *The Phantom Chariot*. Most of his early films are now lost, but those with which he began to build a substantial reputation in Europe, such as *Ingeborg Holm*, *A Man There Was*, and *The Outlaw and His Wife*, still survive. Further international success came with the series of adaptations of the work of Selma Lagerlöf, with whom he shared a common background in Värmland, and belated recognition came from America when *The Phantom Chariot* was released there in 1922.

Sjöström and his Swedish producers seem to have accepted the offer made by the Goldwyn Company in 1922 on a trial basis only, seeing it as a chance to make a distribution agreement with a major American company while giving Sjöström first-hand experience of American production methods. He settled down very well in America, however, and was content to stay there, though he never took part in Hollywood social life to any great extent, preferring the company of his family (he had since remarried) and such fellow Swedes as Lars Hanson and Greta Garbo. He achieved considerable success with his first American film, *Name the Man* (1924), and worked quite happily for what had then become MGM until problems over the release of *The Wind* in 1927–28 led him to believe that it was no longer possible to work in Hollywood with the creative freedom that he required. He completed two more films for MGM before leaving America for good in April 1930.

He devoted himself to both film and theater for the remainder of his life, but directed only two more films: *Markurells i Wadköping* (1930) in Sweden and *Under the Red Robe* (1936) in Britain. After that he worked solely as an actor, partly in films and notably in the role of the Professor in Bergman's *Wild Strawberries* (1957), and partly resuming the life of a touring actor in the provinces with which he had begun his theatrical career. He died on 3 January 1960 at the age of eighty.

Notes

Introduction

1. Two books that examine this process are Thomas J. Saunders, *Hollywood in Berlin: American Cinema and Weimar Germany* and Kristin Thompson, *Exporting Entertainment: America in the World Film Market.*

2. Original names: Sándor Korda, Mihály Kertész, and Pál Fejös.

3. Though I have isolated here three main periods of particularly significant foreign arrivals, there has always been a steady trickle of individual recruits to the Hollywood scene. British, Canadian, and Australian directors, unhampered by problems of language and coming from a somewhat similar cultural background, have perhaps enjoyed a greater overall success rate in the United States than European directors have. There are, of course, many exceptions.

4. Since the original publication of this book in 1985, Sabine Hake's *Passions and Deceptions: The Early Films of Ernst Lubitsch* (Princeton, N.J.: Princeton University Press, 1992) has appeared, offering a similarly positive assessment of many of these films. Her overall concerns, however, are rather different from mine.

Chapter 1

1. I have derived most of my historical information on this period from the following: Frederick Lewis Allen, *Only Yesterday;* Paul A. Carter, *The Twenties in America;* John Higham, *Strangers in the Land: Patterns of American Nativism, 1860–1925;* Richard Hofstadter, *The Age of Reform: From Bryan to F.D.R.;* William E. Leuchtenberg, *The Perils of Prosperity, 1914–1932;* Henry F. May, *The End of American Innocence: A Study of the First Years of Our Own Time, 1912–1917;* Lary May, *Screening Out the Past: The Birth of Mass Culture and the Motion Picture Industry;* Geoffrey Perrett, *America in the Twenties: A History.*

2. Higham, *Strangers in the Land,* 208–9.

3. Higham, *Strangers in the Land,* 230–31.

4. Higham, *Strangers in the Land,* 264–65, 278, 270, 308, 311.

5. Further evidence of hatred of foreigners and immigrants during this period is abundant. Carter in *The Twenties in America* claims that "bigotry and intolerance" were widespread in America during the decade, and not just in "backward" rural areas (102); he adds that "the First World War only interrupted and dampened, but by no

means extinguished, an American rhetoric of 'Nordic,' 'Aryan,' sometimes 'Anglo-Saxon' racial supremacy" (96). Henry May in *The End of American Innocence* speaks of "the storm of hatred that burst in 1917 and 1918 against the German-Americans, the race riots of 1919, the xenophobia of the early twenties" (350). Perrett in *America in the Twenties* describes the frequent calls for "100 percent Americanism" and talks of a "hatred of all things foreign [that] reached a pitch of viciousness" around 1920 (80–81). Hofstadter in *The Age of Reform* quotes an appalling tirade against the alleged vices of immigrants and the threats they posed to "American blood" and American civilization, which was published in 1914 but still carried considerable resonance a decade later; he adds that well-meaning attempts to integrate, educate, and benignly "Americanize" immigrants were unsuccessful during the 1920s (178–80).

6. Lary May, *Screening Out the* Past, 64, 65.
7. For more details see Saunders, *Hollywood in Berlin* and Kristin Thompson, *Exporting Entertainment.*
8. "Germans Shun Films from America," *MPW,* 9 August 1919, 799–800. For further information on American films' ultimately successful penetration of the German market, which continued throughout the remainder of the decade, see Saunders, *Hollywood in Berlin.*
9. "American Film Industry Has Cause to Fear Competition of Foreign Film Producers," *MPW,* 8 May 1920, 848.
10. "Paul Cromelin Is Welcomed Home at Luncheon and He Makes a Hit," *MPW,* 14 August 1920, 861.
11. "With Berlin Foreign Center; Famous Shuffling Directors," *Variety,* 25 November 1921, 44.
12. "The Ogre Who Proves to Be a Pigmy." *Photoplay,* June 1922, 55, 91–92.Not surprisingly, the same magazine commented wearily on Murnau's *Tartuffe* in October 1927: "Another of those artistic German pieces that isn't worth a dime . . . between the queer lighting and the wanderings of the actors this is plain bunk—not art."
13. "Close-ups and Long-Shots," *Photoplay,* November 1927, 27, and "An Open Letter to Erich von Stroheim," *Screenland,* March 1925, 15.
14. I realize this paragraph raises questions about the general critical awareness of directorial identity in the 1920s, and this subject will be examined toward the end of this chapter.
15. "The Screen Year in Review," *MPC,* September 1921, 24–25.
16. Lubitsch's films were not shown in America in the same order they were produced in Germany, and this may account in part for the disappointment with which critics who had been bowled over by *Passion* or *Deception* (for example) greeted the earlier and less accomplished *Eyes of the Mummy* when it finally reached them, doubtless assuming in many cases that this represented the director's latest work. Films released in America in the order *Passion, Deception, Gypsy Blood, One Arabian Night, The Eyes of the Mummy, The Loves of Pharaoh,* and *Montmartre* were originally produced (keeping the American titles) as *The Eyes of the Mummy* (1918),

Gypsy Blood (1918), *Passion*, (1919), *One Arabian Night* (1920), *Deception* (1920), *The Loves of Pharaoh* (1922), and *Montmartre* (1923). Of the many comedies interspersed between these, only *Die Puppe* (1919) seems to have reached the United States (as *The Doll*) and then not till 1928.

17. It is at present virtually impossible to carry out the detailed comparison of the German and American prints of these films which could confirm any suspicions that major alterations might have taken place: apart from the sheer difficulty of examining prints existing on two different continents (as would have to be the case with *One Arabian Night*), no major American archive possesses a print of *The Loves of Pharaoh*, and the most complete German print, in the Munich Film Museum, lacks at least one major sequence. No complete print of *Montmartre* is known to exist anywhere at present.

Chapter 2

1. As trade papers like *Variety* lost no opportunity to point out, the critical enthusiasm for German films was rarely matched by their box-office performance. When describing Lubitsch's abortive first visit to America, the author in the same article remarks about "the very slight effect [German films] have had on American conditions. Bookings of 'The Cabinet of Dr. Caligari' have been only $78,000 up to last week, and the comparative flop of 'Passion,' 'Deception,' 'The Golem,' and others has been commented on" ("German Director, Lubitsch, Regarded Unkindly, He Says," *Variety*, 3 February 1922, 48).

2. "German Director, Lubitsch, Regarded Unkindly, He Says," *Variety*, 3 February 1922, 48.

3. Both Gerald Mast in his discussion of Lubitsch in *The Comic Mind* and Leland Poague in *The Cinema of Ernst Lubitsch* neglect to mention the German comedies. Weinberg's comments on them in *The Lubitsch Touch* are vague and misleading and seem to rely on memories of viewings from several years previous.
The fullest discussion of them to date can be found in Hake's *Passions and Deceptions*, though her claim that films like *Die Austernprinzessin, Die Puppe*, and *Die Bergkatze* are "lesser-known comedies" that "have been largely ignored" itself ignores the sympathetic attention given them in the first edition of this book, several years before her own work appeared, while David Shipman, in *The Story of Cinema, Volume One* and elsewhere, had already championed such films as *Die Bergkatze*. Scott Eyman's more recent *Ernst Lubitsch: Laughter in Paradise* also comments favorably on several of the German comedies.

4. My concern in the original edition of this book to draw attention to the virtues of Lubitsch's German comedies—which had been largely overlooked by English-speaking critics at the time of writing—led me to be unduly harsh concerning some aspects of his historical and Oriental films. Viewings of restored versions of *One*

Arabian Night (Sumurun) at the 1999 Pordenone Silent Film Festival, and *Deception (Anna Boleyn)* at the 1999 Bologna *Cinema Ritrovato* festival have led me to modify my criticisms. *One Arabian Night* still seems to me to suffer—especially in contrast to Lubitsch's comedies of the period—from an inability to decide whether it is a grotesque comedy, a romantic melodrama, or a tragedy, shifting, alarmingly and without warning, from one mode to another throughout. The acting, especially that of Lubitsch himself in the role of a hunchback consumed by unrequited love for a dancing girl played by Pola Negri, is exaggerated well past the point of parody: his character is alternately ridiculous, pathetic, tragic, and heroic with no particular rationale or consistency, and the minor roles are similarly over played and poorly motivated. The sets and costumes, however, and some of the imagery—though conforming to the standard clichés of Orientalist iconography—often display considerable visual flair and imagination.

When seen in a beautifully restored and tinted print, *Deception* is even more visually spectacular, with lavishly detailed sets and costumes and—with the exception of Emil Jannings as Henry VIII—a much more subdued and convincing acting style. Though there is a certain amount of low comedy centered around Henry himself and the court jester, the main role of Anna is performed with considerable dignity by Henny Porten—an interesting choice on Lubitsch's part as this actress, then at the peak of her fame, was seen as the embodiment of middle-class German womanhood, dutiful, loyal, and devoted to the needs of her husband and family, and by no means a typical adulteress. She portrays Anna as a woman seduced by the idea of becoming queen, yet also innocent and trusting. Once she fails to produce a male heir, she sees herself being displaced in Henry's affections in exactly the same manner as she had ousted her predecessor and seeks comfort in a friendship—but not an affair—with one of the courtiers. She is arrested, tried, and condemned on false charges of adultery, extorted through torture of witnesses. Denied a last meeting with her child, she goes to her death, after an initial moment of fear and despair, with calm dignity.

5. See Robert Carringer and Barry Sabath, *Ernst Lubitsch: A Guide to References and Resources*, 58. In an interview given during his first visit to America, Lubitsch named *Die Puppe* as his own favorite among his films to date (Frederick James Smith, "The Photoplay in Stagnant Waters," *MPC*, April 1922, 34).

6. Piotrovskij, "Toward a Theory of Cine-Genres," in Herbert Eagle, ed.

7. Piotrovskij, "Toward a Theory of Cine-Genres," 140.

8. Piotrovskij, "Toward a Theory of Cine-Genres," 140.

9. Piotrovskij, "Toward a Theory of Cine-Genres," 141.

10. Piotrovskij, "Toward a Theory of Cine-Genres," 140.

11. In this chapter I discuss only films that I have actually seen. Most of Lubitsch's German feature-length films survive, as well as all the American films except *Kiss Me Again* (1925) and *The Patriot* (1928). According to Hake, "during the early teens, Lubitsch directed an average of five to eight one- and two-reelers per year,"

(38) most of which are now lost. Plot summaries of all Lubitsch's major films can be found in Carringer and Sabath's *Ernst Lubitsch*.

12. Though both Keaton and Lloyd often "change" in the course of their films, in the sense that they are much more competent at the end than they were at the beginning, this is more a matter of their discovering their own latent or true abilities than a fundamental alteration of values or outlook.

13. A phrase that was in use as early as 1923, even before Lubitsch had made such films as *The Marriage Circle* to which one would naturally expect it to be applied. Reviewing *Rosita*, the critic for *Exceptional Photoplays* commented: "As for direction, nowhere is the picture stamped with the Lubitsch touch as prominently as usual: still his hand is recognizable for the artistry that has made him world famous" (quoted in Anthony Slide, ed., *Selected Film Criticism* 1921–1930, 243).

14. *Variety*, 6 September, 1923, 22; *NYT*, 4 September 1923; *MPW*, 15 September 1923, 262; *MPW*, 15 December 1923, 632.

15. Lubitsch appears to have regarded the film somewhat in the light of a "calling card." Interviewed by Harry Carr for *MPC* while making *The Marriage Circle*, he said: "In my first picture, I had to make all kinds of concessions to what they told me the American people wanted. I made my first one that way. This one I am going to make to please Lubitsch" (*MPC*, February 1924, 38).

16. Carringer and Sabath, *Ernst Lubitsch*, 23.

17. For an interesting discussion of the DeMille "formula" see the chapter "Cecil B. DeMille and the Consumer Ideal" in Lary May's *Screening Out the Past*. In it he comments that "the formula was to take the desires projected onto foreign lovers and bring them into American culture" (209). In contrast to Lubitsch, however, DeMille's solution was that "foreign allures had to be safely integrated into the American family" (211).

18. In Freda Kirchwey, ed., *Our Changing Morality*, 249.

19. The review in *MPC*, May 1924, 48, makes this quite clear when it announced: "We hold the impression that Lubitsch displays a hidden talent, for heretofore he has been the sponsor of ponderous pictures." *MPW*, 16 February, 1924, 581, says that Lubitsch "has shown he is as much at home with an intimate domestic story as with the spectacular and heavily dramatic"—implying that he had not given evidence of this before.

   Similar misconceptions persisted as late as 1980 when Dwight Macdonald, in a review essay of recent books on Buster Keaton (*New York Review of Books*, 9 October 1980, 33), claimed that Lubitsch was "inspired" by *A Woman of Paris* to abandon historical drama and take up comedy instead. See also David Shipman's response to this in the issue of 2 April 1981, 44.

20. Two examples are the opening shots of *A Sailor-Made Man* and *Safety Last*.

21. Already a Lubitsch trademark. Mary Pickford is reported to have complained that he was more interested in directing doors than in directing people. One might, however, set against this widely retailed comment Marie Prevost's much more favorable

assessment, from the *MPC* interview already cited: "I never realized what acting really meant until I began to hear Mr. Lubitsch's voice coming to me from behind the camera. He deals in subtleties that I never dreamed of before. His marvelous technique consists of elements and effects that I never heard of before. At first it was terribly discouraging. He made me do simple scenes—just coming in and out of rooms—fifteen or twenty times. At first it seemed as tho there wasn't any sense to it at all. Then it began to dawn upon me what the art of acting was all about, and it seemed intolerably and impossibly difficult. Then I began to see as he saw it. He is a tremendous and wonderful artist. To act even one scene under his direction is not only an education but a revelation" (February 1924, 80).

22. Carringer and Sabath give a summary of the film that they say is taken from the press book deposited at the Library of Congress; the print they saw is incomplete. The print that I saw (at the George Eastman House) also lacked some scenes, but it differs in some significant aspects from the plot as Carringer and Sabath describe it and is closer to the outline summary given in *MPW*'s review. My own synopsis of the film as I saw it is as follows: The Czarina of a small European country is flirtatious and sophisticated. Alexei, a young officer, learns that some of his fellow soldiers are planning a rebellion; he sets off to warn the Czarina, but is thrown from his horse. He is offered a ride in a motor car by a foreign ambassador, but when the visitors stop at an inn and are sidetracked into watching some gypsy dancers, he appropriates the car and continues his journey. He has to force his way past the skeptical Chamberlain into the Czarina's presence; she treats his warning lightly, but is attracted by his handsome appearance, and when the Ambassador arrives, he is kept waiting till her *tête-à-tête* with Alexei is over. The conspiracy is suppressed and Alexei is promoted; his infatuation with the Czarina leads him to neglect his sweetheart Anna, who is one of the ladies-in-waiting. The Czarina publicly distinguishes him as her current favorite and awards him the Star given to all her lovers. When Alexei sees several other officers wearing the same Star, he is jealous and indignant; he defends his ruler's honor in a duel and tells the Czarina that he will arrest those have maligned her. When she ridicules this suggestion he becomes disillusioned and involves himself in a new conspiracy against her. The rebellion appears to have succeeded and the Czarina is at his mercy in the deserted palace; Alexei gloats over her helplessness, threatens her, and forces he to kneel before him. Meanwhile the cynical Chamberlain has bought off the leaders of the revolt and when the "rebels" arrive in the palace they proclaim their loyalty to the Czarina, and Alexei is arrested. She offers to pardon him if he will become her lover again; he spurns her and says he would prefer to be hanged. Nevertheless she does pardon him, knowing that he will return to Anna. The Czarina appears heartbroken, but when the Ambassador returns for an audience she starts to flirt with him. When the Ambassador leaves her presence, he is wearing a Star.

23. *Variety,* 5 August 1925, 31.

24. The film is based on a French play from the late nineteenth century, but the pattern established by *The Marriage Circle* remained pervasive throughout the remainder of

Lubitsch's career. He even remade the film as *One Hour with You* in 1932, just as *Kiss Me Again* was remade as *That Uncertain Feeling* in 1941. The implications of this reworking of the same material are interesting, but beyond the scope of this study.

25. Lubitsch was to develop this device more extensively in his sound films, most notably in the opening to *Trouble in Paradise*.

26. These complex negotiations are summarized in Carringer and Sabath, *Ernst Lubitsch*, 7–8. Eyman, in *Ernst Lubitsch: Laughter in Paradise*, states that "Lubitsch's series of pictures for Warner Bros. had been profitable, but not by much" (117) and quotes from some rather irritable telegrams exchanged between Jack and Harry Warner and Lubitsch himself at this stage, with Harry claiming that "[Lubitsch's] pictures ARE OVER PEOPLE'S HEADS HERE KISS ME AGAIN TAKEN OFF WHEREVER PLAYED AFTER THREE DAYS" (116) and Lubitsch complaining that he had not been given the chance to make "BIG PICTURES" and that the Warners had only themselves to blame that his talents had been wasted as a result.

27. The most whole-hearted favorable review seems to have been from Welford Beaton in the *Film Spectator*. His review is quoted in full in Slide, *Selected Film Criticism 1921–1930*, 278–80. The film is sometimes given the title *The Student Prince in Old Heidelberg*, or simply *In Old Heidelberg*.

28. The highly laudatory review by Richard Watts, Jr., in *The Film Mercury* is quoted in Slide, *Selected Film Criticism*, 219–21.

29. Though there was no dialogue, synchronized sound effects and a music score had been added to the print reviewed by *Variety*.

30. The phrase in quotation marks is taken from the press sheet for the film, quoted in Carringer and Sabath, 97.

31. The kind of "BIG PICTURE," presumably, that he had reproached Warners for not allowing him to make.

32. Although I have concentrated in this chapter on American responses to Lubitsch's work, it is interesting to note the comments by German critics on his American films, which are given in some detail by Saunders in *Hollywood in Berlin*. To summarize very briefly: *The Marriage Circle* was welcomed by one major critic as "one of the . . . most un-American films ever created" and an encouraging sign that Lubitsch's "German artistic personality is strong enough not to let himself be 'Americanized' and conform to his new home" (203). He was also praised for combining the subtlety and refinement of the German chamber drama with the American knack for popular subjects (204). While *Three Women* was felt to be too much of a compromise with American taste, *Kiss Me Again* was thought to combine once again the best of the European and American traditions and to have retained a degree of subtlety and refinement that was "German" rather than "American" (206). By 1926, however, critics like Georg Mendel were accusing him of having become too American (207) and a final verdict seemed to be that "only *The Marriage Circle* demonstrated constructive American input—the remainder showed America's standardizing influence" (208).

Chapter 3

1. Some typical responses to *Faust* were as follows: "Splendidly pictorial version of Goethe's immortal story" (*MPW*, 11 December 1926, 440); "From the standpoint of taste and photographic brilliance it is doubtful whether there has ever been a production that surpassed it" [*Variety*, 17 November 1926, 16]; "If 'Faust' isn't a 'Last Laugh' then it's the next thing to it. . . . It's a corking picture that holds tension from start to finish. . . . One of the best that Germany has sent over" (*Variety*, 8 December 1926, 16); "Here is a picture which is as far removed from the ordinary movie as a Tintoretto painting. It flashes along, it is true. It inspires with its wealth of imagination, its shadows and soft lights, its astounding camera feats and its admirable portrayals. If any picture is calculated to lift the abused screen out of a rut, it is this radiant jewel" (*NYT*, 9 December 1926).
2. *Variety*, 27 July 1927, 16; *MPW*, 3 September 1927, 50; *NYT*, 25 July 1927.
3. The connection is discussed by Thomas Elsaesser in "Secret Affinities," 35–36, as well as by many other critics.
4. Janet Bergstrom, "Sexuality at a Loss: The Films of F. W. Murnau," 188. The quotations from *Hollywood in Berlin* given in note 32 of chapter 2 also indicate that German critics saw their national cinema as having a stronger artistic tradition than the American one. In chapter 6 of her *Cinema and Painting*, Angela Dalle Vacche discusses in detail Murnau's links with and use of German Romantic painting.
5. *Phantom* was noted briefly—and unfavorably—by Variety in a report from Berlin dated 7 December 1922: "All the old junk from the picture attic is present . . . technically, in casting, direction, and photography, the film is not up to the standard of those made 10 years ago in America. . . . The direction of F. W. Murnau is without ideas." Noting that the film was popular in Germany, probably because it touched "some vague type of sentimentality," it added sourly that it hoped no one would be "so stupid as to waste any time trying to sell it to America" (*Variety*, 6 January 1923, 43). Apparently nobody was.
6. "The Ideal Picture Needs No Titles," *Theatre Magazine*, January 1928, 72.
7. "Films of the Future," *McCall's Magazine*, September 1928, 90.
8. "F. W. Murnau Comes to America. The German Genius of the Films Talks of Movies and Men," *MPC*, October 1926, 16.
9. For those who wish them, nevertheless, plot summaries of these films are given in Lotte Eisner's *Murnau*.
10. The word was in general use at the period, though it can cause confusion for modern readers. An interesting contemporary explanation of the use of subtitles, for both aesthetic and pragmatic effect, can be found in "Motion Picture Sub-Titles," *MPW*, (8 June 1928, 1415).
11. Asked about that film by Matthew Josephson, Murnau replied tactfully: "It was frankly an experiment. It was *aufregend* (stimulating), aroused wider interest in motion pictures, showed what might be done" (*MPC*, October 1926, 84).
12. The stills in Eisner's *Murnau* collect some of these images (112–13).

13. My comments on the film are based throughout on the "definitive" version prepared by Enno Patalas for the Munich Film Museum.

14. An account of how some of these sequences were set up is given in Eisner, *Murnau*, 99–100.

15. A similarly strange coexistence of a traditional "timeless" village setting and an ultra-modern city just across the lake is found later in *Sunrise*.

16. A re-viewing of *Der Gang in die Nacht* at Bologna in 1999 leads me to modify somewhat my dismissal of it as a "stilted melodrama." Though the convoluted plot and much of the acting could be characterized as "melodramatic" in the pejorative sense, the pervasive imagery of the natural world—especially of storm-tossed seas and windswept headlands—and the linking of this with the emotions of the characters, provides a strong link with such later works as *Sunrise* and *Tabu*. Much of the action takes place out of doors, on cliff tops and at the seaside, and the most strongly dramatic scene of the film, as Egil, the doctor, waits to see if his cure of the painter's blindness has been successful and Lily dances seductively and passionately before him, is intercut with shots of stormy seas and windswept clouds, followed by shots of a calm sea as the painter recovers his sight. When Egil realizes that Lily is leaving him for the painter, his emotions are externalized in more scenes of stormy weather. Imagery of light and darkness is also found throughout, often in strikingly dramatic contrasts, as in the scene where the painter recovers his sight, in which shafts of light dominate ("You gave him light," Lily tells Egil later). When, however, the cure proves to be only temporary, the final confrontations take place in near darkness. Accepting his fate, the painter stoically writes a note to Egil: "We are all guilty. I return to my night. Don't condemn yourself. You gave me light." An interesting visual parallel between the two men is seen in virtually identical shots of the painter's initial arrival, standing upright in a small boat, and a later scene in which Egil, just before he realizes that he has been abandoned by Lily, returns from a visit to town in exactly the same manner.

17. *MPW*, 7 February 1925, 555.

18. *MPC*, October 1926, 84.

19. Although Murnau was justified in claiming in the interview for *McCall's Magazine* that the meaning of *The Last Laugh* was perfectly clear even without titles, it is my experience that spectators (not least myself) are often puzzled as to the identity of the elderly lady who brings the meal at this point: she seems to be the character called "his aunt" in the credits that Eisner gives for the film, but whom she refers to as "a neighbor" in her text.

20. Though he is credited with the script, Mayer did not in fact accompany him.

21. "Murnau's Trip to Hollywood," *MPC*, July 1927, 36–37, 74, 86. Detailed discussions of the circumstances of the film's making and reception can be found in Robert C. Allen, "William Fox Presents 'Sunrise,'" and Dudley Andrew, "The Gravity of 'Sunrise.'"

22. *MPC*, October 1926, 84.

23. *McCall's Magazine*, September 1928, 27.

24. As John Cawelti points out in *Adventure, Mystery, and Romance*, these include some of the staple ideas of the American melodramatic tradition and can be traced through much popular culture of the nineteenth and early twentieth centuries.

25. *McCall's Magazine*, September 1928, 90.

26. *Theatre Magazine*, January 1928, 41, 72.

27. "Murnau, for a matter of fact, has composed a complete musical score for the Sundermann-inspired picture. This will be orchestrated by some more technical and more musicianly educated composer" (*MPC*, July 1927, 74).

28. *MPC*, July 1927, 73.

29. *Film Spectator*, 24 December 1927, 4–5. Though this particular quotation may not make the point immediately evident, Beaton was in fact one of the most shrewd and interesting reviewers of the period, running and writing, virtually single-handed, what was essentially a full trade paper, for several years. Other critical responses, both favorable and unfavorable, are given in Steven N. Lipkin, "'Sunrise': A Film Meets Its Public." German critics quoted in Saunders, *Hollywood in Berlin* (214, 218) seem to have had mixed reactions to the film, though an Austrian critic quoted by Lipkin was ecstatic: "the symphonic welding together of the advantages of American and European films. The final fulfillment of the dream of film perfection" (352).

30. *Theatre Magazine*, January 1928, 72.

31. *McCall's Magazine*, September 1928, 90.

32. The title is written this way in most contemporary reviews.

33. *MPC*, October 1926, 17.

34. A synopsis of the film can also be found in Frank Thompson, *Lost Films: Important Movies that Disappeared*.

35. *NYT*, 7 October 1928.

36. *Variety*, 10 October 1928, 15. This is from a review of the sound version of the film.

37. For a discussion of these problems in relation to Paul Fejös's *Lonesome*, see p. 181 in this volume.

38. My comments are based on the print of *City Girl* held by the Museum of Modern Art in New York.

39. Even John and Mary, in King Vidor's contemporaneous (and relatively "realistic" and "un-Hollywood") *The Crowd* (1929), decide to get married after their first date.

40. See Eisner's account of the making of the film in *Murnau*, 207–18.

41. The ideology of the *films* need not always, in this case, reflect the ideology of the *man:* as a homosexual, Murnau may not necessarily have shared the enthusiasm for the married heterosexual couple or the nuclear family that is found throughout his films. Nevertheless the films present both—powerfully and movingly—in a favorable light (with the exception, chiefly, of the patriarch in *City Girl* before his change of heart).

42. Bergstrom, "Sexuality at a Loss," 202.

Chapter 4

1.   "The Saga of Sjöström," *The Picturegoer,* April 1922, 12–13, 56. Like almost all other interviewers, this one commented, somewhat despairingly, on Sjöström's shy and reticent personality and his obvious dislike of being interviewed.
2.   See especially the letter quoted in Bengt Forslund, *Victor Sjöström: His Life and His Work,* 119–20.
3.   Also known as *The Phantom Carriage, The Stroke of Midnight,* and *Thy Soul Shall Bear Witness.* Few other Sjöström films had been shown in the United States: they included *The Girl from the Marsh Croft* (made in 1917 and shown in the United States in 1919); *A Man There Was* (made in 1916 and shown in 1920); and *The Outlaw and His Wife* (made in 1917 and shown, with an added Prologue and Epilogue and under the title of *You and I,* in 1921). In contrast, Sjöström's films from *Ingeborg Holm* onwards had been remarkably successful in Europe and Britain.
4.   Bengt Idestam-Almquist, "Origin of the Swedish Cinema," 11.
5.   Hans Pensel's filmography of Sjöström in *Seastrom and Stiller in Hollywood* lists forty-four Swedish titles. I saw eleven of these, which I was told represented virtually all the surviving work, on a visit to the Swedish Film Institute in Stockholm in 1977. John Gillett's article "Swedish Retrospective," 152–53, mentions one film, *Cloisters of Sendomir* (1920), that I have not seen, and a reviewer (Jack Lodge) of the original edition of this book pointed out that an early Sjöström film, *Sea Vultures,* was shown at the London Film Festival in 1981. Forslund (36–37) gives a description of Sjöström's first film as director, *The Gardener* (1912), based on an English-language version called *The Broken Spring Rose* held by the Library of Congress. Almost all the lost Swedish films date from the period before 1916; everything after *Terje Vigen* survives, with the apparent exception of Sjöström's last Swedish film, *Det Omringade Huset* (1922).
6.   On the other hand, Elsaesser in "Secret Affinities" sees an influence of Scandinavian cinema in Murnau's use of locations in his German films, especially *Nosferatu.*
7.   From the English-language summary appended to Idestam-Almquist's *När Filmen Kom Till Sverige,* 583–609. The quotations are from pages 595–96.
8.   Pensel lists it as his ninth film overall.
9.   Idestam-Almquist, *När Filmen Kom Till Sverige,* 606.
10. Idestam-Almquist, *När Filmen Kom Till Sverige,* 606.
11. Gösta Werner, *Dens Svenska Filmens Historia,* quoted in the Museum of Modern Art's program notes for its showing of *Terje Vigen* (3 and 6 February 1977).
12. The story is told by Idestam-Almquist in *När Filmen Kom Till Sverige,* 608, and rather more elaborately in his chapter of *Classics of the Swedish Cinema* called "Victor Sjöström and his 'Conversion.'"
13. Pensel, *Seastrom and Stiller in Hollywood,* 21.
14. Idestam-Almquist, *Classics of the Swedish Cinema,* 42–43.

15. The American-made *The Tower of Lies* was based on a Lagerlöf novel.

16. This becomes very clear when the plot summary given in the *Variety* review (9 June 1922) is compared with the events of the original film. The reviewer's complaint about the arbitrariness of the happy ending becomes much more understandable when, instead of seeing a David Holm brought into constant contact with his past misdeeds and their consequences throughout the film, the audience simply sees an unregenerate brute who is miraculously reformed after a brief ride in a ghostly carriage.

17. To (perhaps) clarify the various possibilities: (1) If David is merely unconscious, not dead, why do we (and Sister Edit) see his spirit? (2) If it is all a dream, how can we account for Sister Edit seeing David's spirit and dying happy as a result, and why does his dream tell him so accurately what his wife is doing? (3) If it is all the product of supernatural intervention, with time standing still while David comes to terms with his past life, why do some aspects of time still progress in the meantime, and why are some of the consequences of this irreversible and some not?

18. Idestam-Almquist in *När Filmen Kom Till Sverige* suggests that such an attempt was doomed to failure in any case in the face of American film companies' determination to establish a stranglehold over film distribution in Europe (609).

19. The sinking itself was apparently unscheduled and not provided for in the script. The ending, as filmed, was not that originally envisaged by Sjöström either.

20. See Forslund, *Victor Sjöström*, 125–26. His name had already been anglicized to Seastrom for the credits of *The Stroke of Midnight*, but I will continue to use the original Swedish name throughout.

21. Forslund, 127.

22. Despite this provision, however, *Name the Man* was substantially shortened by June Mathias before its release.

23. Forslund in *Victor Sjöström* makes an explicit parallel with Lagerlöf's work: "Like her stories, it deals with conflicts of conscience and the misery of young girls when they get pregnant against their will. As in Lagerlöf's fiction also, the men are often careless charmers or seducers or cruel alcoholics, while the women are pure, innocent and strong" (179).

24. A film that Sjöström named as the finest he had seen since coming to America; see the interview with Jim Tully cited above.

25. *Variety*, 17 January 1924, 26.

26. *MPC*, April 1924, 17–18, 85.

27. Forslund, *Victor Sjöström*, 182.

28. Forslund, *Victor Sjöström*, 189.

29. Paul introduces yet another overtly masochistic element into his performance in a routine that has him trying to climb on to Consuelo and Bezano's horse as they ride together; he falls off, and is dragged along behind them while clutching the horse's tail.

30. Not into a shot of the circus ring, as Pensel in *Seastrom and Stiller in Hollywood* describes it (33). This comes later.

31. *NYT*, 10 November 1924. Pensel quotes this same review, but very inaccurately, in *Seastorm and Stiller in Hollywood*, 35.

32. The script was written by Frances Marion (though Sjöström certainly had a hand in it too). Her original continuity was published in Frances Taylor Paterson, *Motion Picture Continuities*. The film follows this script very closely in such matters as the ordering of events and the concept of the characters (Patterson stresses that the role of Hester was written to suit Lillian Gish's screen personality); but the visual elements that give the film its real distinction are nowhere provided for in the script and must have been developed by Sjöström during shooting.

33. Louis B. Mayer and Irving Thalberg were so pleased with the film that Sjöström was awarded double the normal five-thousand-dollar bonus on its completion.

34. Pensel, *Seastrom and Stiller in Hollywood*, 40.

35. A synopsis is given in Frank Thompson's *Lost Films*, 210–17.

36. She had also been responsible for his being hired as director on *The Scarlet Letter*: "Irving [Thalberg] asked me which director I would like, and I suggested Victor Seastrom. He had come from Sweden a few years earlier and I had admired his work since seeing his *Stroke at* [sic] *Midnight.*" (Lillian Gish, *The Movies, Mr. Griffith, and Me*, 286). In Albert Bigelow Paine's biography of her, *Life and Lillian Gish*, she paid glowing tribute to Sjöström as a director:

    He got the spirit of the story [The Scarlet Letter] *exactly, and was himself a fine actor, the finest that ever directed me. I never worked with anyone I liked better than Seastrom. He was Scandinavian—thorough and prompt. If Mr. Seastrom said we would start at eight, or half-past, the camera was ready at that time, and so were we.*

    His direction was a great education for me. In a sense, I went through the Swedish school of acting. . . . The Italian school is one of elaboration; the Swedish is one of repression. Mr. Vidor's method—of the American school, if there is such a thing—leaned to self-expression, which has its advantages. (225)

37. Gish, *The Movies*, 292. In Paine's biography (which also offers a vivid picture of the problems involved in trying to shoot and develop film at a temperature of 120 degrees in the shade), she says much the same thing, but with a touch of bitterness: "It was the very worst experience I ever went through. Temperature 120 in the shade. In the sun . . . ? One man burned his hand quite badly opening the door of a motor. We had eight wind machines, and in the studio, to match up with the blowing sand outside (supposed to be blowing in the doors and windows), we used sulphur pots, the smoke giving the effect of sand blowing in. The sand itself was bad enough, but the pots were worse. I was burned all the time, and was in danger of having my eyes put out. The hardships of making *Way Down East* were nothing to it. My hair was burned and nearly ruined by the sulphur smoke. I could not get it clean for months. Such an experience is not justified by any picture" (239).

38. A restored print of the film was included recently in the admirable Thames Silents series of reissues of classic and neglected silent films and this has helped considerably to confirm its status as one of the major works of its period.
39. The film was released earlier, in 1927, in Europe and received a much better reception there.
40. *Film Spectator,* 1 June 1929, 7.
41. *Variety,* 7 November 1928, 15; *MPC,* January 1929; *NYT,* 5 November 1928.
42. Herring, "Film Imagery: Seastrom," *Close-Up* 4, no. 1, 1929.
43. *MPC,* February 1929, 53; *NYT,* 27 November 1928; *Variety,* 28 November 1928, 15; *Photoplay,* December 1928, 54; *Film Weekly,* 23 December 1929, 24.
44. MGM, however, apparently expected him to return. Forslund in *Victor Sjöström* quotes a letter from Irving Thalberg giving him permission to film a "short subject" (based on Strindberg's *Miss Julie*) during his absence, but otherwise binding him exclusively to MGM (232).
45. Forslund, *Victor Sjöström,* 230. This is from an interview originally printed in the Swedish newspaper *Dagens Nyheter* on 21 May 1933.
46. Stern, "Hollywood and Montage: The Basic Fallacies of American Film Technique" (*Experimental Cinema,* no. 4, 1931, 47–52). This remarkable article contains a detailed indictment of "the lies and illusions in which the Hollywood producers place their faith," and Stern's listing of eleven "false methods . . . of filmic construction" anticipates with startling exactness the methodology of current investigations into the ideological function of the "Hollywood style." J. M. Valdes-Rodriguez's article in the same issue, "Hollywood: Sales Agent of American Imperialism" (18–20, 52–53) explores similar, still relevant, issues, also from a Marxist perspective.
47. *Photoplay,* December 1927, 52.
48. See especially pages 46 and 47.

Chapter 5

1. Originally Mihály Kertész. He left Hungary in 1919 and came to America in 1926 to work for Warner Brothers, after working for UFA in Europe for some years. His first major film for Warners was *Noah's Ark* (1928), but his career as a whole flourished after 1930 and thus falls outside the scope of this study.
2. Gillett, "The Mysterious X," 99–100.
3. The biographical information is taken largely from the booklet *Benjamin Christensen* by John Ernst, published by the Danish Film Museum in 1968. An unpublished translation of this booklet by Ron Mottram is held by the Film Department of the Museum of Modern Art in New York, and I am grateful to the Department for allowing me to consult it.
4. *Blind Justice* (with the direction attributed to Benjamin Christie) was reviewed and highly praised in *Variety,* 22 September 1916, 37. *The Mysterious X,* with the

American title *Under Sealed Orders,* was given favorable mention in the same review, though it had been released earlier.

5. It was not shown publicly in the United States until 1929, when the *NYT* (28 May 1929) found it "for the most part, fantastically conceived and directed, holding the onlooker in a sort of medieval spell." The film's title is usually spelled as Häxan when it is mentioned by American sources.

6. Quoted in Ernst, *Benjamin Christensen,* from a letter by Christensen.

7. *MPW,* 10 April 1926, 436; *Variety,* 31 March 1926, 42; *NYT,* 31 March 1926.

8. *NYT,* 22 August 1927.

9. *Variety,* 24 August 1927, 23; *MPW,* 10 September 1927, 115; *Picture Play,* December 1927, 62.

10. *MPC,* November 1927, 66.

11. A nice Technicolor print of the film (lacking, however, the final reel) exists in the Czech Film Archive.

12. *Variety,* 27 June 1928, 34.

13. *NYT,* 23 December 1928; *Film Spectator,* 8 December 1928, 10.

14. *Variety,* 19 June, 1929, 32.

15. Ernst, *Benjamin Christensen,* 28–29 (42–43 of Mottram's translation). Ernst, citing but not specifying "interviews" given by Christensen, says that this was first used on *The Haunted House.*

16. Information on Fejös's career is taken from Dodds, *The Several Lives of Paul Fejös,* and Philippe Haudiquet, *Paul Fejös.* Dodds's book is based on interviews with Fejös now lodged in the Columbia Oral History Research Center, which I have also consulted. For more detailed information on Fejös's career and his post-Hollywood films, see my articles "Fejos," and "Paul Fejos in America," As with Sjöström and Christensen, I have kept the original spelling of his name rather than the anglicized Fejos.

17. Shamroy went on to enjoy a distinguished career as one of the finest of Hollywood cameramen. His credits include *The Black Swan* (1942), *Leave Her to Heaven* (1946), and *The Robe* (1953).

18. A synopsis and supporting materials can be found in Frank Thompson, *Lost Films,* 151–65.

19. George G. Pratt, *Spellbound in Darkness,* 425–26.

20. *Variety,* 14 March 1928, 25.

21. For more details of the various prints of the film still in existence, see my "Paul Fejos in America," 31, 36.

22. *Photoplay,* September 1929, 54. Though it was made before *Broadway,* it was not released until shortly after *Broadway* had opened.

23. *Broadway* was billed as the "first million dollar talkie" and Universal spent $225,000 to acquire the rights to the play. Fejös's assertion to Dodds that the rights alone cost a million dollars and that he had a total budget of $5 million for the film must contain a degree of exaggeration, though the film was certainly very expensive

to make. Richard Koszarski's interview with Hal Mohr, Fejös's cameraman on *Broadway, The Last Performance,* and *The Captain of the Guard,* in *Film Comment,* September/October 1974, 48–53, provides valuable information on this stage of Fejös's career and on his working methods.

24. Dodds, *The Several Lives of Paul Fejös,* 42.

25. The working title was *La Marseillaise,* and the film is called this in the report of Fejös's accident given in *Film Weekly,* 16 December 1929, 5. Mohr hints in the *Film Comment* interview (53) that Fejös may have faked the accident in order to get out of completing a film in which he had lost interest.

26. Dodds, *The Several Lives of Paul* Fejös, 48.

27. For an account of the "discovery" of this film, long thought to be lost, see: István Nemeskürty, "Sentence of the Lake: A Film by Paul Fejos and Peverell Marley Rediscovered," *Hungarian Quarterly* no. 139, Autumn 1995, 141–43.

28. Information on Leni's early career is found in Freddy Buache, *Paul Leni.*

29. A useful reminder (like the equally absurdly named Lord Clancharlie of *The Man Who Laughs*) that European concepts of Anglo-Saxon life and social behavior are often as wildly inaccurate as Hollywood's presentation of what it conceives to be typically European activities and characters.

30. *Variety,* 9 June 1926, 17.

31. Lang's film, under the title *Between Two Worlds,* opened in New York in July 1923.

32. *NYT,* 19 March 1926. The American title at this stage was *The Three Wax Works.*

33. *MPW,* 14 May 1927, 133. See also *Variety,* 14 September 1927, 22; *NYT,* 10 September 1927.

34. *NYT,* 2 January 1928.

35. *Picture Play,* August 1928, 68; *Film Spectator,* 31 March 1928, 7–8.

36. *Variety,* 2 May 1928, 14; *NYT,* 28 April 1928.

37. *Variety,* 9 January 1929, 34; *NYT,* 7 January 1929.

38. Interview in *Film Comment,* 10, no. 2 (1974), 49.

39. Information on Stiller's life and career can be found in Idestam-Almquist, *Classics of the Swedish Cinema* and *Mauritz Stiller;* Pensel, *Seastrom and Stiller in Hollywood;* Alexander Walker, *Garbo;* and Werner, *Mauritz Stiller och hans filmer,* 1912–1916.

40. None of the sources explains how someone who was presumably classed as a deserter could have returned so easily to work in Finland.

41. Werner, *Mauritz Stiller,* 353.

42. Virtually all of Stiller's early films and most of Sjöström's were destroyed in a fire in the vaults of Svensk Filmindustri in 1941. For more information on Stiller's "lost" films, see: Martin Sopocy, "Beyond Realism: Reconstructing Some Lost Stiller Films at the Library of Congress."

43. Werner, *Mauritz Stiller,* 354.

44. Sopocy in "Beyond Realism" suggests that Werner's 1980 "reconstruction" of the scenario for a now lost film called *The Wings* (1916) establishes it as "an art film of remarkable sophistication for its date" (82).

45. Obvious examples include *The Awful Truth* (1937) and *The Philadelphia Story* (1940). The film might, in fact, be classed as one of the earliest examples of what Stanley Cavell calls "the comedy of re-marriage" in *Pursuits of Happiness* (Cambridge, Mass.: Harvard University Press, 1981).

46. It was based on a novel by the Finnish writer Johannes Linnankoski. Lagerlöf's unhappiness with Stiller's handling of her books is mentioned in Idestam-Almiquist, *Classics of the Swedish Cinema*, 32.

47. *Variety*, 2 December 1921, 43; *MPW*, 10 December 1921, 711; *NYT*, 10 January 1928.

48. The two-part silent version was first shown in Sweden in March 1924. Stiller prepared a shorter, one-part version for the Berlin premiere in September 1924, and this was in turn altered for the later Swedish sound copy. American prints of the film are presumably based on Stiller's "Berlin" version, doubtless with additional tampering by U.S. distributors, and give no real idea of the film's scope and the rhythm with which the action is developed. The Swedish Film Institute's restoration program has also produced beautifully tinted prints of *Johan* and *Song of the Scarlet Flower* that enhance even further the strong visual qualities of both films. For information on Garbo's early career and her discovery by Stiller, see, especially, Walker, *Garbo*. *Gösta Berling* was the only film that Stiller and Garbo made together.

49. For a detailed account of these negotiations, see Walker, *Garbo*, 27–28.

50. *Variety*, 31 October 1928, 31; *NYT*, 29 October 1928.

51. Walker, *Garbo*, 30.

52. Pola Negri, *Memoirs of a Star*, 225.

53. Accounts of the problems on *The Temptress* can be found in Walker, *Garbo*, 42, 46; and Pensel, *Seastrom and Stiller*, 58–59.

54. Walker, *Garbo*, 22.

55. Negri, *Memoirs*, 255.

56. Walker, *Garbo*, 54.

57. Negri, *Memoirs*, 280; and Pensel, *Seastrom and Stiller*, 60.

58. *Variety*, 5 January 1927, 16; *MPW*, 8 January 1927, 142; *Photoplay*, January 1927, 53.

59. Walker in *Garbo* for example calls *Barbed Wire* Stiller's "second Paramount picture" and implies that he was responsible for directing all of it (70). He makes no mention of *The Woman on Trial*. Pensel in *Seastrom and Stiller* says that *The Woman on Trial* was Stiller's "second feature with Pola Negri" (and thus his second Paramount picture) and mentions that he was replaced by Lee on *Barbed Wire* because of bad health (62). Negri makes no mention of any association with Stiller after *Hotel Imperial*, makes no reference to *The Woman on Trial*, and does not say who directed her on *Barbed Wire* (which is the next film she discusses after *Hotel Imperial*). Walker says that Stiller left Sweden in November 1927; Pensel dates this to December of that year. Idestam-Almquist, perhaps wisely under the circumstances, disposes of Stiller's career after *Hotel Imperial* in less than a page, and with minimal attention to facts and dates.

The print of *Barbed Wire* that I saw at the Czech Film Archive is officially credited to Lee. Pensel's summary of its plot (101) is ambiguous, and a more accurate account is as follows: Negri is a French peasant woman who is saved by a German prisoner-of-war from rape at the hands of a French officer. She testifies in the prisoner's favour at the subsequent court-martial and is labeled a traitor for doing so. After the war, she and the German are on the point of being driven out of the village by their neighbors when her war-blinded brother returns home and urges reconciliation and forgiveness. The film ends with a vision of universal brotherhood.

60. *NYT,* 26 September 1927; *MPW,* 1 October 1927, 311; *Variety,* 28 September 1927, 25.

61. Walker, *Garbo,* 79.

62. *NYT,* 28 May 1928; *MPW,* 1 October 1927, 311. The film starred Emil Jannings as a cockney burglar and Fay Wray as a Salvation Army girl who attempts to reform him.

63. Victor Sjöström, "As I Remember," 7.

64. Stiller's Swedish films still await a fuller reassessment than there has been space for here. Shipman's *The Story of Cinema* devotes a whole chapter to a welcome rehabilitation of Sjöström, who is hailed as "The Screen's First Master." Unfortunately (and suffering perhaps from a variant of the if-Keaton-is-good-Chaplin-must-be-bad syndrome) he reinforces his praise of Sjöström by denigrating Stiller's work (especially on pages 64–65). A fairer treatment of Stiller is given in Cowie's *Swedish Cinema,* and a very brief article by Mark Langer in *1000 Eyes Magazine* (March 1977) shows a sensitive awareness of Stiller's achievement.

65. Jacques Feyder came to America in 1929 after a successful—and, in the case of *Les Nouveaux Messieurs,* controversial—decade of filmmaking in France. He signed a contract with MGM and directed Garbo in her last silent film, *The Kiss,* a film of considerable visual beauty and subtlety. Most of his subsequent assignments, however, involved directing foreign-language versions of early sound films (including Garbo's *Anna Christie*), and he was given only two original projects, *Daybreak* and *Son of India.* Disillusioned, like so many others, he returned to France, where he worked and made such films as *La Kermesse Héroique* (1935) until shortly before his death in 1948.

66. Dupont has been mentioned earlier as director of *Der Weisse Pfau* on which Leni worked as set designer. The international success of *Variety* brought him a contract with Universal, but his first film for the company, *Love Me and the World is Mine,* was extensively re-edited against Dupont's wishes before its release. Disillusioned (a word which occurs with depressing frequency when outlining his and other careers), he went to Britain, where he made the masterly *Moulin Rouge* (1928) and *Piccadilly* (1929), and two sound films, and directed the first all-sound film to be made in Europe, *Atlantic* (1929). After a couple of years back in Germany, he returned to the United States, where he worked for the remainder of his life, steadily declining from relatively prestigious productions, to B films, to television, and then to low-budget quickies such as *The Neanderthal Man* in the 1950s. He died in Los

Angeles in 1956. More information about his career can be found in Herbert G. Luft, *E. A. Dupont.*

67. Luft, *E. A. Dupont,* 176.

68. Chaplin conflates the pattern of *He Who Gets Slapped* and *Variety* by making his heroine a bareback rider and her successful lover a trapeze artist.

69. Eisner, *Murnau,* 187–97. She says that the actors were doubled by a professional act called the Four Codonas; *Variety's* actors were doubled by the Three Codonas—presumably the same group. A synopsis and further information about the film can be found in Frank Thompson, *Lost Films,* 263–73.

70. The synopsis in Frank Thompson's *Lost Films* gives the characters' names as Charles and Marion and gives a somewhat different, ambiguously happy, ending.

71. An interesting shot at this stage of the film invites comparison, possibly deliberately, with *Variety.* Carl takes Mary to his room and plies her with drink and chocolates prior to making advances to her. One factor that induces him to change his mind is a sense of compassion when he becomes aware of her poverty—which is signaled by a hole in her stocking. The still from *Variety* on pages 182–83 of Luft's booklet on Dupont shows Jannings leering knowingly as the girl stretches her leg provocatively toward him; a toe emerges from a hole in her crumpled stockings. This blatantly erotic image demonstrates graphically the gulf between Continental treatments of sexuality and the limitations placed on American directors even at a period of relative freedom. *Variety* was first shown in America in November 1925; *The Devil's Circus* was released in March 1926.

72. For a more detailed discussion of Fejös's innovations with sound in this film, see my "Paul Fejös in America," 35.

73. *Film Comment,* 10, no. 5 (1974), 52. Mohr also describes in detail the design and use of the "Broadway crane."

74. A print of *Broadway* that includes the Technicolor sequence is held by the Royal Danish Film Museum.

75. *Film Comment,* 10, no. 5 (1974), 49.

76. As described by Mohr on page 50 of the *Film Comment* interview.

77. That the original story of the film was by a Hungarian, Lajos Biro, and that the producer, Erich Pommer, was German is obviously relevant but is not in itself the whole explanation.

78. For a fuller analysis of the film's structure, see my "Paul Fejos in America," 32–33.

79. As has been mentioned above, *Lonesome* was released both as a silent and as a part-talkie, with sound effects, music, and two short dialogue sequences.

Conclusion

1. It could be argued that a later opportunity occurred between, roughly, 1967 and 1977, when the early films of Robert Altman, Martin Scorsese, Terrence Malick,

Francis Ford Coppola, Arthur Penn, Sam Peckinpah, and some others seemed to point to a similar accommodation between art and commerce—in this case largely inspired rather than created by European filmmakers (though the early American films of Roman Polanski and Milos Forman were also significant at the period). Here too, however, after initial critical and even popular approval, a reaction set in against work that was too "downbeat," "esoteric," or "depressing" and most of the directors involved either modified their work to suit popular taste or were punished by commercial oblivion.

2.   Brian Attebery, *The Fantasy Tradition in American Literature*, 32.

Works Cited and Consulted

Periodicals, Magazines, and Newspapers of the 1920s

Close-Up
Exceptional Photoplays
Experimental Cinema
Film Spectator
Film Weekly
Motion Picture Classic (MPC)
Motion Picture Magazine
Moving Picture World (MPW)
New York Times (NYT)
Photoplay
Picture Play Magazine
Screenland
Variety

Books and Recent Magazine Articles

Allen, Frederick Lewis. *Only Yesterday.* New York: Harper Brothers, 1931.

Allen, Robert C. "William Fox Presents 'Sunrise.'" *Quarterly Review of Film Studies* 2, no. 3 (1977): 327–38.

Andrew, Dudley. "The Gravity of 'Sunrise.'" *Quarterly Review of Film Studies* 2, no. 3 (1977): 356–87.

Attebery, Brian. *The Fantasy Tradition in American Literature.* Bloomington: Indiana University Press, 1980.

Bergstrom, Janet. "Sexuality at a Loss: The Films of F. W. Murnau." *Poetics Today* 6, nos. 1–2 (1985): 185–203.

Brewster, Ben and Lea Jacobs. *Theatre to Cinema: Stage Pictorialism and the Early Feature Film.* Oxford: Oxford University Press, 1997.

Buache, Freddy. *Paul Leni.* Paris: *Anthologie du Cinéma,* no. 33, March 1968.

Carringer, Robert, and Barry Sabath. *Ernst Lubitsch: A Guide to References and Resources.* Boston: G. K. Hall, 1978.

Carter, Paul A. *The Twenties in America.* 2nd ed. Arlington Heights, Ill.: AHM Publishing. 1975.

Cawelti, John. *Adventure, Mystery, and Romance.* Chicago: University of Chicago Press, 1976.

Cowie, Peter. *Swedish Cinema.* London: Zwemmer's, 1966.

Dalle Vacche, Angela. *Cinema and Painting: How Art Is Used in Film.* Austin: University of Texas Press, 1996.

Dodds, John. W. *The Several Lives of Paul Fejos.* New York: Wenner-Gren Foundation, 1973.

Eagle, Herbert, ed. *Russian Formalist Film Criticism.* Ann Arbor: University of Michigan Press, 1981.

Eisner, Lotte. *The Haunted Screen.* Berkeley: University of California Press, 1969.

———. *Murnau.* Berkeley: University of California Press, 1973.

Elsaesser, Thomas. "Secret Affinities." *Sight & Sound* (winter 1988–89): 33–39.

Ernst, John. *Benjamin Christensen.* Copenhagen: Danish Film Museum, 1968.

Eyman, Scott. *Ernst Lubitsch: Laughter in Paradise.* New York: Simon and Schuster, 1993.

Forslund, Bengt. *Victor Sjöström: His Life and Work.* Trans. Peter Cowie, et al. New York: Zoetrope, 1988. Original Swedish edition, 1980.

Gillett, John. "Swedish Retrospective." *Sight & Sound* (summer 1974): 152–53.

———. "The Mysterious X." *Sight & Sound* (spring 1966): 99–100.

Gish, Lillian. *The Movies, Mr. Griffith, and Me.* Englewood Cliffs, N.J.: Prentice-Hall, 1969.

Guillermo, Gilberto Perez. "F. W. Murnau." *Film Comment* 7, no. 2 (1971): 12–15.

Gunning, Tom. "'A Dangerous Pledge': Victor Sjöström's Unknown Masterpiece, *Mästerman.*" In John Fullerton and Jan Olsson (eds.). *Nordic Explorations: Films Before 1930,* pp. 204–231. Sydney, Australia: John Libbey & Company, 1999. [Originally published as *Aura. Film Studies Journal* 5, nos. 1/2, 1999].

Hake, Sabine. "Lubitsch's Period Films as Palimpest." In Bruce A. Murray and Christopher J. Wickham, *Framing the Past: The Historiography of German Cinema and Television.* Carbondale: Southern Illinois University Press, 1992.

———. *Passions and Deceptions: The Early Films of Ernst Lubitsch.* Princeton, N.J.: Princeton University Press, 1992.

Haskell, Molly. "Sunrise." *Film Comment* 7, no. 2 (1971): 16–19.

Haudiquet, Philippe. *Fejos.* Paris: *Anthologie du Cinéma,* no. 40, December 1968.

Higham, John. *Strangers in the Land: Patterns of American Nativism 1860–1925.* New Brunswick, N.J.: Rutgers University Press, 1955. Reprint. New York: Atheneum, 1965.

Hofstadter, Richard. *The Age of Reform: From Bryan to F. D. R.* New York: Alfred A. Knopf, 1972.

Idestam-Almquist, Bengt, ed. *Classics of the Swedish Cinema.* Stockholm: Swedish Institute, 1952.

———. *När Filmen Kom Till Sverige.* Stockholm: P. A. Norstedt and Söners Förlag, 1959.

———. *Mauritz Stiller.* Paris: *Anthologie du Cinéma,* no. 25, May 1967.

Jansen, Jytte, ed. *Benjamin Christensen: An International Dane.* New York: Museum of Modern Art, 1999.

Kirchwey, Freda, ed. *Our Changing Morality.* New York: Albert and Charles Boni, 1930.

Koszarski, Richard. "City Girl." *Film Comment* 7, no. 2 (1971): 20–22.

————. Interview with Hal Mohr. *Film Comment* 10, no. 5 (1974): 48–53.

Leuchtenberg, William E. *The Perils of Prosperity, 1914–1932.* Chicago: University of Chicago Press, 1958.

Lipkin, Steven N. "'Sunrise': A Film Meets Its Public." *Quarterly Review of Film Studies* 2, no. 3 (1977): 339–55.

Luft, Herbert G. *E. A. Dupont.* Paris: *Anthologie du Cinéma,* no. 54, April 1970.

Lynd, Robert S., and Helen Merrill Lynd. *Middletown: A Study in Contemporary American Culture.* New York: Harcourt, Brace and Company, 1929.

Mast, Gerald. *The Comic Mind.* 2nd. ed. Chicago: University of Chicago Press, 1979.

May, Henry F. *The End of American Innocence: A Study of the First Years of Our Own Time 1912–17.* London: Jonathan Cape, 1960.

May, Lary. *Screening Out the Past: The Birth of Mass Culture and the Motion Picture Industry.* New York: Oxford University Press, 1980.

Mayne, Judith. "Dracula in the Twilight: Murnau's *Nosferatu* (1922)." In *German Film and Literature: Adaptations and Transformations,* edited by Eric Rentschler, 25–39. New York: Methuen, 1986.

Negri, Pola. *Memoirs of a Star.* New York: Doubleday, 1970.

Paine, Albert Bigelow. *Life and Lillian Gish.* New York: Macmillan, 1932.

Patterson, Frances Taylor, ed. *Motion Picture Continuities.* New York: Columbia University Press, 1929.

Paul, William. *Ernst Lubitsch's American Comedy.* New York: Columbia University Press, 1983.

Pensel, Hans. *Seastrom and Stiller in Hollywood.* New York: Vantage Press, 1969.

Perrett, Geoffrey. *America in the Twenties: A History.* New York: Simon and Schuster, 1982.

Petrie, Graham. "Fejos." *Sight & Sound* (Summer 1978): 175–77.

————. "Paul Fejos in America." *Film Quarterly* (Winter 1978–79):28–37.

Petro, Patrice. *Joyless Streets: Woman and Melodramatic Representation in Weimar Germany.* Princeton, N.J.: Princeton University Press, 1989.

Poague, Leland. *The Cinema of Ernst Lubitsch.* Cranbury, N.J.: Barnes and Noble, 1978.

Pratt, George. *Spellbound in Darkness.* Rochester, N.Y.: University of Rochester Press, 1966.

Saunders, Thomas J. *Hollywood in Berlin: American Cinema and Weimar Germany.* Berkeley: University of California Press, 1994.

Shipman, David. *The Story of Cinema, Volume One.* London: Hodder and Stoughton, 1982.

Sklar, Robert, ed. *The Plastic Age, 1917–1930.* New York: Braziller, 1970.

Slide, Anthony, ed. *Selected Film Criticism 1921–1930.* Metuchen, N.J.: Scarecrow Press, 1982.

Sopocy, Martin. "Beyond Realism: Reconstructing Some Lost Stiller Films at the Library of Congress." *Quarterly Review of Film & Video* 11 (1989): 79–83.

Thompson, Frank. *Lost Films: Important Movies That Disappeared.* Secaucus, N.J.: Carl Publishing, 1996. (Contains synopses and other information for *The Divine Woman, Four Devils, The Last Moment,* and *The Patriot.*)

Thompson, Kristin. *Exporting Entertainment: America in the World Film Market.* London: BFI Publishing, 1985.

Walker, Alexander. *Garbo.* London: Weidenfeld and Nicolson, 1980.

Weinberg, Herman. *The Lubitsch Touch.* New York: Dutton, 1968.

Werner, Gösta. *Mauritz Stiller och hans filmer, 1912–1916.* Stockholm: P.A. Norstedt and Söners Förlag, 1969.

Wood, Robin. "F. W. Murnau." *Film Comment* 12, no. 3 (1976): 4–19.

———. "Tabu." *Film Comment* 7, no. 2 (summer 1971): 23–27.

Illustration Credits

Photographs on pages 13 (bottom), 20, 22, 52 (top), 61, 63, 70, 78, 97, 105 (top), 107, 137, 153, 157, 164, 167, 182, 184, 201, 211 (bottom), 214, 219 (bottom), 223, 224, and 227 courtesy of the Museum of Modem Art/Film Stills Archive.

Photographs on pages 110, 115, 116, 129, 192, 196, and 206 courtesy of the Swedish Film Institute.

Photographs on pages 170 and 172 courtesy of the Danish Film Museum.

Photographs on pages 52, 132, 176, 216, and 219 (top) courtesy of the Academy of Motion Picture Arts and Sciences and the Academy Foundation.

Photographs on pages 13 (top), 41, 85, 105 (bottom), 139, 211 (top), and 221 courtesy of the Wisconsin Center for Film and Theater Research.

Photographs on pages 33, 37, and 88 (top) courtesy of Gerhard Ullman.

Index of film Titles

Index of Names

Aho, Juhani, 195
Altman, Robert, ix, 269n. 1
American Legion, 5
Anderson, John Murray, 183
Andreyev, Leonid, 135, 141
Antonioni, Michelangelo, ix
Arzner, Dorothy, 243, 244
Attebery, Brian, 232

Bang, Hermann, 100
Banky, Vilma, 160
Barrymore, John, 67
Bartlett, Randolph, 16
Beaton, Welford, 99, 156–57, 178
Bell, Monta, 199, 206
Bergman, Hjalmar, 118, 126, 127, 131
Bergman, Ingmar, 8, 128, 232, 250
Bergstrom, Janet, 72, 109
Bern, Paul, 131
Bernhardt, Sarah, 149
Bing, Herman, 91
Blasco Ibáñez, Vicente, 199
Blue, Monte, 47, 238
Blumenthal, Ben, 4
Borgström, Hilda, 114, 126
Borzage, Frank, 99
Bresson, Robert, 232
Brown, Clarence, 16, 149
Brownlow, Kevin, xiii
Brunius, Jacques, 240
Buache, Freddy, 187

Caine, Hall, 131, 134
Capra, Frank, 98
Carringer, Robert, 44, 57, 65, 256n. 22
Chaney, Lon, 136, 141, 142, 173, 174, 188, 222

Chaplin, Charles: xii, 35, *Circus, The,* 209;
  Dog's Life, A, 39; Fejos and, 177, 178;
  influence on Lubitsch, 44, 205;
  Josephson on, 19, 235, 236; Lubitsch
  compared with, 39, 40; Pietrovskij on,
  30–31; reputation as director, 16, 19;
  Sjöström, his opinion of, 134; *Woman of
  Paris, A,* 24, 44, 47, 57, 133, 205
Cherkassov, Nikolai, 187
Chevalier, Maurice, 38, 248
Christensen, Benjamin: x, 69, 168–77; as
  actor, 168, 173; brought to US, 19, 169,
  173; comic relief, 226; *Devil's Circus,
  The,* 168, 173, 210–12; *Heksen,* 8, 168,
  170–71; Hollywood career, 69, 165, 166,
  175; 'lost' films, 168, 174; *Mockery,* 168,
  173, 175, 221–24; *Mysterious Island,
  The,* 174; *Mysterious X, The,* 168–69;
  Night of Revenge, 169; reputation in US,
  19; *Seine Frau, die Unbekannte,* 171–73;
  Seven Footprints to Satan, 168, 174, 175,
  218; technical innovations, 175;
  Witchcraft review, 8
Christianson. *See* Christensen
Clair, René, x
Cody, Lew, 53, 55
Collins, John, 17
Conklin, Chester, 174, 175
Coppola, Francis Ford, 269n. 1
Cromelin, Paul, 5–6
Cruze, James, 16, 19, 235
Curtiz, Michael, x, 165, 177, 185
Czinner, Paul, 243

Daniels, Bebe, 244
D'Arrast, Harry D'Abbadie, 31, 57, 206
Daudet, Alphonse, 141

Books in the Contemporary Film and Television Series

Cinema and History, by Marc Ferro, translated by Naomi Greene, 1988

Germany on Film: Theme and Content in the Cinema of the Federal Republic of Germany, by Hans Gunther Pflaum, translated by Richard C. Helt and Roland Richter, 1990

Canadian Dreams and American Control: The Political Economy of the Canadian Film Industry, by Manjunath Pendakur, 1990

Imitations of Life: A Reader on Film and Television Melodrama, edited by Marcia Landy, 1991

Bertolucci's 1900: *A Narrative and Historical Analysis,* by Robert Burgoyne, 1991

Hitchcock's Rereleased Films: From Rope *to* Vertigo, edited by Walter Raubicheck and Walter Srebnick, 1991

Star Texts: Image and Performance in Film and Television, edited by Jeremy G. Butler, 1991

Sex in the Head: Visions of Femininity and Film in D. H. Lawrence, by Linda Ruth Williams, 1993

Dreams of Chaos, Visions of Order: Understanding the American Avant-garde Cinema, by James Peterson, 1994

Full of Secrets: Critical Approaches to Twin Peaks, edited by David Lavery, 1994

The Radical Faces of Godard and Bertolucci, by Yosefa Loshitzky, 1995

The End: Narration and Closure in the Cinema, by Richard Neupert, 1995

German Cinema: Texts in Context, by Marc Silberman, 1995

Cinemas of the Black Diaspora: Diversity, Dependence, and Opposition, edited by Michael T. Martin, 1995

The Cinema of Wim Wenders: Image, Narrative, and the Postmodern Condition, edited by Roger Cook and Gerd Gemünden, 1997

New Latin American Cinema: Theory, Practices, and Transcontinental Articulations, Volume One, edited by Michael T. Martin, 1997

New Latin American Cinema: Studies of National Cinemas, Volume Two, edited by Michael T. Martin, 1997

Giving Up the Ghost: Spirits, Ghosts, and Angels in Mainstream Comedy Films, by Katherine A. Fowkes, 1998

Bertolucci's The Last Emperor: *Multiple Takes,* edited by Bruce H. Sklarew, Bonnie S. Kaufman, Ellen Handler, and Diane Borden, 1998

Alexander Kluge: The Last Modernist, by Peter C. Lutze, 1998

Tracking King Kong: A Hollywood Icon in World Culture, by Cynthia Erb, 1998

Documenting the Documentary: Close Readings of Documentary Film and Video, edited by
    Barry Keith Grant and Jeannette Sloniowski, 1998

Mythologies of Violence in Postmodern Media, edited by Christopher Sharrett, 1999

Feminist Hollywood: From Born in Flames *to* Blue Steel, by Christina Lane, 2000

Reading Cavell's The World Viewed: *A Philosophical Perspective on Film,* by William
    Rothman and Marian Keane, 2000

Writing in Light: The Silent Scenario and the Japanese Pure Film Movement, by Joanne
    Bernardi, 2001

Hollywood Destinies: European Directors in America, 1922–1931, by Graham Petrie, 2002